MODERN CHINESE

现代中文 SECOND EDITION

TEXTBOOK 1B
SIMPLIFIED CHARACTERS

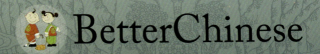
BetterChinese

MODERN CHINESE 现代中文

Textbook Volume 1B

Second Edition

Project Director:	James P. Lin
Editorial Consultant:	Li-Hsiang Yu Shen
Project Manager:	Angel Yeh
Assistant Editors:	Sue-Ann Ma and Christopher Peacock
Curriculum Advisors:	Norman Masuda and Rebecca Starr
Executive Publisher:	Chi-Kuo Shen
Illustrations:	Better World Ltd

Library of Congress Cataloging-in-Publication Data: To be Assigned

ISBN: 978-1-60603-578-8

2 3 4 XLA 16 15 14

For more information about our products, contact us at:

United States

640 Waverley Street

Palo Alto, CA 94301

Tel: 888-384-0902

Fax: 888-384-0901

Email: usa@betterchinese.com

Contents 目录

We are so grateful for the warm reception *Modern Chinese* received in its first year. It confirmed our belief that there is a real need for a refreshing and relevant beginner-level college program that is engaging, encouraging, and intuitive, and that includes empowering technology.

We were encouraged by the professors' positive feedback and university adoptions. This Second Edition incorporates many suggestions based on classroom experiences. We are especially grateful to Professor Hong Jiang of Northwestern University and Professor Hong Zeng of Stanford University. They have helped to make this Second Edition more engaging and relevant to students through their detailed feedback. We also took this opportunity to strike a better balance between delivering authentic text and achieving learning goals.

The creation of *Modern Chinese* incorporates all of the pedagogical experiences that have made us the leading Chinese curriculum publisher in the world. We researched what teachers liked about our existing K-12 programs and what they looked for in a college program: the result was *Modern Chinese*.

The program is revolutionary in many ways. The lessons appear in a complete story-based format that scaffolds vocabulary and grammar patterns from prior lessons to instill confidence in new learners. We take a new approach to the presentation of grammar, focusing on simple explanations and offering practical examples. In addition, we include enriching cultural spotlights to cultivate cultural awareness as well as a variety of exercises to encourage real-life communication. An accompanying website also offers supplemental learning tools such as lesson animations, audio recordings, and online practices.

We are thankful to all those who have helped us with the creation of *Modern Chinese*. Special thanks go to our Executive Publisher, Chi-Kuo Shen, for supporting this project; Chief Educator, Li-Hsiang Shen, for sharing her love of education and inspiration; Norman Masuda for sharing his years of classroom teaching experience and expertise in the area of language acquisition; Professor Rebecca Starr for her invaluable insights as a linguist and providing a non-native learner's perspective; and some of the early team members who contributed to the research and pilot of the program, including Stephanie Puk, Sandra Tung, Chung Trung, and Hope Tammany. We would like to express our gratitude to the professors who provided feedback through numerous rounds of reviews: Wenhui Chen of Washing University in St. Louis; Hong Li of Emory University; Xianmin Liu of Vanderbilt University; Xuehong Lu of State University of New York at Buffalo; Christopher Lupke of Washing State University; Michelle DiBello, Youping Zhang, and Chao Fen Sun of Stanford University. We also wish to thank our advisory board professors for their insightful and constructive feedback: Yujie Ge of Santa Clara University; Li Ma of Florida International University; Hong Jiang of Northwestern University; Cynthia Hsien Shen of University of Florida. Most importantly, Better Chinese would like to recognize the core *Modern Chinese* team: Project Manager, Angel Yeh, for her creative story-telling abilities and critical eye in overseeing every detail of the *Modern Chinese* project; Cheuk-Yue Fung, Sue-Ann Ma, Christopher Peacock, Tiantian Gao, Lauren Chen, and Bin Yan for their relentless pursuit of editorial perfection; and Roger Hsieh for his technical support.

Finally, on a personal note, I would like to thank my wife, Clarissa Shen, for her support and my wonderful children, Maia and Lucas, for inspiring me to make this world a better place. I hope that by making *Modern Chinese* engaging, relevant, and effective, we will encourage more students to continue their studies of Chinese language and culture, empowering them to bring the world a little closer together.

James P. Lin
Project Director
December 2013

MODERN CHINESE 现代中文
Scope and Sequence

Units	Communication Goals	Structure Notes	Language Notes & Cultural Spotlights
中文 **Prelude:** **The Chinese Language**	• Learn the pinyin romanization system • Speak Chinese characters with standard tones and sentence inflection • Understand Chinese tonal changes (tone sandhi)	1. *Understand the 4 Chinese tones* 2. *Learn the Chinese phonetic system, pinyin* 3. *Understand the rules of Chinese stroke order*	• Understand the history of the Chinese language • Identify where the Chinese language is spoken today • Learn about the development of written Chinese, including simplified and traditional Chinese characters
我 **UNIT 1** **Me**	• Greet and say goodbye to people • Introduce yourself and exchange names with others • Ask and answer questions pertaining to age and nationality • Count from 1 to 99	1. *Use an adjective phrase to describe a subject* 2. *Use 们 to convert a pronoun or noun (people only) to its plural form* 3. *Use 也 to express "also"* 4. *Use 吗 to turn a statement into a question* 5. *Use 呢 to ask "What about…?"* 6. *Use 叫 to state one's name* 7. *Use 什么 to ask "what?" questions* 8. *Use 多大 to ask about somone's age* 9. *Add 岁 after a number to state one's age* 10. *Use 是 to indicate equivalency* 11. *Use 哪国人 to ask about nationality and country + 人 to state nationality* 12. *Use 不 to negate a verb* 13. *Use Verb + 不 + Verb to form affirmative-negative questions* 14. *Use Verb or 不 + Verb to answer affirmative-negative questions*	• Understand how Chinese greet and address one another • Learn the structure of Chinese names • Learn about the Chinese diaspora • Learn how to ask for someone's age politely • Learn how to count the numbers from 11 to 99 • Understand the rationale behind Chinese names for countries • Learn Chinese hand gestures for numbers 1 to 10 • Learn the connotations of the numbers 4 and 8 in Chinese culture • Learn about the Chinese Zodiac
家 **UNIT 2** **Family**	• Identify family members and ask others about their families • Ask whether someone has pets • Ask and answer questions regarding quantity • Inquire about someone's occupation • Ask and answer questions about what languages one can speak	1. *Use 有 to express possession* 2. *Use 没有 to express "not have"* 3. *Use 有没有 to form a "have or not have" question* 4. *Use 有什么 to ask what one has* 5. *Use 的 to indicate possession* 6. *Use number + measure word to quantify a noun* 7. *Use 几 + measure word to ask how many and number + measure word to answer* 8. *Use 这 or 那 to express "this" or "that"* 9. *Use 谁 to ask "who?"* 10. *Use 还 to express "also"* 11. *Use 会 to state what one knows how to do* 12. *Use 会不会 to ask whether or not one knows how to do something* 13. *Use 只 to express "only"*	• Learn how to address different family members in Chinese • Understand the evolution of the traditional Chinese family • Learn how people regard pets in China • Learn about the giant pandas in China • Understand the difference between 语 and 文 • Understand the global response to studying Chinese as a world language • Learn about other varieties of spoken Chinese • Learn about the traditional professions of China

Units	Communication Goals	Structure Notes	Language Notes & Cultural Spotlights
时 **UNIT 3** **Time**	• State and ask the time • Talk about future events • Make appointments • Apologize for tardiness • Ask and answer questions about days of the week and months • State and ask for the date • Wish someone "happy birthday" and offer gifts	1. Use 会 to indicate the possibility of an action taking place in the future 2. Use 什么时候 to ask "when" 3. Use 星期几 to ask "what day of the week" and 星期 + number to state the day of the week 4. Use 几点 to discuss time 5. Use 差不多 to express "almost" 6. Use 还没(有) to express "not yet" or "still have not" 7. Use 吧 to make a suggestion 8. Use 几 to ask "what month" and "what day" 9. Use 都 to mean "both" or "all" 10. Use 了 to indicate a change of state or situation 11. Use the verb 送 in the context of gift giving 12. Use 的 to modify nouns	• Learn how to say the different days of the week in Chinese • Learn about how to tell time in Chinese • Compare the differences between the lunar and Western calendars • Learn about auspicious dates in the Chinese calendar • Learn how to read a Chinese calendar • Learn how to use a timeframe to indicate tense in Chinese • Look at the ways in which birthdays are celebrated in China • Understand the symbolism of certain gifts in China
食 **UNIT 4** **Food**	• Inquire and express preferences for food and drink • Express hunger • Order food and drinks at a restaurant • Discuss various dishes and their flavors • Offer to pay for a meal	1. Use 想 to indicate a desired action 2. Use 给 to mean "to give" 3. Use 喜欢 to express liking something or someone 4. Use Verb + 不 + Verb with two-character verbs to form affirmative-negtaive questions 5. Use 那(么) to mean "Well then" or "In that case" 6. Use 好 + Verb to form a compound adjective 7. Use 怎么样 to ask for an opinion of something 8. Use 太……了 to describe an exaggerated attribute 9. Use 要 to indicate desire 10. Use 为什么 and 因为 to ask questions and give explanations respectively 11. Use 一下 to express the brevity of an action	• Look at special pronouns in Mandarin Chinese and when to omit them • Learn about regional Chinese cuisines • Learn about symbolism in Chinese cuisine • Learn about Chinese uses of onomatopoeia • Learn about the Chinese equivalents of foreign names and locations • Learn about Chinese dining etiquette • Discover the art of tea
住 **UNIT 5** **Daily Lives**	• Make simple introductions of others • Be able to state where you or others live • Name buildings and facilities on campus • Be able to describe relative locations • Name furniture and rooms in a house	1. Use 在 to indicate location 2. Use 在 as a verb complement 3. Use 哪里 to ask "where" 4. Use 要 to talk about future events 5. Use 跟……一起 to express doing things together 6. Use 可以 to express permission 7. Use 在 with an action verb to indicate the location of an activity 8. Use 到 as a resultative complement to indicate completion of an action 9. Use 得 or 不 and a resultative complement to indicate whether it is possible or not possible to reach a result	• Learn about introductions in Chinese • Know about verb-object compounds • Learn about traditional Chinese architecture (Si He Yuan) • Discover some of the universities with study abroad opportunities in China • Learn about telephone greetings in Chinese

Units	Communication Goals	Structure Notes	Language Notes & Cultural Spotlights
	• Use the appropriate expressions on the telephone • Ask and answer questions about relative locations	10. Use 可能 to express likelihood 11. Use completion 了 to describe completed actions 12. Use 就 to indicate "right" or "precisely"	• Review some spatial location words used in Chinese • Learn some of the contemporary slang used for texting • Learn about the art of Feng Shui and its modern applications
买 **UNIT 6** **Shopping**	• Ask about the availability and cost of different items or products in a store • Understand and use different denominations and amounts of money • Negotiate prices • Indicate that you wish to pay for an item with either cash or credit card • Use the correct expressions when paying with cash and receiving change	1. Use 有 to express existence rather than possession 2. Use 得 to express "must" 3. Use 给 as the preposition "to" 4. Use 多少 to ask "how many" or "how much" 5. Use Adjectives with (一)点(儿) to express "a little more" 6. Use 还是...吧 to express a suggested alternative 7. Use 再 to indicate a repeating action 8. Use 因为…所以… to express causal relationships 9. Use 不用 to say "need not" 10. Use 这么 or 那么 to intensify adjectives 11. Use Verb + 了 to describe specific completed actions 12. Use 已经 to express "already" 13. Use 要是…(的话)…就 to say "if… then…" 14. Use (是)…还是… to express either-or questions	• Learn about Chinese currency • Learn about counting from 100 and above • Know about the Silk Street • Learn how to bargain in Chinese markets • Learn about words used in financial transactions • Learn about the currencies of different countries • Learn about trade along the Silk Road • Learn about how Western stores have impacted China
行 **UNIT 7** **Travel & Navigation**	• Ask and answer questions about vacation plans • Give information about one's hometown and family background • Describe the attractions of China's capital • Express the distance between two places • Give and receive directions • Describe different modes of transportation	1. Use 的时候 to create "when" expressions 2. Use 才 to indicate an action occurring later than anticipated 3. Use 从 with a place word to indicate origin 4. Use 是……的 to emphasize the time, locale, or manner of a completed action 5. Use 送……去 to mean "take" 6. Use 离 to express location relative to a reference point 7. Use 到 with place words to indicate destination 8. Use 怎么 to ask how something is done 9. Use 往 to indicate directional movement 10. Use 先…, 再…, 然后… to indicate a sequence of events	• Learn the meaning of hometown in Chinese • Discover the relationship between seasons and how it classifies vacations • Learn about various modes of transportation in China • Discover activities done during China's "Golden Weeks" • Learn common direction expressions • Discover some of Beijing's historical hotspots

Units	Communication Goals	Structure Notes	Language Notes & Cultural Spotlights
学 **UNIT 8** **Academics**	• Discuss classes and school subjects • Express interest in something • Indicate levels of difficulty • Discuss exams, homework, and classroom situations • Ask to borrow something • Express subjective opinions	1. Use 懂 as a resultative complement to indicate ability to understand 2. Use 多 or 少 to express doing an activity more or less often 3. Use 只好 to indicate the best course of action among limited options 4. Use Verb + 完 to describe completed actions 5. Use 以后 to express "after doing something" 6. Use Verb + 了 to describe a sequence of events 7. Use 把 to indicate an action performed on a specific object 8. Use 怎么 to ask "how come" questions 9. Use 怎么这么/那么 to express incredulity or amazement regarding a situation 10. Use 一…就… to express "as soon as A, B" 11. Use 觉得 to express subjective opinions 12. Use 还是 with adjectives to compare qualities 13. Use 第 to express ordinal numbers 14. Use (正)……在(呢) to indicate ongoing actions	• Review previously learned radicals and phono-semantic compounds • Learn about China's Four Great Inventions • Learn about homographs in the Chinese language • Review the use of interjections in Chinese • Learn about examinations in China • Learn about the Four Treasures of the Study
衣 **UNIT 9** **Fashion**	• Name different articles of clothing • Discuss and find appropriate sizes • Make comparisons and express sameness • List and express preferences for different colors • Make use of some basic loan words • Express superlatives	1. Use 或者 to express choices and options 2. Use 看/听 +起来 to express a subjective impression 3. Use 比 to make comparisons 4. Use 更 to say "even more" 5. Use (一)点(儿) to describe small differences 6. Use 又…又… to express "both . . . and . . ." 7. Use …跟…一样 (Adjective) to express sameness 8. Use Verb 一 Verb to describe casual or brief activities 9. Use 最 to express superlatives 10. Use reduplication to intensify adjectives or adverbs 11. Use Verb reduplication to describe casual or brief activities 12. Use 看 to mean "and see" 13. Use 有(一)点(儿) to express "somewhat" 14. Use 好 as an intensifier	• Review use of adjectives • Learn about color symbolism in Chinese • Learn about clothing terms • Explore Chinese fashion trends • Learn the history of foot-binding

Units	Communication Goals	Structure Notes	Language Notes & Cultural Spotlights
娱 **UNIT 10** **Hobbies &** **Activities**	• Inquire about what people like to do in their free time • Discuss sports and leisure activities • Express how often you like to do something • Discuss musical performances and instruments • Describe how well somebody does something • Indicate time periods and duration	1. Use 一边…一边… to describe simultaneous actions 2. Use 什么 to mean "any" 3. Use topic-comment sentences 4. Use 有的 to mean "some" 5. Use 对……有兴趣 to express interest in something 6. Use 常(常)to express "often" 7. Use 能 to describe ability 8. Use name + 他们 to refer to a group of people 9. Use 得 to describe the manner of actions 10. Use 每…都… to express "every" 11. Use time periods to indicate duration 12. Use multiple numbers to estimate amounts 13. Use 不是……吗? to ask a rhetorical question 14. Use 对 as the preposition "to, towards"	• Learn about pictographs and ideographs in the evolution of Chinese characters • Learn about the culture of Karaoke or Chinese KTV • Learn about Mahjong • Learn about Chinese Martial Arts
情 **UNIT 11** **Relationships** **& People**	• Arrange to go on a date with someone • Describe a person's qualities and attributes • Discuss relationships, marriage, and break-ups • Describe your emotions • Refer to something using the passive voice • Talk about past experiences	1. Use 得 to indicate degree or result 2. Use 次 to express number of times 3. Use 让 to express to "let" or "make" someone do something 4. Use 记住 to describe keeping something in mind 5. Use 被 to form the passive voice 6. Use 一直 to express "constantly" 7. Use Verb + 过 to express a past experience	• Review loan words and associative compounds • Learn about Chinese Valentine's Day and the story of Qixi • Learn about China's tallest couple • Discuss relationship terms • Examine Chinese punctuation • Observe Chinese wedding traditions
医 **UNIT 12** **Medicine**	• Inquire after a person's health • Describe the symptoms of an illness • Talk about the weather and the seasons • Name illness and afflictions • Refer to different parts of the body • Describe some of the differences between Chinese and Western medicine	1. Use 最好 to make suggestions 2. Use 带 to express bringing objects or people 3. Use noun or measure word reduplication to express "every" 4. Use name/pronoun + 那儿 to talk about someone's location or home 5. Use 地 to express the manner in which an action is performed 6. Use 帮 to mean "for" 7. Use 好 as a resultative complement to describe a properly completed action 8. Use 又……了 to say "again"	• Review intensifiers used in the Chinese language • Learn about expressions used to discuss the weather • Learn about massages and Chinese morning exercises • Identify body parts in Chinese • Understand the difference between 等一会儿 and 一下 • Review different ways to talk about weeks • Learn about Western versus Eastern medicinal differences • Understand the importance of hot and cold foods in Chinese medical tradition

Units	Communication Goals	Structure Notes	Language Notes & Cultural Spotlights
商 **UNIT 13** **Business**	• Talk about your full- or part-time job • Offer words of encouragement • Indicate that something is unexpected • Discuss internships and working in China • Talk about your employment experience and resume • Discuss your post-graduation plans • Learn about the importance of *guanxi* or "connections"	1. Use 没想到 *to introduce an unexpected event* 2. Use 难怪 *to express "no wonder"* 3. Use 什么样的 *to ask "what kind?"* 4. Use 不但… 而且… *to express "not only...but also..."* 5. Use 虽然… 但是… *to express "although . . . however . . ."* 6. Use 从…到… *to express length of time* 7. Use 想要 *to express a desire* 8. Use 极了 *as an intensifier* 9. Use 跟……有关 *to express relevance to a subject* 10. Use Noun + 这样/那样 *to say "this/that type of . . ."*	• Identify different work titles • Learn about the concept of *guanxi*, or business relationships/networking in China • Review different professions • Examine basic characteristics of a Chinese resume • Learn about China's Special Economic Zones and state-owned enterprises in China
节 **UNIT 14** **Festivals**	• Talk about the customs and traditions of Chinese New Year • Use the appropriate expressions to convey New Year's greetings and wishes • Compare and contrast various Chinese and Western holidays • Discuss the different foods that are eaten during Chinese holidays • Expand on a topic by providing examples	1. Use 用…(来)… *to describe the means of doing something* 2. Use 着 *to indicate an ongoing action* 3. Use 快要……了 *to say "be about to"* 4. Use 到时候 *to express "when the time comes"* 5. Use 像 *to express "resemble" or "is like"* 6. Use 越来越 *to mean "increasingly"* 7. Use 比方说 *to say "for example"* 8. Use 连……都 *to say "even . . ."*	• Observe greetings performed during Spring Festival • Learn about the use of idioms in the Chinese language • Learn about customs related to Tomb Sweeping Festival, the Dragon Boat Festival, and the Mid-Autumn Festival • Identify important foods related to Chinese holidays • Learn about the development of writing horizontal and vertical text in Chinese • Understand customs used during Chinese New Year and the Lantern Festival

Units	Communication Goals	Structure Notes	Language Notes & Cultural Spotlights
礼 **UNIT 15** **Chinese Ways**	• Politely ask someone to do something • Understand and follow Chinese social conventions • Use correct etiquette towards one's elders • Name some features of traditional Chinese culture • Express that one has "just" done something • Make basic comparisons between ancient and modern Chinese culture • Indicate that something is an ongoing process	1. Use 麻烦 *to make requests* 2. Use 来 *before verbs to express commencing an activity* 3. Use 要不然 *to say "or else" or "otherwise"* 4. Use 正好 *to express "as it happens"; "happen to . . ."* 5. Use 刚 *or* 刚刚 *to express "just now"* 6. Use *nouns with* 化 *to form "-ize" verbs or "-ized" adjectives* 7. Use 比如(说) *to say "for instance" and give examples* 8. Use *double-*了 *to describe an action continuing up to the present*	• Understand the Chinese concept of "face" • Compare the difference between 客气 and 礼貌 • Learn about Confucius and his teachings • Learn about the difference between classical and modern Chinese language usage • Learn about Daoism • Understand the meaning of resilience found in Confucian philosophy and Daoist beliefs
@ **UNIT 16** **Technology & Modern China**	• Use expressions related to computers and the internet • Discuss city lifestyles • Understand and use the "besides" construction • Express that you will miss someone • Use terms for posting letters and packages as well as sending emails • Wish someone a safe trip	1. Use 除了……以外 *to say "besides…"* 2. Use *question words with* 都 *to express "any" or "every"* 3. Use 自己 *to refer to oneself or another* 4. Use 等 *to express "at the point when/by the time"* 5. Use *Verb Phrase* 给 *Someone* 看/听 *to express doing something to show someone else* 6. Use 陪 *to express keeping someone company* 7. Use 会……的 *to stress that something will be the case* 8. Use 死 *to mean "extremely" or "to death"*	• Learn about internet cafes • Review learned measure words • Explore modern Beijing architecture • Learn about internet use in China • Review sentence-final particles • Learn about cell phone use in China • Learn more about the Maglev Train and China's high-speed rail

衣

Fashion

第九单元
UNIT 9

Communication Goals

Lesson 1: 买衣服 **Shopping for Clothes**
- Name different articles of clothing.
- Discuss and find appropriate sizes.
- Make comparisons and express sameness.

Lesson 2: 你喜欢什么颜色? **What Colors Do You Like?**
- List and express preferences for different colors.
- Make use of some basic loan words.
- Express superlatives.

买衣服
Shopping for Clothes

欢迎光临!

你想买什么衣服?

我想买毛衣和
衬衫,还想买裙子。
máo yī
chèn shān
qún zi

走,我们先去看毛衣。
máo yī

这件毛衣太大了,你应该穿中号的或者小号的。
jiàn máo yī
chuān zhōng hào
huò zhě xiǎo hào

LESSON TEXT 9.1

Shopping for Clothes 买衣服

Sun Mali and Zhang Anna are shopping for a sweater, shirt, and skirt for Sun Mali. After consdering different items, Sun Mali finds a sweater and a matching skirt.

售货员：	欢迎光临！	Huānyíng guānglín!
张安娜：	你想买什么衣服？	Nǐ xiǎng mǎi shénme yīfu?
孙玛丽：	我想买毛衣和衬衫，还想买裙子。走，我们先去看毛衣。	wǒ xiǎng mǎi máoyī hé chènshān, hái xiǎng mǎi qúnzi. Zǒu, wǒmen xiān qù kàn máoyī.
张安娜：	这件毛衣太大了，你应该穿中号的或者小号的。	Zhèi jiàn máoyī tài dà le, nǐ yīnggāi chuān zhōnghào de huòzhě xiǎohào de.

孙玛丽：	这件很漂亮，你觉得呢？	Zhèi jiàn hěn piàoliang, nǐ juéde ne?
张安娜：	我觉得这件看起来比那件更大！	Wǒ juéde zhèi jiàn kànqilai bǐ nèi jiàn gèng dà!
孙玛丽：	可是这件比那件便宜一点儿。	Kěshì zhèi jiàn bǐ nèi jiàn piányi yì diǎnr.
张安娜：	你看，这件红色的毛衣有中号的，又漂亮又便宜。	Nǐ kàn, zhèi jiàn hóngsè de máoyī yǒu zhōnghào de, yòu piàoliang yòu piányi.
孙玛丽：	不错啊！裙子呢？	Bú cuò a! Qúnzi ne?
张安娜：	这条裙子跟那件毛衣一样便宜，也很配。你买这条吧！	Zhèi tiáo qúnzi gēn nèi jiàn máoyī yíyàng piányi, yě hěn pèi. Nǐ mǎi zhèi tiáo ba!

字 词 VOCABULARY

LESSON VOCABULARY 9.1

	SIMPLIFIED	TRADITIONAL	PINYIN	WORD CATEGORY	DEFINITION
1.	毛衣		máoyī	n	sweater
2.	衬衫	襯衫	chènshān	n	shirt
3.	裙子		qúnzi	n	skirt; dress
4.	件		jiàn	mw	(used for articles of clothing such as shirts, dresses, jackets, and coats)
5.	穿		chuān	v	to wear
6.	中号	中號	zhōnghào	adj	medium size
	中		zhōng	adj	middle
	号	號	hào	n	size
7.	或者		huòzhě	cj	or
8.	小		xiǎo	adj	small; little
9.	漂亮		piàoliang	adj	pretty, beautiful
10.	看起来	看起來	kànqilai	ie	it appears, it seems
11.	比		bǐ	prep	compared to
12.	更		gèng	adv	even more
13.	红色	紅色	hóngsè	n	red
14.	又…又…		yòu…yòu…	adv	both . . . and . . .
15.	一样	一樣	yíyàng	adj	same
16.	配		pèi	v, adj	to match, suit

REQUIRED VOCABULARY 9.1

SIMPLIFIED	TRADITIONAL	PINYIN	WORD CATEGORY	DEFINITION
WORDS RELATED TO CLOTHING				
17. 双	雙	shuāng	*adj, mw*	double, two; a pair
18. 鞋(子)		xié (zi)	*n*	shoes
19. 袜子	襪子	wàzi	*n*	socks
20. 戴		dài	*v*	to wear (for glasses and hats)
21. 帽子		màozi	*n*	hat
22. 眼镜	眼鏡	yǎnjìng	*n*	glasses
23. 墨镜	墨鏡	mòjìng	*n*	sunglasses

OPTIONAL VOCABULARY 9.1

SIMPLIFIED	TRADITIONAL	PINYIN	WORD CATEGORY	DEFINITION
WORDS RELATED TO CLOTHING				
24. 顶	頂	dǐng	*mw*	(used for hats)
25. 外套		wàitào	*n*	coat, jacket
26. 大衣		dàyī	*n*	overcoat
27. 西装	西裝	xīzhuāng	*n*	suit
28. T-恤衫		T-xùshān	*n*	T-shirt

 ONLINE RESOURCES

Visit *http://college.betterchinese.com* for a list of other words related to clothing.

Review of Adjectives

In this lesson, adjectives are used to compare the qualities of two things. The following are some useful comparative adjectives which have appeared in the lessons so far.

好	hǎo	good
差	chà	poor
大	dà	big; old
小	xiǎo	small; young
贵	guì	expensive
便宜	piányi	cheap; inexpensive
漂亮	piàoliang	pretty
有意思	yǒu yìsi	interesting
难	nán	difficult
容易	róngyi	easy
近	jìn	close
远	yuǎn	far
好玩（儿）	hǎowán(r)	fun
简单	jiǎndān	simple
辣	là	spicy
好吃	hǎo chī	tasty

Remember that when an adjective is used in its regular form to describe something, it is generally presented with a modifier such as 很, as in:

他做的菜很辣。   The food he made is spicy.
Tā zuò de cài hěn là.

However, when adjectives are used in comparisons, they must appear either by themselves or with special modifying phrases used for comparisons:

他做的菜比你做的辣。   The food he made is spicier than the food you made.
Tā zuò de cài bǐ nǐ zuò de là.

他做的菜比你做的辣一点。   The food he made is a bit spicier than the food you made.
Tā zuò de cài bǐ nǐ zuò de là yì diǎn.

STRUCTURE NOTE 9.1
Use 或者 *to express choices and options*

In Structure Notes 6.14 and 8.12, 还是 *was introduced as a way to ask either-or questions. However, this pattern cannot be used as an equivalent for "or" in other types of sentences. To express "or" in a statement as opposed to a question, one must use* 或者 *(huòzhě).*

> Subject + Option A + 或者 + Option B

> Subject + Option A + 、+ Option B + , + 或者 + Option C

From the Lesson Text:

你应该穿中号的或者小号的。
Nǐ yīnggāi chuān zhōnghào de huòzhě xiǎohào de.
You should be wearing a medium or a small.

Other examples:

我想去法国或者德国。
Wǒ xiǎng qù Fǎguó huòzhě Déguó.
I want to go to France or Germany.

你可以买毛衣、衬衫，或者裙子。
Nǐ kěyǐ mǎi máoyī, chènshān, huòzhě qúnzi.
You can buy a sweater, a shirt, or a skirt.

Practice: Create complete sentences with 或者 using the information provided below.

Example: 他 / 想 / 学 / 汉语 / 法语 → 他想学汉语或者法语。

1. 我 / 想 / 喝 / 茶 / 咖啡

   _____

2. 明天下午 / 我 / 想 / 去 / 健身房 / 图书馆

   _____

3. 今年 / 孙玛丽 / 打算 / 去 / 中国 / 加拿大

   _____

4. 我 / 要 / 去商店 / 买 / 毛衣 / 衬衫 / 鞋子

   _____

5. 我的书 / 可能 / 在桌子上 / 在沙发上

   _____

STRUCTURE NOTE 9.2
Use 看/听 + 起来 *to express a subjective impression*

To express that something seems to be a particular way, the phrases 看起来 *(kànqilai: "looks") and* 听起来 *(tīngqilai: "sounds") can be used.*

> Subject + 看/听 + 起来 + Adjective Phrase

From the Lesson Text:

我觉得这件看起来比那件更大！
Wǒ juéde zhèi jiàn kànqilai bǐ nèi jiàn gèng dà!
I think this one looks even bigger than that one!

Other examples:

那本书听起来很有意思。
Nèi běn shū tīngqilai hěn yǒu yìsi.
That book sounds very interesting.

他做的菜看起来不太好吃。
Tā zuò de cài kànqilai bú tài hǎo chī.
The food he made doesn't look very tasty.

NOTE: *Normally, the characters* 起来 *carry the tones qǐ and lái and mean "to rise" and "to come," respectively. When certain phrases like* 起来 *become part of fixed grammatical patterns, they lose their original meaning and are pronounced with unstressed neutral tones.*

Practice: Transform the sentences below into Chinese using 看起来 or 听起来.

Example: That bowl of Hot and Sour Soup looks very spicy.
→ 那碗酸辣汤看起来很辣。

1.   The grammar in lesson fourteen looks very easy.

_____

2.   The sweater that you talked about sounds very expensive.

_____

3.   That pair of black socks looks very big.

_____

4.   Beijing sounds like a lot of fun!

_____

5.   That new book that he has written looks interesting.

_____

STRUCTURE NOTE 9.3
Use 比 *to make comparisons*

To express a comparison between two things that are of an unequal value, Chinese uses the character 比 *(bǐ: "compared to"). In this pattern,* 比 *connects an item A that has more of some quality than item B, meaning "A is more (adjective) than B." To say "A is not more (adjective) than B," simply add* 不 *before* 比.

> A + 比 + B + Adjective

> A + 不 + 比 + B + Adjective

From the Lesson Text:
我觉得这件看起来比那件更大！
Wǒ juéde zhèi jiàn kànqilai bǐ nèi jiàn gèng dà!
I think this one looks even bigger than that one!

Other examples:

我不比他大。
Wǒ bù bǐ tā dà.
I am not older than him. (i.e., I am as old as or younger than him)

这本书比那本书有意思。
Zhèi běn shū bǐ nèi běn shū yǒu yìsi.
This book is more interesting than that book.

NOTE: *In a comparative sentence, the adjective appears either on its own or with certain special modifiers (see Structure Notes 9.4 and 9.5).* 很 *or other standard intensifiers may not be used with adjectives in a* 比 *sentence. As illustrated in the examples, optional modifying phrases such as* 看起来 *are located before* 比.

To express the idea "A is not as (adjective) as B," use 没有 *(那么).*

> A + 没有 + B (+ 那么) + Adjective

Examples:

我没有他大。
Wǒ méiyǒu tā dà.
I am not as old as him.

这件毛衣没有那件那么贵。
Zhèi jiàn máoyī méiyǒu nèi jiàn nàme guì.
This sweater is not as expensive as that one.

Practice: Use 比, 不比, or 没有(那么) and the information provided below to create comparative sentences.

Example: 李中平/陈大东/大 → 李中平比陈大东大。

1. 音乐会/生日派对/好玩儿 _____
2. 生词/语法/难 _____
3. 烤鸭/烧鸡/好吃 _____
4. 袜子/鞋子/便宜 _____
5. 中文/英文/有意思 _____

STRUCTURE NOTE 9.4

Use 更 to say "even more"

更 (gèng) is an adverb that modifies comparative adjectives. It is used to express that something is even more (adjective) than something else.

> Subject + 更 + Adjective

From the Lesson Text:

我觉得这件看起来比那件更大！
Wǒ juéde zhèi jiàn kànqilai bǐ nèi jiàn gèng dà!
I think this one looks even bigger than that one!

Other examples:

那只狗很小，可是这只狗更小。
Nèi zhī gǒu hěn xiǎo, kěshì zhèi zhī gǒu gèng xiǎo.
That dog is small, but this dog is even smaller.

我想找一本更有意思的书。
Wǒ xiǎng zhǎo yì běn gèng yǒu yìsi de shū.
I want to find an even more interesting book.

Practice: Turn the following statements into comparative sentences using 比 and 更, following the example provided.

Example: 茶很好喝。（咖啡）
→ 茶很好喝，可是咖啡比茶更好喝。

1. 这件衬衫很贵。（那件衬衫）

   _____

2. 我的汉语很好。（英语）

   _____

3. 波士顿很大。（北京）

   _____

4. 这杯茶很苦。（那杯茶）

   _____

5. 学校离我家很远。（博物馆）

   _____

STRUCTURE NOTE 9.5

Use （一）点（儿）to describe small differences

When describing to what extent two things are different in a comparative sentence, special modifying phrases are added after the adjective. This lesson features the modifying phrase （一）点（儿）, which is used to express "A is a little more (adjective) than B."

> A + 比 + B + Adjective Phrase + （一）点（儿）

From the Lesson Text:　可是这件比那件便宜一点儿。
Kěshì zhèi jiàn bǐ nèi jiàn piányi yì diǎnr.
But this one is a bit cheaper than that one.

Other examples:

我比他小点儿。
Wǒ bǐ tā xiǎo diǎnr.
I am a bit younger than he is.

他写的字比我写的好一点儿。
Tā xiě de zì bǐ wǒ xiě de hǎo yì diǎnr.
The character he wrote was a bit better than the one I wrote.

Practice: Using the information given below, create comparative sentences with（一）点（儿）.

Example: 烧鸡 / 烤鸭 / 好吃 → 烧鸡比烤鸭好吃一点。

1. 第九课 / 第八课 / 容易　　　＿＿＿＿＿＿＿＿＿＿
2. 毛衣 / 衬衫 / 贵　　　　　　＿＿＿＿＿＿＿＿＿＿
3. 这条裙子 / 那条裙子 / 漂亮　＿＿＿＿＿＿＿＿＿＿
4. 饭馆 / 商店 / 近　　　　　　＿＿＿＿＿＿＿＿＿＿
5. 哥哥 / 弟弟 / 大　　　　　　＿＿＿＿＿＿＿＿＿＿

STRUCTURE NOTE 9.6
Use 又···又··· *to express "both . . . and . . ."*

In Chinese, 和 *is generally used to join two nouns. To join related adjectives, the pattern* 又···又··· *(yòu… yòu…) can be used to express "both (adjective) and (adjective)."*

> Subject + 又 + Adjective + 又 + Adjective

From the Lesson Text:　这件红色的毛衣有中号的，又漂亮又便宜。
Zhèi jiàn hóngsè de máoyī yǒu zhōnghào de, yòu piàoliang yòu piányi.
There's a medium in this red sweater; it's pretty and inexpensive too.

Other Examples:

她的房间看起来又大又漂亮。
Tā de fángjiān kànqilai yòu dà yòu piàoliang.
It looks like her room is large and also pretty.

我今天买的饺子又便宜又好吃。
Wǒ jīntiān mǎi de jiǎozi yòu piányi yòu hǎo chī.
The dunmplings I bought today was inexpensive and also delicious.

Practice: Construct sentences in Chinese using 又…又… and the information provided below.

    Example: This cake is both sweet and delicious. → 这个蛋糕又甜又好吃。

1. After he finished class, he was both tired and hungry.

    _____

2. The restaurant on campus is inexpensive and delicious.

    _____

3. This Hot and Sour Soup is spicy and delicious.

    _____

4. Her cellphone looks new and expensive.

    _____

5. Let's go eat. I'm hungry and thirsty!

    _____

STRUCTURE NOTE 9.7

Use …跟…一样 *(adjective) to express sameness*

So far, this lesson has described a range of patterns that cover comparisons. The final pattern in this group is that which expresses sameness, or in other words, "A is as (adjective) as B." To create such a sentence, take the phrase "A is the same as B" (A 跟 B 一样) and add an an adjective to the end.

A + 跟 + B + 一样 + Adjective

From the Lesson Text:

这条裙子跟那件毛衣一样便宜。
Zhèi tiáo qúnzi gēn nèi jiàn máoyī yíyàng piányi.
This skirt is just as cheap as that sweater.

Other examples:

我跟他一样大。
Wǒ gēn tā yíyàng dà.
I am the same age as he is.

你觉得你们的老师跟我们的一样好吗？
Nǐ juéde nǐmen de lǎoshī gēn wǒmen de yíyàng hǎo ma?
Do you think your teacher is as good as ours?

Practice: Using the lists below, match the noun pairs with an appropriate adjective to form whole sentences.

这个墨镜跟这个眼镜		难	Example: 烧鸡跟烤鸭一样好吃。
烧鸡跟烤鸭		便宜	_____
玛丽跟安娜		有意思	_____
这本书跟那本书	一样	好吃	_____
中文跟英文		漂亮	_____
那家饭馆跟那家餐厅		大	_____

PRACTICE 9.1

You go shopping for clothes with your friend. Write the name of the product below the picture and choose which items you want to buy. Ask your friend what he or she wants to buy.

Example:

A: 你今天想买什么？

B: 我想买毛衣和衬衫。你呢？

PRACTICE 9.2

You and your friend try on some clothes at a department store. Describe each item and comment on each other's clothes. Tell your friend which items you would like to buy and give the reason why. Talk about each of your preferences in terms of size, color, and price. Use the vocabulary you have learned, including the words and patterns provided in the box below.

Example:

A: 这件毛衣很漂亮，你觉得呢？

B: 我觉得这件看起来比那件更大！

看起来　不错　很配　又…又…　应该　或者　比　更

	Radical	Stroke Order
比	比 bǐ compare	一　　ﾋ　　ﾋ　　比
号	口 kǒu mouth	丶　　口　　口　　吕　　号
样	木 mù wood	一　十　才　木　术　栏　栏　栏　栏　样
衣	衣 yī clothing	丶　二　广　衣　衣　衣
毛	毛 máo fur	ノ　二　三　毛
条	夂 zhǐ follow	ノ　夕　夂　冬　条　条　条
穿	穴 xué cave	丶　八　宀　宀　空　空　穿　穿
件	亻(人) rén person	ノ　亻　亻　仁　件　件
漂	氵(水) shuǐ water	丶　氵　氵　沪　沪　沪　泗　泗　泗　洒　漂　漂　漂
亮	亠 tóu lid	丶　二　广　亩　亩　亩　亭　亮
更	一 yī one	一　厂　戸　百　百　更　更
红	纟(丝) sī silk	乚　纟　纟　纟　红　红
色	色 sè color	ノ　夕　夕　名　负　色
配	酉 yǒu wine vessel	一　厂　厅　丙　西　酉　酉　酌　配
又	又 yòu again	フ　又

PRACTICE 9.4

Make an audio recording and send it to your teacher. Discuss what you would wear if you were going to a formal party. Talk about what accessories and colors you would wear to make your outfit match.

PRACTICE 9.5

Type the following sentences on your computer.

1. 这件毛衣比那件便宜一点儿。
2. 你应该穿中号的或者小号的。
3. 我觉得这条裙子看起来比那条更漂亮。
4. 这件衬衫跟那条裙子很配。
5. 欢迎光临！

PRACTICE 9.6

Write the size of each sweater on the tag and create sentences to describe them.

Example:

这件红色的毛衣是中号的。

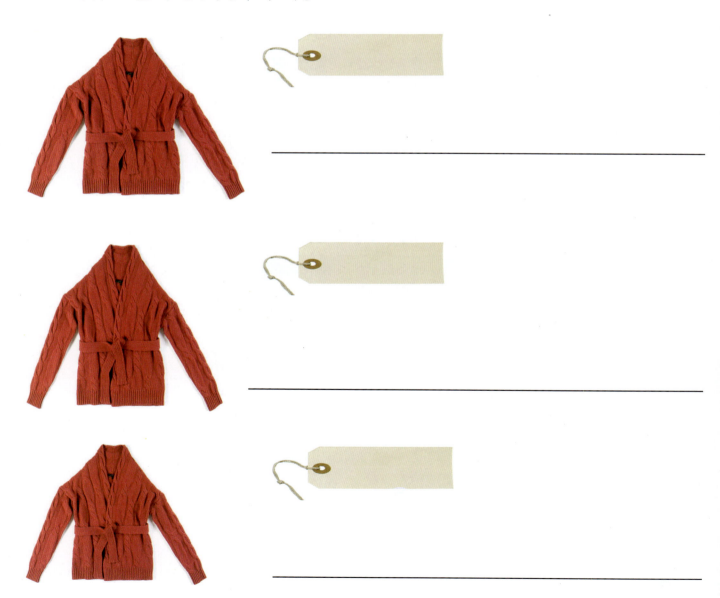

PRACTICE 9.7

我和安娜今天去百货公司。我想买一件红色的毛衣，可是红色的太大了。我问售货员有没有小号的，售货员说没有了，小号的红色毛衣都卖完了。安娜买了一条裙子，又漂亮又便宜。

Read Sun Mali's diary and answer the following questions.
1. Why couldn't Sun Mali buy the sweater?
2. What did Zhang Anna buy?

PRACTICE 9.8

售货员：欢迎光临！

李中平：我想买一件衬衫。

售货员：是你自己穿吗？

李中平：对，有中号或小号的吗？

售货员：有，这件衬衫是中号的。

李中平：哦！看起来不错！请问多少钱？

售货员：十六块九毛九。

Read the dialogue and answer the following questions.
1. What does Li Zhongping want to buy?
2. Which size does the salesperson show Li Zhongping?

PRACTICE 9.9

| Sender | 玛丽 |
| Subject | 买衣服 |

小美：

我听大东说中国的衣服比美国的便宜，你这次去中国可不可以帮我去商店买衣服？我要一件小号的红色毛衣，还有一件小号的衬衫，我还要一条大号的裙子，价钱不要太贵。你回来以后我会把钱给你。谢谢！

Read Sun Mali's e-mail and answer the following questions.
1. What color does Sun Mali want for her sweater?
2. What size does she want for her skirt?

Color Symbolism in Chinese

Red

The most prominent color in Chinese culture is red. Red represents celebration, good luck, and happiness. Traditionally, brides wore red clothing and veils for marriage ceremonies. Many still do, although it has also become popular to wear Western-style white dresses. Wedding ceremonies also involve the presentation of 红包 (hóngbāo: "red envelope"), a small packet filled with money. The positive associations with the color red have led to the meaning of the word 红 itself expanding to include success, popularity, and happiness.

White

In the West, black is typically identified as the color of funerals and mourning. In China, one conversely finds white objects and attire at funerals, as this color is associated with concepts such as pureness and immortality. Consequently, one should never send white flowers to a Chinese person unless mourning a loss.

Yellow

Tradition has it that Chinese civilization began in the Yellow River basin. The Yellow River, China's second longest river, is thought to have nurtured Chinese culture from the very beginning. The color also lent itself to the title of the Yellow Emperor, the legendary ruler of Chinese mythology who is said to be the ancestor of the Han race. From that period onward, many dynasties reserved yellow for the imperial house and forbade common people from using it.

Blue-Green

Blue and green are typically associated with nature, prosperity, and harmony. The usage of blue can symbolize immortality, with dark blue frequently used on somber occasions like funerals. A man should also take care to never wear a green hat or to present a man with a green hat as a gift because the Chinese expression 戴绿帽子 (dài lǜ màozi: "to wear a green hat") means that a man has been fooled.

售货员：	欢迎光临！	Welcome!
王小美：	你想买什么衣服？	What clothes do you want to buy?
孙玛丽：	我想买毛衣和衬衫，还想买裙子。走，我们先去看毛衣。	I want to buy a sweater, a shirt, and a skirt. Come on, let's go look at sweaters first.
张安娜：	这件毛衣太大了，你应该穿中号的或者小号的。	This sweater is too big. You should be wearing a medium or a small.
孙玛丽：	这件很漂亮，你觉得呢？	This one is very pretty. What do you think?
张安娜：	我觉得这件看起来比那件更大！	I think this one looks even bigger than that one!
孙玛丽：	可是这件比那件便宜一点儿。	But this one is a bit cheaper than that one.
张安娜：	你看，这件红色的毛衣有中号的，又漂亮又便宜。	Look, this red sweater is a medium; it's pretty and cheap too.
孙玛丽：	不错啊！裙子呢？	Not bad! What about the skirt?
张安娜：	这条裙子跟那件毛衣一样便宜，也很配。你买这条吧！	This skirt is as cheap as that sweater and they match as well. You should buy this one!

What Can You Do?

Interpretive
- I can distinguish between different articles of clothing and their appearances.
- I can understand comparisons and expressions of sameness.

Interpersonal
- I can compare clothing sizes with others.
- I can discuss the relative merits of different items.

Presentational
- I can give a presentation of clothing which includes sizes, personal preferences, and specific comparisons.

你喜欢什么颜色?
What Colors do You Like?

嗨，祥安，
进来吧！

我看，你应该
买新裤子了。

不用，这条还
好好的。我很喜欢
这条长裤——

安娜，我先走了，祥安
需要帮忙，帮他找一找吧！

没问题！祥安，
你喜欢什么颜色?

我最喜欢蓝色。黑色，灰色或者黄色也可以。

明白了。

这条黑色的牛仔裤怎么样？大小合适吗？试试看！

这条有一点儿短……

不短！我觉得很合适，你看起来真的好酷。

是吗？好！就买这条。

LESSON TEXT 9.2

What Colors Do You Like?　你喜欢什么颜色？

Sun Mali and Zhang Anna see Huang Xiang'an in a clothing store. Sun Mali enlists Zhang Anna's help to find a new pair of jeans for Huang Xiang'an, despite his reluctance.

孙玛丽：	嗨，祥安，进来吧！我看，你应该买新裤子了。	Hēi, Xiáng'ān, jìnlai ba! Wǒ kàn, nǐ yīnggāi mǎi xīn kùzi le.
黄祥安：	不用，这条还好好的。我很喜欢这条长裤 ——	Búyòng, zhèi tiáo hái hǎohāo de. Wǒ hěn xǐhuan zhèi tiáo chángkù —
孙玛丽：	安娜，我先走了，祥安需要帮忙，帮他找一找吧！	Ānnà, wǒ xiān zǒu le, Xiáng'ān xūyào bāngmáng, bāng tā zhǎo yi zhǎo ba!
张安娜：	没问题！祥安，你喜欢什么颜色？	Méi wèntí! Xiáng'ān, nǐ xǐhuan shénme yánsè?

___

黄祥安：	我最喜欢蓝色。黑色、灰色或者黄色也可以。	Wǒ zuì xǐhuan lánsè. Hēisè, huīsè huòzhě huángsè yě kěyǐ.
张安娜：	明白了。这条黑色的牛仔裤怎么样？大小合适吗？试试看！	Míngbai le. Zhèi tiáo hēisè de niúzǎikù zěnmeyàng? Dàxiǎo héshì ma? Shìshi kàn!
黄祥安：	这条有一点儿短……	Zhèi tiáo yǒu yì diǎnr duǎn……
张安娜：	不短！我觉得很合适，你看起来真的好酷。	Bù duǎn! Wǒ juéde hěn héshì, nǐ kànqilai zhēnde hǎo kù.
黄祥安：	是吗？好！就买这条。	Shì ma? Hǎo! Jiù mǎi zhèi tiáo.

字 词 VOCABULARY

LESSON VOCABULARY 9.2

	SIMPLIFIED	TRADITIONAL	PINYIN	WORD CATEGORY	DEFINITION
1.	嗨		hēi	*ie*	hi
2.	进来	進來	jìnlai	*dc*	to come in
3.	裤子	褲子	kùzi	*n*	pants, trousers
4.	长裤	長褲	chángkù	*n*	pants, trousers (lit. "long pants")
5.	需要		xūyào	*v*	to need; to want
6.	帮忙	幫忙	bāngmáng	*vo*	to help
7.	颜色	顏色	yánsè	*n*	color
8.	最		zuì	*adv*	most (used to describe superlative degree)
9.	蓝色	藍色	lánsè	*n*	blue
10.	黑色		hēisè	*n*	black
11.	灰色		huīsè	*n*	gray
12.	黄色		huángsè	*n*	yellow
13.	明白		míngbai	*v*	to understand
14.	牛仔裤	牛仔褲	niúzǎikù	*n*	jeans (lit. "cowboy pants")
15.	大小		dàxiǎo	*n*	size
16.	合适	合適	héshì	*adj*	suitable
17.	看		kàn	*v*	(after a reduplicated verb) try and see, do something and see
18.	短		duǎn	*adj*	short
19.	真的		zhēnde	*adv, ie*	really
20.	酷		kù	*adj*	cool

REQUIRED VOCABULARY 9.2

	SIMPLIFIED	TRADITIONAL	PINYIN	WORD CATEGORY	DEFINITION
COLORS					
21.	白色		báisè	n	white
22.	绿色	綠色	lǜsè	n	green

OPTIONAL VOCABULARY 9.2

	SIMPLIFIED	TRADITIONAL	PINYIN	WORD CATEGORY	DEFINITION
COLORS					
23.	紫色		zǐsè	n	purple
24.	橙色		chéngsè	n	orange
25.	咖啡色		kāfēisè	n	coffee color; brown

ONLINE RESOURCES
Visit *http://college.betterchinese.com* for a list of other words related to clothing.

Clothing Terms

帽子*
màozi

大衣
dàyī

裙子
qúnzi

眼镜*
yǎnjìng

西装
xīzhuāng

牛仔裤
niúzǎikù

衬衫
chènshān

T-恤衫
T-xùshān

袜子
wàzi

毛衣
máoyī

裤子
kùzi

鞋子
xiézi

外套
wàitào

Colors

红色
hóngsè

橙色
chéngsè

黄色
huángsè

绿色
lǜsè

蓝色
lánsè

紫色
zǐsè

黑色
hēisè

白色
báisè

咖啡色
kāfēisè

灰色
huīsè

Measure Words

Chinese	Pinyin	Used For
条	tiáo	裤子、裙子、牛仔裤
双	shuāng	鞋子、袜子
顶	dǐng	帽子
件	jiàn	衬衫、毛衣、外套、大衣、T-恤衫
套	tào	西装
副	fù	眼镜

* To talk about wearing hats and glasses, use the verb 戴 rather than 穿

STRUCTURE NOTE 9.8

Use Verb 一 Verb to describe casual or brief activities

When making suggestions or requests in Chinese, it is polite to soften the verb in order to suggest that the activity will be brief or casual. One way to do this is by inserting 一 between a repeated single-character verb. When the verb is part of a verb-object pair, the object is placed after the second verb.

> Subject + Verb + 一 + Verb (+ Object)

From the Lesson Text:
帮他找一找吧！
Bāng tā zhǎo yi zhǎo ba!
Why don't you help him look for a bit.

Other examples:
你试一试吧。
Nǐ shì yi shì ba.
Why don't you give it a try.

你看一看这件毛衣。
Nǐ kàn yi kàn zhèi jiàn máoyī.
Take a look at this sweater.

Practice: Use the Verb 一 Verb construction to soften the tone of the sentences below, following the example given.

Example: 你去跟朋友说。→ 你去跟朋友说一说吧。

1. 请看这本书。

   _____

2. 你进来坐吧。

   _____

3. 我想试这双鞋。

   _____

4. 我找不到钱包，你可以帮我找吗？

   _____

5. 有事吗？你跟我说。

   _____

STRUCTURE NOTE 9.9

Use 最 to express superlatives

最 (zùi) *means "the most" or "-est" and can be placed before adjectives or certain verbs that can be expressed with different degrees such as* 想, 喜欢, 要, 需要, *etc., to form superlatives.*

> Subject + 最 + Adjective / Verb Phrase

From the Lesson Text:	我最喜欢蓝色。
	Wǒ zuì xǐhuan lánsè.
	I like blue the most.

Other examples:

我最喜欢蓝色。

哪件毛衣最便宜？
Něi jiàn máoyī zuì piányi?
Which of these sweaters is the
cheapest?

我最想去的地方就是北京。
Wǒ zuì xiǎng qù de dìfang jiù shì Běijīng.
The place that I want to go to the most is
Beijing.

Practice: Express the following statements in Chinese using 最.

Example: I like dumplings the most. → 我最喜欢吃饺子。

1.   Yellow is my favorite color.

_____

2.   This airport is the biggest one in China.

_____

3.   I want to take literature classes the most.

_____

4.   This is her favorite skirt.

_____

5.   This is the cheapest cellphone.

_____

STRUCTURE NOTE 9.10
Use reduplication to intensify adjectives or adverbs

When an adjective is reduplicated, a more intense or emphatic effect is created. Monosyllabic adjectives are simply repeated, so 好, *for example, becomes* 好好. *With disyllabic adjectives, the characters are doubled in an AABB pattern, so* 漂亮 *becomes* 漂漂亮亮. *Reduplicated adjectives have special tone patterns. If a single-character adjective is reduplicated, the second character generally switches to a first tone, as in* 好好 *(hǎohāo). Two-character adjectives with neutral tones, like* 漂亮 *(piàoliang), have their tones reinstated, as in* 漂漂亮亮 *(piàopiàoliàngliàng). Intensifiers such as* 很 *are not used when the adjective is reduplicated. Be aware that not all adjectives can be reduplicated.*

Character A + Character A (+ Character B + Character B)

From the Lesson Text:	这条还好好的。
	Zhèi tiáo hái hǎohāo de.
	This pair is still good.

Other examples:

我想买一条短短的裙子。
Wǒ xiǎng mǎi yì tiáo duǎnduǎn de qúnzi.
I want to buy a short skirt.

大家正在考试，教室里安安静静的。
Dàjiā zhèngzài kǎoshì, jiàoshì lǐ ān'ān-jìngjìng de.
Everyone is currently taking a test; the classroom is very quiet.

Practice: Complete the sentences below by adding the reduplicated form of the adjective in parentheses into the spaces provided.

Example:　你穿这件衬衫看起来（　　　　）。（酷）

→ 你穿这件衬衫看起来酷酷的。

1.　他做了几个（　　　　）的菜，但是都很好吃。（简单）
2.　她家的猫（　　　　），很可爱。（小）
3.　今天的酸辣汤（　　　　），很好喝。（酸，辣）
4.　这个蛋糕（　　　　），很好吃。（甜）
5.　现在大家都喜欢穿（　　　　）的牛仔裤。（短）

STRUCTURE NOTE 9.11
Use Verb reduplication to describe casual or brief activities

In Structure Note 9.8, the pattern Verb + 一 *+ Verb was introduced as a way of describing casual or brief activities. An even more common way to express this same meaning is to reduplicate the verb. This pattern can also be used when making suggestions or requests. Unlike two-character adjective reduplication, where an AABB sequence is used, reduplicated verbs follow an ABAB structure, so* 练习 *is reduplicated as* 练习练习. *Be careful to only use this ABAB pattern for true two-character verbs. For verb-object compounds, repeat the verb only, as in* 看看书.

> Subject + Verb + Verb (+ Object)

From the Lesson Text:　试试看！
Shìshi kàn!
Go try them on!

Other examples:

跟我一起练习练习吧。
Gēn wǒ yìqǐ liànxi liànxi ba.
Why don't you practice a bit with me.

睡觉前我喜欢看看书。
Shuìjiào qián wǒ xǐhuan kànkan shū.
Before sleeping, I like to do a bit of reading.

Practice: Use the information given below to create sentences containing reduplicated verbs, following the example provided.

Example:　用筷子 / 简单 / 试 → 用筷子很简单，你来试试吧！
1.　今天的作业 / 难 / 帮忙 _____
2.　明天 / 小考 / 准备 _____
3.　今晚 / 听 / 音乐 _____
4.　跟 / 朋友 / 说话 _____
5.　进来 / 坐 / 吧 _____

STRUCTURE NOTE 9.12
Use 看 to mean "and see"

The verb 看 can be added after a reduplicated verb to add the meaning ". . . and see (how it is)." Essentially, this pattern means to see or find out by means of the preceding verb.

Subject + Reduplicated Verb + 看 (+ Object)

From the Lesson Text:

试试看！
Shìshi kàn!
Go try them on!

Other Examples:

请帮我找找看。
Qǐng bāng wǒ zhǎozhǎo kàn.
Please help me look around and see.

老师想听听看我的中文怎么样。
Lǎoshī xiǎng tīngtīng kàn wǒ de Zhōngwén zěnmeyàng.
The teacher wants to hear how I speak Chinese.

Practice: Answer the following questions in Chinese using reduplicated verbs and 看, in the manner of the example provided.

Example:　我的手机在哪里呢？（找）→ 不知道，我帮你找找看。

1.　这家饭馆怎么样？（试）

_____

2.　第九课的录音容易懂吗？（听）

_____

3.　你觉得那条裤子会太短吗？（试）

_____

4.　这张沙发怎么样？（坐）

_____

5.　你觉得这件毛衣好不好看？（穿）

_____

STRUCTURE NOTE 9.13
Use 有(一)点(儿) to express "somewhat"

In Unit 2, Lesson 2, （一）点（儿）*was used before an object as a way to describe "a bit of something," as in* 喝一点咖啡, *"drink a bit of coffee." In this pattern,* 有（一）点（儿）*is placed before adjectives or verbs such as* 想 *and* 喜欢 *to mean "a little" or "somewhat."*

```
Subject + 有（一）点（儿）+ Adjective / Verb Phrase
```

From the Lesson Text:
这条有一点儿短••••••
Zhèi tiáo yǒu yì diǎnr duǎn......
This pair is a little short . . .

Other examples:
我觉得他有点喜欢我。   我的卧室有点儿小。
Wǒ juéde tā yǒu diǎn xǐhuan wǒ.   Wǒ de wòshì yǒu diǎnr xiǎo.
I think he likes me a little.   My bedroom is kind of small.

NOTE: *In Structure Note 9.5,* （一）点（儿）*was placed after the adjective to describe the degree to which something was different from something else, as in* 我比他大一点. *When this phrase is placed after an adjective, it has a comparative meaning of "a bit more." In this pattern,* 有（一）点（儿）*is placed before the adjective and does not have a comparative meaning.*

Practice: Respond to the following questions using 有（一）点（儿）and the words provided in parentheses.

Example: 波士顿好玩吗？（小）→ 很好玩，可是有点小。

1.   你昨天买的茶好喝吗？（贵）

_____

2.   她怎么在图书馆里睡觉呢？（累）

_____

3.   那条黑色的牛仔裤怎么样？（大）

_____

4.   你昨天晚上为什么没有去她家？（远）

_____

5.   这个学期你选的课难吗？（难）

_____

STRUCTURE NOTE 9.14
Use 好 as an intensifier

好 can be interchangeable with 很 as an intensifier meaning "very." Different Chinese-speaking regions use 好 and 很 with different frequencies, and certain expressions are conventionally said using either one or the other. In general, 好 is a more casual intensifier than 很.

好 + Adjective / Verb

From the Lesson Text:

你看起来真的好酷。
nǐ kànqilai zhēnde hǎo kù.
You look really cool.

Other examples:

我好喜欢他。
Wǒ hǎo xǐhuan tā.
I like him a lot.

你的女朋友好漂亮啊！
Nǐ de nǚ péngyou hǎo piàoliang a!
Your girlfriend is very pretty!

Practice: Turn the following sentences into Chinese using 好 as an intensifier.

Example: He really likes listening to music. → 他好喜欢听音乐。

1. Yesterday's homework was really easy.

   _____

2. I was very tired after I finished class yesterday.

   _____

3. The stationery in this shop is so cheap.

   _____

4. These noodles are really salty; I don't want to eat anymore.

   _____

5. These medium-size pants are really short.

   _____

PRACTICE 9.10

Look around the classroom at the clothes your classmates are wearing. Identify as many of the different articles of clothing and their colors as you can.

Example: 陈大东今天穿红色的毛衣、黑色的裤子跟灰色的鞋子。

PRACTICE 9.11

You and your friends are reading a fashion magazine. Comment on the pictures you see below (e.g., price, color, size, length).

Example:

A: 你觉得这件怎么样?

B: 我觉得太短了。

PRACTICE 9.12

With a partner, practice words for colors by discussing which pairs of glasses below you would and would not want to buy. Take turns to ask each other about each pair.

Example:

A: 你想买绿色的眼镜吗？

B: 我想买绿色的眼镜。/ 我不想买绿色的眼镜。

PRACTICE 9.13

Conduct a survey to determine what color is the most popular among your classmates. Record your findings below.

Color	Number of Students

PRACTICE 9.14

Type the following sentences on your computer and provide answers to the questions.

1. 你想买什么颜色的裤子？
2. 你觉得这条灰色的牛仔裤怎么样？
3. 他穿那条牛仔裤看起来很酷！
4. 我想试试看这件中号的裙子。
5. 我觉得这件黄色的衬衫大小很合适。

PRACTICE 9.15

Make an audio recording and send it to your teacher. In the recording, talk about your favorite clothes and colors. On what occasion would you wear the kind of outfit you are describing?

	Radical	Stroke Order
帮	巾 jīn cloth	一 二 三 丰 丰ﾞ 邦 帮 帮
忙	忄 (心) xīn heart	丶 八 忄 忙 忙 忙
进	辶 chuò walk	一 二 丰 井 ㄧ井 讲 进
需	雨 yǔ rain	一 厂 广 丙 雨 雨 雪 雪 雪 雪 雪 需 需 需
颜	页 yè page	丶 丷 亠 立 产 产 彦 彦 彦 彦 彦 颜 颜 颜
最	日 yuē say	丶 口 曰 日 旦 旦 旦 旦 旦 最 最 最
蓝	艹 (草) cǎo grass	一 ꩖ 艹 ꭗ 艹 莎 莎 蓝 蓝 蓝 蓝 蓝
黑	黑 hēi black	丶 口 ロ 四 四 甲 里 黑 黑 黑 黑
灰	火 huǒ fire	一 ナ 太 太 灰 灰
黄	黄 huáng yellow	一 十 ꭗ 共 苦 苦 苗 苗 黄 黄
或	戈 gē spear	一 一 戸 可 豆 或 或 或
者	耂 (老) lǎo old	一 十 土 尹 者 者 者
合	口 kǒu mouth	丿 人 ㅅ 今 合 合
适	辶 chuò walk	丿 二 千 舌 舌 舌 适 适
短	矢 shǐ arrow	丿 ㅗ 上 牛 矢 矢 矩 知 知 知 短 短

PRACTICE 9.17

Sender 小美	**Sender** 玛丽
Subject 颜色	**Subject** re: 颜色

玛丽：
昨天我在中国的一家商店买了一件小号的红色毛衣给你。可是我忘了你要什么颜色的衬衫和裙子。我看到了一件白色衬衫和一条灰色的裙子，你喜欢吗？

小美：
我喜欢绿色，我要一条绿色或者白色的裙子。可是我不要绿色或者白色的衬衫，我觉得黑色的衬衫会跟红色的毛衣比较配。

Read the e-mails and answer the following questions.
1. What color does Sun Mali want for her skirt?
2. What color does Sun Mali want for her shirt?

PRACTICE 9.18

售货员：先生，需要帮忙吗？
陈大东：是的，可以帮我找一件中号的衬衫吗？
售货员：没问题！这件黄色的怎么样？
陈大东：我觉得这件看起来有一点儿小。
售货员：这件蓝色的比黄色的大一点儿，你试试看吧。
陈大东：不错！好！我就要这件蓝色的衬衫。

Read the dialogue and answer the following questions.
1. What size shirt does Chen Dadong initially want to buy?
2. What is color of the shirt that he buys?

PRACTICE 9.19

我很喜欢我的蓝色裤子，可是因为玛丽说那条裤子看起来有一点儿短，所以我们就去商店看一看别的长裤。商店里有一条黑色的牛仔裤看起来很酷，跟我的T-恤衫很配。玛丽也说这条牛仔裤又好看又好配衣服，可是因为价钱太贵了，我没有买。

Read Li Zhongping's diary and answer the following questions.
1. Why did Li Zhongping decide to buy a new pair of pants?
2. Did he end up buying a new pair of pants? Why?

Chinese Fashion Trends

Like all fashions throughout the world, clothing trends in China have changed along with the times.

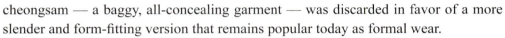

During the Qing Dynasty (1644 – 1912 AD), the Manchu elite demanded that all males adopt the 长衫 (chángshān: "long gown") and a long braid known in English as a queue. Han women also adopted the Manchu 旗袍 (qípáo: "cheongsam"), the female equivalent of the male robe, commonly known in English by the Cantonese term "cheongsam."

After the Qing Dynasty fell in 1912, Han men were ordered to sever their queues in order to symbolize a break with the past. Modernized men began to adopt a Western-style suit of jacket and trousers. For women, the old version of the cheongsam — a baggy, all-concealing garment — was discarded in favor of a more slender and form-fitting version that remains popular today as formal wear.

The rise of Communism saw yet another shift in China's fashions. The four-pocketed tunic worn by Mao Zedong, known in the West as the "Mao suit," became the standard for people all over the country, eventually becoming a sort of national uniform.

When China reopened its doors to the world in the 1980s, Western fashions became influential once again. The situation in modern-day China is now much like that in the West, with popular trends from Asia, along with domestic fashions, starting out in urban centers like Shanghai and spreading outwards.

Foot Binding

The practice of foot binding is one of the most well-known of imperial China's fashions. Tiny feet were considered beautiful on a woman, and thus a long process of shrinking a girl's feet was begun in infancy. A gruesome and excruciatingly painful procedure, foot binding entailed breaking the toes, curling them into the sole, and wrapping the feet in bandages until they were reduced to a miniature size.

By the Qing dynasty, foot binding had become widespread among all strata of society, but in the twentieth century it became a major political issue in the debates over China's modernization. Bound feet kept women at home and subservient to both men and their families, and so the practice became a magnet for criticism of misogyny in Chinese society. While the practice was formally banned under the Nationalist government, it was not until the foundation of the People's Republic that the policy was truly implemented and foot binding was made a thing of the past.

孙玛丽：	嗨，祥安，进来吧！我看，你应该买新裤子了。	Hi, Xiang'an, come in! It looks to me like you should buy a new pair of pants.
黄祥安：	不用，这条还好好的。我很喜欢这条长裤 ——	No need, this pair is still good. I like this pair of pants a lot —
孙玛丽：	安娜，我先走了，祥安需要帮忙，帮他找一找吧！	Anna, I have to leave. Xiang'an needs some help. Why don't you help him look around!
张安娜：	没问题！祥安，你喜欢什么颜色？	No problem. Xiang'an, what colors do you like?

黄祥安：	我最喜欢蓝色。黑色、灰色或者黄色也可以。	I like blue the most. Black, gray, or yellow are okay too.
张安娜：	明白了。这条黑色的牛仔裤怎么样？大小合适吗？试试看！	Got it. What do you think of this pair of black jeans? Does the size fit? Go try them on!
黄祥安：	这条有一点儿短……	This pair is a little short . . .
张安娜：	不短！我觉得很合适，你看起来真的好酷。	They're not short! I think they suit you well. You look really cool.
黄祥安：	是吗？好！就买这条。	Really? OK, then I'll buy this pair.

What Can You Do?

INTERPRETIVE
- I can understand a range of different colors.
- I can understand superlatives.

INTERPERSONAL
- I can use some basic colloquial loan words in conversation.
- I can complement someone on his or her appearance.

PRESENTATIONAL
- I can describe the colors of different items.
- I can present information about someone's appearance.

ACT IT OUT

Working in groups, compose an original three-minute skit that utilizes the vocabulary and structures introduced in Unit 9. Each of you should assume a role and have a roughly equal number of lines in the skit. Be prepared to perform your skit in class. You can either come up with your own story or choose from one of the following situations:

A) You and a friend are at the mall. You discuss what stores you plan to go to and what you plan to buy there.

B) You and a group of friends are casually discussing campus fashion, including what is currently popular among the students.

C) You are trying on different articles of clothing and ask a sales associate for her opinion regarding style, size, color, and other features.

CHECK WHAT YOU CAN DO

RECOGNIZE

Adjectives
- [ ] 中
- [ ] 小
- [ ] 漂亮
- [ ] 一样
- [ ] 双
- [ ] 合适
- [ ] 短
- [ ] 酷

Adverbs
- [ ] 更
- [ ] 又…又…
- [ ] 最

Conjunction
- [ ] 或者

Directional Complement
- [ ] 进来

Idiomatic Expressions
- [ ] 看起来
- [ ] 嗨
- [ ] 真的

Measure Word
- [ ] 件

Nouns
- [ ] 毛衣
- [ ] 衬衫
- [ ] 裙子
- [ ] 号
- [ ] 红色
- [ ] 鞋(子)
- [ ] 袜子
- [ ] 帽子
- [ ] 眼镜
- [ ] 墨镜
- [ ] 裤子
- [ ] 长裤

- [ ] 颜色
- [ ] 蓝色
- [ ] 黑色
- [ ] 灰色
- [ ] 黄色
- [ ] 牛仔裤
- [ ] 大小
- [ ] 白色
- [ ] 绿色

Preposition
- [ ] 比

Verbs
- [ ] 穿
- [ ] 配
- [ ] 戴
- [ ] 需要
- [ ] 帮忙
- [ ] 明白
- [ ] 看

WRITE
- [ ] 比
- [ ] 号
- [ ] 样
- [ ] 衣
- [ ] 毛
- [ ] 条
- [ ] 穿
- [ ] 件
- [ ] 漂亮
- [ ] 更
- [ ] 红色
- [ ] 配
- [ ] 又

- [ ] 帮忙
- [ ] 进
- [ ] 需
- [ ] 颜
- [ ] 最
- [ ] 蓝
- [ ] 黑
- [ ] 灰
- [ ] 黄
- [ ] 或者
- [ ] 合适
- [ ] 短

USE

- [ ] 或者 to express choices and options.
- [ ] 看/听 + 起来 to express a subjective impression.
- [ ] 比 to make comparisons.
- [ ] 更 to say "even more."
- [ ] (一)点(儿) to describe small differences.
- [ ] 又…又… to express "both . . . and . . ."
- [ ] …跟…一样 (adjective) to express sameness.

- [ ] Verb 一 Verb to describe casual or brief activities.
- [ ] 最 to express superlatives.
- [ ] Reduplication to intensify adjectives or adverbs.
- [ ] Verb reduplication to describe casual or brief activities.
- [ ] 看 to mean "and see."
- [ ] 有(一)点(儿) to express "somewhat."
- [ ] 好 as an intensifier.

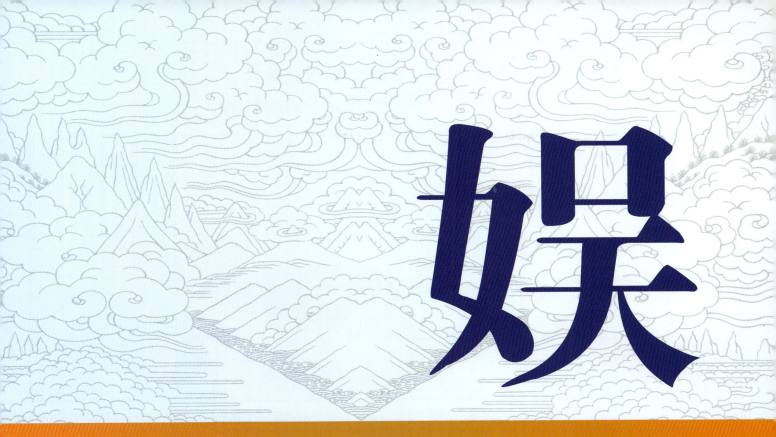

娱

Hobbies & Activities

第十单元
UNIT 10

Communication Goals

Lesson 1: 星期六的活动 **Plans for Saturday**
- Inquire about what people like to do in their free time.
- Discuss sports and leisure activities.
- Express how often you like to do something.

Lesson 2: 在音乐会 **At a Concert**
- Discuss musical performances and instruments.
- Describe how well somebody does something.
- Indicate time periods and duration.

星期六的活动
Plans for Saturday

怎么大家都这么忙！
máng

看看祥安有没有空。
yǒu kòng

喂，安娜！你好！

嗨，祥安，你在做什么？

我一边吃饭一边跟你说话啊！
yì biān
yì biān　　shuō
huà

哈哈，我是说，今天是星期六，你有什么活动吗？
hā hā
huó dòng

没什么活动。你呢？玛丽他们呢？

他们……有的去打球，有的去游泳，还有的去跑步了，可是我对这些活动都没有兴趣。

那你喜欢做什么？

跳舞、唱歌我都喜欢，我也常常去看电影。

是吗？我今天晚上八点要去看一部新电影，是功夫片。

你想跟我一起去吗？

哦！听起来很有意思。

好吧，你能不能七点五十分在电影院门口等我？

行，晚上见。

LESSON TEXT 10.1

Plans for Saturday 星期六的活动

Zhang Anna cannot find anyone to go out with because they are all busy. She decides to call Huang Xiang'an to see what he is doing.

张安娜：	怎么大家都这么忙！看看祥安有没有空。	Zěnme dàjiā dōu zhème máng! Kànkan Xiángān yǒu méiyǒu kòng.
黄祥安：	喂，安娜！你好！	Wèi, Ānnà! Nǐ hǎo!
张安娜：	嗨，祥安，你在做什么？	Hēi, Xiáng'ān, nǐ zài zuò shénme?
黄祥安：	我一边吃饭一边跟你说话啊！	Wǒ yìbiān chī fàn yìbiān gēn nǐ shuōhuà a!
张安娜：	哈哈，我是说，今天是星期六，你有什么活动吗？	Hāhā, wǒ shì shuō, jīntiān shì Xīngqī liù, nǐ yǒu shénme huódòng ma?
黄祥安：	没什么活动。你呢？玛丽他们呢？	Méi shénme huódòng. Nǐ ne? Mǎlì tāmen ne?
张安娜：	他们……有的去打球，有的去游泳，还有的去跑步了，可是我对这些活动都没有兴趣。	Tāmen ……yǒude qù dǎ qiú, yǒude qù yóu yǒng, hái yǒude qù pǎobù le, kěshì wǒ duì zhèixiē huódòng dōu méiyǒu xìngqu.

黄祥安：	那你喜欢做什么？	Nà nǐ xǐhuan zuò shénme?
张安娜：	跳舞、唱歌我都喜欢，我也常常去看电影。	Tiàowǔ, chàng gē wǒ dōu xǐhuan, wǒ yě chángcháng qù kàn diànyǐng.
黄祥安：	是吗？我今天晚上八点要去看一部新电影，是功夫片。你想跟我一起去吗？	Shì ma? Wǒ jīntiān wǎnshang bā diǎn yào qù kàn yí bù xīn diànyǐng, shì gōngfu piàn. Nǐ xiǎng gēn wǒ yìqǐ qù ma?
张安娜：	哦！听起来很有意思。	Ò! Tīngqilai hěn yǒu yìsi.
黄祥安：	好吧，你能不能七点五十分在电影院门口等我？	Hǎo ba, nǐ néng bu néng qī diǎn wǔshí fēn zài diànyǐngyuàn ménkǒu děng wǒ?

张安娜：　行，晚上见。

Xíng, wǎnshang jiàn.

LESSON VOCABULARY 10.1

	SIMPLIFIED	TRADITIONAL	PINYIN	WORD CATEGORY	DEFINITION
1.	忙		máng	adj	busy
2.	有空		yǒu kòng	vo	to have free time
3.	一边	一邊	yìbiān	conj	on the one hand; at the same time
4.	说话	説話	shuōhuà	vo	to talk
5.	哈哈		hāhā	on	(sound of laughter)
6.	活动	活動	huódòng	n	activity
7.	打球		dǎ qiú	vo	to play ball
8.	游泳		yóuyǒng	vo	to swim
9.	跑步		pǎobù	vo	to jog
10.	对	對	duì	prep	at; toward
11.	这些	這些	zhèixiē	n	these
	些		xiē	mw	some
12.	兴趣	興趣	xìngqù	n	interest
13.	跳舞		tiàowǔ	vo	to dance
14.	唱歌		chàng gē	vo	to sing
15.	常常		chángcháng	adv	often
16.	部		bù	mw	(used for movies)
17.	电影	電影	diànyǐng	n	movie
18.	功夫片		gōngfu piàn	n	kung fu movie
	功夫		gōngfu	n	kung fu
19.	听起来	聽起來	tīngqilai	ie	to sound like
20.	能		néng	av	can; be able to
21.	电影院	電影院	diànyǐngyuàn	n	cinema, movie theater
22.	门口	門口	ménkǒu	n	entrance
23.	等		děng	v	to wait

LESSON VOCABULARY 10.1 (continued)

	SIMPLIFIED	TRADITIONAL	PINYIN	WORD CATEGORY	DEFINITION
24.	行		xíng	*adj*	OK, all right

REQUIRED VOCABULARY 10.1

OTHER

25.	玩		wán	*v*	to play
26.	游戏	遊戲	yóuxì	*n*	game
27.	很少		hěn shǎo	*adv*	very infrequently; rarely

OPTIONAL VOCABULARY 10.2

MOVIE GENRES

28.	喜剧	喜劇	xǐjù	*n*	comedy
29.	悲剧	悲劇	bēijù	*n*	tragedy
30.	恐怖片		kǒngbù piàn	*n*	horror movie

HOBBIES & ACTIVITIES

31.	乒乓球		pīngpāngqiú	*n*	ping pong
32.	羽毛球		yǔmáoqiú	*n*	badminton
33.	骑马	騎馬	qí mǎ	*vo*	to ride a horse
34.	高尔夫球	高爾夫球	gāo'ěrfūqiú	*n*	golf
35.	排球		páiqiú	*n*	volleyball
36.	踢		tī	*v*	to kick

OTHER

37.	不常		bù cháng	*adv*	not often; seldom

 ONLINE RESOURCES

Visit *http://college.betterchinese.com* for a list of other words related to hobbies and activities.

Pictographs

Most Chinese characters are "phono-semantic compounds," meaning that they are comprised of a radical, which relates to the character's meaning, and a phonetic component, which hints at its pronunciation. Some characters, however, are structured differently. Pictographs are characters that originated as actual graphic representations of the things they signify. The modern forms of these characters do not always have a strong visual link to their subject, but we can still trace their development and perceive the resemblance. The following are some examples of pictographs starting from their origin in bone script, to seal script, and then to their modern day forms.

	Bone Script	Seal Script	Modern Script		Bone Script	Seal Script	Modern Script
mù: "eye"				yuè: "moon"			
rén: "person"				shuǐ: "water"			
rì: "sun"				shān: "mountain"			

Ideographs

Another category of Chinese characters, and one that is also comparatively rare, is the ideograph. Unlike pictographs, ideographs are an abstract representation of the concept that they signify. The following are some examples of ideographs.

Character		Meaning	Derivation
一	yī	one	a single stroke
二	èr	two	two strokes
三	sān	three	three strokes
上	shàng	above	above a horizontal line
下	xià	below	below a horizontal line
中	zhōng	center	a line through the center
凸	tū	convex	a protruding component
凹	āo	concave	a sunken component

STRUCTURE NOTE 10.1
Use 一边···一边··· *to describe simultaneous actions*

To indicate that someone is doing one action at the same time as doing another, add 一边 *(yìbiān: "at the same time") before each of the actions that is occurring simultaneously. In English, this pattern is usually translated as "while" or "at the same time as," or even simply as "and."*

> Subject + 一边 + Verb Phrase A + 一边 + Verb Phrase B

From the Lesson Text:

我一边吃饭一边跟你说话啊。
Wǒ yìbiān chī fàn yìbiān gēn nǐ shuōhuà a.
I'm talking to you while eating.

Other examples:

我常常一边看电视一边吃饭。
Wǒ chángcháng yìbiān kàn diànshì yìbiān chī fàn.
I often watch television and eat at the same time.

他不能一边跳舞一边唱歌。
Tā bù néng yìbiān tiàowǔ yìbiān chàng gē.
He can't dance and sing at the same time.

Practice: Use the 一边···一边··· construction and the verb phrases provided to create complete sentences in Chinese.

Example: 大东 / 上课 / 说话 → 大东一边上课一边说话。

1. 你 / 开车 / 打电话 _____
2. 弟弟 / 做功课 / 唱歌 _____
3. 他 / 看书 / 听音乐 _____
4. 我 / 工作 / 喝咖啡 _____
5. 我们 / 运动 / 看电视 _____

STRUCTURE NOTE 10.2
Use 什么 *to mean "any"*

什么 *has already been introduced as a question word meaning "what," but it can also be used before nouns to mean "some" or "any." When it is negated, this pattern means "not much/not many" or "none/nothing in particular."*

> 什么 + Object

From the Lesson Text:

今天是星期六。你有什么活动吗?
Jīntiān shì Xīngqī liù, nǐ yǒu shénme huódòng ma?
Today is Saturday. Do you have any plans?

没什么活动。你呢?
Méi shénme huódòng. Nǐ ne?
Not really. And you?

Other examples:

他说他要去买什么东西。
Tā shuō tā yào qù mǎi shénme dōngxi.
He said he had to go buy something or other.

这儿没什么人。
Zhèr méi shénme rén.
There aren't many people here.

NOTE: *Look out for the use of* 吗 *in questions in which* 什么 *appears. In questions in which* 什么 *is used to mean "any,"* 吗 *is used to turn the statement into a question, while in questions where* 什么 *means "what,"* 吗 *cannot be used.*

Examples:

你今天有什么活动？
Nǐ jīntiān yǒu shénme huódòng?
What plans do you have today?

你今天有什么活动吗？
Nǐ jīntiān yǒu shénme huódòng ma?
Do you have any plans today?

Practice: Respond to the following questions in the negative using 什么, following the example shown below.

Example: 这有好玩儿的活动吗？ → 这没什么好玩儿的活动。

1. 你今天有时间吗？ _____
2. 那边有很多人吗？ _____
3. 我可以借点钱吗？ _____
4. 有事吗？ _____
5. 你对数学有兴趣吗？ _____

STRUCTURE NOTE 10.3
Use topic-comment sentences

Chinese is characterized by linguists as a topic-comment language. This means that, although the basic sentence structure is subject-verb-object, many sentences have an alternative structure in which the topic of the sentence is put first, followed by a comment that says something about that topic. There is a pattern in English that is similar to this, although it is rarely used: "Bagels, I like. Muffins, not so much." The topic is generally a definite noun phrase that would have been the object in a regular sentence pattern.

Topic + Comment

From the Lesson Text: 跳舞、唱歌我都喜欢。
Tiàowǔ, chàng gē wǒ dōu xǐhuan.
I like dancing and singing.

Other examples:

那本书我很喜欢。
Nèi běn shū wǒ hěn xǐhuan.
I really like that book.

汉字他觉得很难写。
Hànzì tā juéde hěn nán xiě.
He thinks that Chinese characters are difficult to write.

Practice: Rewrite the following sentences as topic-comment sentences, following the example provided.

Example: 我很喜欢吃中国菜。 → 中国菜我很喜欢吃。

1. 我很想去中国。

   _____

2. 中平有的时候听不懂中文课。

   _____

3. 我听不懂你说的话。

   _____

4. 我今天早上就做中文作业了。

   _____

5. 她最喜欢唱歌。

   _____

STRUCTURE NOTE 10.4
Use 有的 to mean "some"

In Unit 2, Lesson 1, 有 *was introduced as the verb "to have" or "there is/are." In this lesson,* 有的 *is introduced as a means to say "some." In this construction, the subject normally appears following* 有的, *as in* 有的 人 *("some people"). However, if the subject of conversation is already clear, the* 有的 *can appear on its own. In the example from the Lesson Text, the subject has been topicalized (see Structure Note 10.3), so it is not repeated.*

> 有的 (+ Subject) + Verb Phrase

From the Lesson Text:
他们……有的去打球，有的去游泳，还有的去跑步。
Tāmen……yǒude qù dǎ qiú, yǒude qù yóuyǒng, hái yǒude qù pǎobù.
Well . . . some of them went to play sports, some went swimming, and others went running.

Other examples:
有的人喜欢吃肉，有的人不喜欢吃肉。
Yǒude rén xǐhuan chī ròu, yǒude rén bù xǐhuan chī ròu.
Some people like to eat meat, and some people don't.

学生们有的学中文，有的学英语，还有的学法语。
Xuéshēngmen yǒude xué Zhōngwén, yǒude xué Yīngyǔ, hái yǒude xué Fǎyǔ.
Some of the students study Chinese, some study English, and some study French.

Practice: Use the following sets of words and 有的 to create complete sentences in Chinese.

Example: 人 / 打球 / 游泳 / 跳舞
→有的人喜欢打球，有的人喜欢游泳，还有的人喜欢跳舞。

1. 人 / 吃肉 / 吃素
   _____

2. 小孩子 / 蓝色 / 黄色
   _____

3. 人 / 吃酸的 / 吃辣的 / 吃甜的
   _____

4. 人 / 开车 / 火车 / 公共汽车
   _____

5. 这些人 / 美国人 / 加拿大人
   _____

STRUCTURE NOTE 10.5

Use 对……有兴趣 *to express interest in something*

The phrase 有意思 *(yǒu yìsi), though ostensibly a verb and an object ("to have interest"), is actually used as an adjective meaning "interesting." The word* 兴趣 *(xìngqù), however, does mean "interest" and is paired with* 有 *only as part of a set pattern to indicate something that one is interested in. To express that someone is (or is not) interested in something,* 对 *is placed before the object, and* 有兴趣 *follows.*

Subject + 对 + Object + 有 / 没(有) + 兴趣

From the Lesson Text: 可是我对这些活动都没有兴趣。
Kěshì wǒ duì zhèi xiē huódòng dōu méiyǒu xìngqù.
But I'm not interested in any of these activities.

Other examples:
他对功夫很有兴趣。
Tā duì gōngfu hěn yǒu xìngqù.
He is very interested in kung fu.

你对法文有没有兴趣？
Nǐ duì Fǎwén yǒu méiyǒu xìngqù?
Are you interested in French?

Practice: Change the following sentences into Chinese. Pay particular attention to when you should use 有兴趣 and when you should use 有意思.

Example: I'm very interested in languages. → 我对语言很有兴趣。

1.   This book isn't very interesting.   _____

2.   Xiang'an is interested in soccer.   _____

3.   Are you interested in cooking?   _____

4.   Do you think she's interested in me?   _____

5.   They have no interest in movies.   _____

STRUCTURE NOTE 10.6
Use 常 (常) to express "often"

Adverbial expressions of frequency, like 常常 *(chángcháng), are placed between the subject and the verb phrase. While the reduplicated form* 常常 *is used more frequently, the expression can also be abbreviated to the single character* 常*. Other useful expressions of frequency are* 不常 *(bùcháng: "not often") and* 很少 *(hěnshǎo: "very infrequently").*

> Subject + 常 (常) + Verb Phrase

From the Lesson Text: 我也常常去看电影。
Wǒ yě chángcháng qù kàn diànyǐng.
I also often go to see movies.

Other examples:

我常常跟朋友一起去看电影。
Wǒ chángcháng gēn péngyou yìqǐ qù kàn diànyǐng.
I often go see movies with my friends.

你常给爸爸妈妈打电话吗？
Nǐ cháng gěi bàba māma dǎ diànhuà ma?
Do you call your parents often?

Practice: Use the information below to create sentences with 常 (常), 不常, or 很少.

Example: 中平 / 下课以后 / 去图书馆
→ 中平下课以后常常去图书馆。

1.   爸爸 / 去饭馆 / 喝酸辣汤   _____

2.   妹妹 / 早上 / 运动   _____

3.   我 / 上课的时候 / 睡觉   _____

4.   他 / 周末 / 去听音乐会   _____

5.   姐姐 / 看电影 / 看书   _____

STRUCTURE NOTE 10.7
Use 能 to describe ability

能 (néng) *means "can," describing physical ability to do something. Just as in English, where "can" is often used to mean "may," in Chinese* 能 *and* 可以 *can often be used interchangeably, although* 能 *corresponds more closely to "can" and* 可以 *corresponds more to "may."*

> Subject + 能 + Verb Phrase

From the Lesson Text:

你能不能七点五十分在电影院门口等我？
Nǐ néng bu néng qī diǎn wǔshí fēn zài diànyǐngyuàn ménkǒu děng wǒ?
Can you wait for me at the entrance to the theater at 7:50?

Other examples:

她今天不能跟我们一起去跳舞。
Tā jīntiān bù néng gēn wǒmen yìqǐ qù tiàowǔ.
She can't go dancing with us today.

现在太晚了，我不能再等了。
Xiànzài tài wǎn le, wǒ bù néng zài děng le.
It's too late now; I can't wait anymore.

NOTE: 能 *can sometimes be confused with* 会. *In English, we can say "Can you speak English?" or "Do you know how to speak English?" but in Chinese, this is usually expressed with* 会, *not with* 能. *A good rule to keep in mind is that* 会 *refers to general knowledge of how to do something, while* 能 *refers to ability to do something in a specific instance.*

Practice: Use 能, 会, or 可以 to fill in the gaps in the sentences below.

Example:　你__跳舞吗？ → 你会跳舞吗？

1. 我太累了，不 __ 做作业了。 _____
2. 服务员，我们 __ 点菜吗？ _____
3. 你 __ 说中文吗？ _____
4. 她们 __ 吃辣吗？ _____
5. 这么贵的东西我不 __ 买。 _____

STRUCTURE NOTE 10.8
Use name + 他们 *to refer to a group of people*

When a plural pronoun (most often 他们*) is added after a name it indicates that the speaker is referring to a particular person and the people associated with him or her. This is similar to English expressions such as "Mali and the others," and "Mali and the rest of them."*

Name + Plural Pronoun

From the Lesson Text:

玛丽他们呢?
Mǎlì tāmen ne?
What about Mali and the others?

Other examples:

安娜她们都喜欢跳舞。
Ānnà tāmen dōu xǐhuan tiàowǔ.
Anna and the rest of them all like dancing.

我不知道大东他们在哪里。
Wǒ bù zhīdào Dàdōng tāmen zài nǎli.
I don't know where Dadong and the others are.

Practice: Express the following sentences in Chinese using the name + 他们 pattern.

Example: Xiang'an and the others have all gone to the library.
→ 祥安他们都去图书馆了。

1. What do Dadong and the rest of them have for lunch?

   _____

2. Do Mali and the others like soccer?

   _____

3. Anna and the others will wait for you at school.

   _____

4. Zhongping and the others have an important test next week.

   _____

5. Xiang'an and the rest all went swimming.

   _____

PRACTICE 10.1

In the spaces provided, write the activity that matches the picture.

PRACTICE 10.2

Working with a partner, use the information in the table below to engage in a dialogue about what each of the characters did last weekend and what their plans for this weekend are.

Example:

A: 陈大东上个周末有什么活动？

B: 大东上个星期去打球了。

A: 他这个星期六有什么计划？

B: 他要跟玛丽吃晚饭。

名字	上个周末	这个星期六
1. 陈大东	打球	跟玛丽吃晚饭
2. 李中平	在图书馆看书	练功夫
3. 王小美	吃饺子	吃北京烤鸭
4. 黄祥安	看足球比赛	看功夫片
5. 孙玛丽	做中文功课	跟大东吃饭
6. 张安娜	买东西	给祥安打电话

PRACTICE 10.3

Working with a partner, practice the following conversation in which you make a phone call to your friend to invite him or her to go to a movie with you.

Example:

A: 喂？你这个周末有空吗？

B: 有什么事吗？

A: 星期天我想去看电影。你想跟我一起去吗？

B: 你想看什么电影？

A: 我想看功夫片。

B: 好啊。电影几点开始？

A: 电影下午三点开始。

B: 好。那，我下午两点三刻在电影院门口等你。

PRACTICE 10.4

Interview your classmates about their hobbies and fill out the chart below. What are their favorite things to do? What did they do last weekend? Did they enjoy it?

Example:

A: 你上个周末有什么活动？

B: 我上个星期六去看电影了。

A: 电影怎么样？

B: 很有意思。

名字	喜欢什么活动？	上个周末做什么了？	怎么样？

PRACTICE 10.5

Do a survey of the class to find out what weekend activity is most common among your classmates. Record the most popular answer below.

Activity	Number of Students

✏️ PRACTICE 10.6

	Radical	Stroke Order
说	讠(言) yán speech	丶 讠 讠 讠 讠 讠 讠 说 说
打	扌(手) shǒu hand	一 十 扌 扌 打
球	王 wáng king	一 二 干 王 玎 玎 玎 球 球 球
口	口 kǒu mouth	丨 口 口
空	穴 xué cave	丶 丷 宀 宀 穴 空 空 空
边	辶 chùo walk	乛 力 力 边 边
活	氵(水) shuǐ water	丶 丶 氵 汇 汇 汗 汗 活 活
动	力 lì power	一 二 云 云 动 动
些	止 zhǐ stop	丨 卜 止 止 止 此 此 些
常	巾 jīn cloth	丨 丷 丷 丷 丷 常 常 常 常 常
部	阝(邑) yì city	丶 亠 亠 立 立 音 音 部 部
夫	大 dà big	一 二 丰 夫
影	彡 shān hair	丶 口 口 日 旦 早 昌 昌 景 景 景 影 影 影
院	阝(阜) fù hill	了 阝 阝 阝 阼 阼 阼 院
等	竹(竹) zhú bamboo	丿 ⺮ ⺮ ⺮ 竹 竹 竺 竺 竺 筌 等 等

💬 PRACTICE 10.7

Make an audio recording and send it to your teacher. In the recording, talk about your plans for the coming weekend.

PRACTICE 10.8

Type the following sentences on your computer and provide answers to the questions.

1. 他一边吃饭一边看电视。
2. 这个周末你有什么活动吗？
3. 我对这些活动都没什么兴趣。
4. 你想跟我一起去看一部新的功夫片吗？
5. 明天晚上八点十五分我在电影院门口等你。

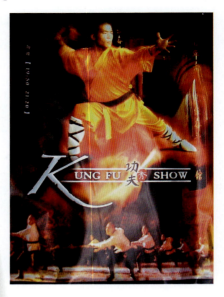

PRACTICE 10.9

今天我想找朋友一起去听音乐会，可是大家都很忙，有的准备考试，有的做作业，只有祥安有空，他今天没什么活动。晚上七点十五分，祥安会在图书馆门口等我，然后我们去听音乐会。

Read Zhang Anna's diary and answer the following questions.
1. Why can't Zhang Anna's friends go to the concert with her?
2. Where will Huang Xiang'an meet Zhang Anna?

PRACTICE 10.10

李中平：你喜欢做什么活动？

孙玛丽：我喜欢游泳，每天早上我都去游泳。

李中平：我对游泳没兴趣，可是我喜欢打球。

孙玛丽：周末我还喜欢和朋友一起吃饭、跳舞、看电影。

李中平：是吗？那我们这个星期六中午一起去中国饭馆吃饭，怎么样？

孙玛丽：行，吃完午饭后，我请你去看电影。

李中平：看什么电影？

孙玛丽：一部新的电影《功夫熊猫》。

李中平：听起来很有意思。

Read the dialogue and answer the following questions.
1. What activity does Li Zhongping like doing?
2. What will Li Zhongping and Sun Mali do after having lunch?

Karaoke or Chinese KTV

Karaoke or 卡拉OK (kǎlā-OK) might be known throughout the world, but this entertainment sensation from Japan is especially popular in contemporary China. While many Westerners view the experience as an embarrassing public display of talent (or lack there of), in China karaoke has developed into a more serious social activity. The interactive sing-a-long game first emerged on China's social scene via upscale hotels in Hong Kong, Beijing, and Shanghai in the late 1980s. The appellation KTV (short for "karaoke television") was later adopted to denote the Chinese version of karaoke. In their early years, the first KTV bars acquired a bad reputation as somewhat seedy places. However, the widespread expansion of KTV in the 1990s gradually built a legitimate reputation for the pastime, establishing it as one of China's most widespread and popular social activities.

Mahjong

There is much debate over the exact origins of the Chinese game 麻将 (májiàng: "Mahjong"). One of the most popular myths suggests that the game was invented by the Chinese philosopher Confucius in around 500 BC. As the story goes, Confucius was fond of birds, hence the game's original name of 麻雀 (máquè: "sparrow").

Mahjong consists of a set of 144 tiles based on Chinese characters and symbols and typically involves four players. The game is a favorite pastime in China as well as in Chinese-speaking communities around the world. Today, when strolling about narrow alleys in any part of China, one can often hear clacking tiles and catch a glimpse of four competitors seated around a square table playing this time-honored game.

Chinese Martial Arts

According to legend, the genesis of Chinese 武术 (wǔshù: "martial arts") dates back more than 4,000 years to when the Yellow Emperor introduced the earliest fighting systems to China. Legend also has it that he was a great general who wrote lengthy treatises on ancient forms of martial arts. Later, the subject began to crop up in famed texts such as 《庄子》 (Zhuāngzǐ: "*Zhuangzi*"), 《道德经》 (Dàodéjīng: "*Daodejing*"), and 《孙子兵法》 (Sūnzǐ Bīngfǎ: "*The Art of War*"), all of which refer to martial arts being more than merely a sport or a means of physical combat. These works define the discipline as a philosophy, an art, and a means to cultivate the unity of body, soul, and universe. The true goal of martial arts is thus not to inflict pain on others, but to attain spiritual enlightenment for oneself through the strict physical and mental discipline that it demands. It is still a significant aspect of China's cultural heritage, and hundreds of forms of martial arts — some of which are referred to as 功夫 (gōngfu: "kung fu"), others as 武术 — continue to be practiced both in China and throughout the rest of the world.

张安娜：	怎么大家都这么忙！看看祥安有没有空。	Why is everyone so busy! Let's see if Xiang'an is free.
黄祥安：	喂，安娜！你好！	Hello Anna!
张安娜：	嗨，祥安，你在做什么？	Hi Xiang'an, what are you doing?
黄祥安：	我一边吃饭一边跟你说话啊！	I'm talking to you while eating.
张安娜：	哈哈，我是说，今天是星期六，你有什么活动吗？	Haha, I mean, today is Saturday, do you have any plans?
黄祥安：	没什么活动。你呢？玛丽他们呢？	Not really. And you? What about Mali and the others?
张安娜：	他们……有的去打球，有的去游泳，还有的去跑步了，可是我对这些活动都没有兴趣。	Well . . . some went to play sports, some went swimming, and others went running, but I'm not interested in any of those activities.

黄祥安：	那你喜欢做什么？	Then what do you like to do?
张安娜：	跳舞、唱歌我都喜欢，我也常常去看电影。	I like dancing and singing. I also often go to see movies.
黄祥安：	是吗？我今天晚上八点要去看一部新电影，是功夫片。你想跟我一起去吗？	Oh really? At 8 o'clock tonight, I'm going to see a new movie; it's a kung fu film. Would you like to go with me?
张安娜：	哦！听起来很有意思。	Oh! Sounds interesting.
黄祥安：	好吧，你能不能七点五十分在电影院门口等我？	OK, can you wait for me at the entrance to the movie theatre at 7:50?
张安娜：	行，晚上见。	Sure, see you tonight.

What Can You Do?

INTERPRETIVE
- I can understand different terms for sports, hobbies, and leisure activities.

INTERPERSONAL
- I can discuss leisure activities with others.
- I can make arrangements to play sports or go to the movies with someone.

PRESENTATIONAL
- I can give a basic presentation about my hobbies.
- I can express how frequently I do something.

在音乐会
At a Concert

大东，中平，你们下个周末有空吗？

有什么 tè bié 特别的事吗？

星期六小美会在音 biǎo yǎn 乐会表演，我们一起去看，好不好？

哇，小美真 tiān cái 是个天才！

niàn shū niàn de   wǎng qiú   de   huà   huàr
念书念得好，网球打得好，画画儿
yīn yuè jiā ya
也画得好，还是个音乐家呀！

她今天 biǎo yǎn 表演什么呢?

tán jí tā zuì jìn měi
弹吉他。她最近每天都
rèn zhēn
练习五六个小时，很认真!

玛丽，你不是
lā xiǎo tí qín
会拉小提琴吗?
tiān cái
你也是个天才!

nǎ lǐ nǎ lǐ lā de
哪里，哪里! 大东拉得比我好!

chū lai
小美出来了!

xiào duō kāi xīn
你们看，她笑得多开心。

喂，大东，为什么
xiào
小美只对你笑呢?

LESSON TEXT 10.2

At a Concert 在音乐会

Sun Mali, Li Zhongping, and Chen Dadong make plans to go to Wang Xiaomei's concert the following Saturday. They attend, then chat about hobbies and music.

孙玛丽：	大东，中平，你们下个周末有空吗？	Dàdōng, Zhōngpíng, nǐmen xià gè zhōumò yǒu kòng ma?
李中平：	有什么特别的事吗？	Yǒu shénme tèbié de shì ma?
孙玛丽：	星期六小美会在音乐会表演，我们一起去看，好不好？	Xīngqī liù Xiǎoměi huì zài yīnyuèhuì biǎoyǎn, wǒmen yìqǐ qù kàn, hǎo bu hǎo?

陈大东：	哇，小美真是个天才！念书念得好，网球打得好，画画儿也画得好，还是个音乐家呀！	Wā, Xiǎoměi zhēn shì gè tiāncái! Niàn shū niàn de hǎo, wǎngqiú dǎ de hǎo, huà huàr yě huà de hǎo, hái shì gè yīnyuèjiā ya!
李中平：	她今天表演什么呢？	Tā jīntiān biǎoyǎn shénme ne?
孙玛丽：	弹吉他。她最近每天都练习五六个小时，很认真！	Tán jítā. Tā zuìjìn měi tiān dōu liànxí wǔ liù gè xiǎoshí, hěn rènzhēn!
李中平：	玛丽，你不是会拉小提琴吗？你也是个天才！	Mǎlì, nǐ bú shì huì lā xiǎotíqín ma? Nǐ yě shì gè tiāncái!
孙玛丽：	哪里，哪里！大东拉得比我好！	Nǎlǐ, nǎlǐ! Dàdōng lā de bǐ wǒ hǎo!
孙玛丽：	小美出来了！你们看，她笑得多开心。	Xiǎoměi chūlai le! Nǐmen kàn, tā xiào de duō kāixīn.

字 词 VOCABULARY

李中平： 喂，大东，为什么小美只对
你笑呢？

Wèi, Dàdōng, wèishénme Xiǎoměi zhǐ duì nǐ xiào ne?

LESSON VOCABULARY 10.2

	SIMPLIFIED	TRADITIONAL	PINYIN	WORD CATEGORY	DEFINITION
1.	特别	特别	tèbié	adj	special
2.	表演		biǎoyǎn	v, n	to perform; performance
	演		yǎn	v	to perform, to act
3.	天才		tiāncái	n	genius; talent
4.	念书	念書	niàn shū	vo	to study; to read
5.	网球	網球	wǎngqiú	n	tennis
6.	画画(儿)	畫畫(兒)	huà huà(r)	vo	to paint; to draw
	画儿	畫兒	huàr	n	painting; drawing
7.	音乐家	音樂家	yīnyuèjiā	n	musician
8.	呀		ya	p	(used to express surprise like 啊 but follows vowels)
9.	弹	彈	tán	v	to play (a musical instrument); to pluck
10.	吉他		jítā	n	guitar
11.	最近		zuìjìn	adv	recently
12.	每		měi	pr	every, each
13.	认真	認真	rènzhēn	adj	serious; conscientious; diligent
14.	拉		lā	v	to play (an instrument with a bow); to pull
15.	小提琴		xiǎotíqín	n	violin
16.	哪里哪里	哪裏哪裏	nǎlǐ nǎlǐ	ie	not at all (a polite reply to a compliment)
17.	出来	出來	chūlai	dc	to emerge; come out
18.	笑		xiào	v	to smile; to laugh
19.	多		duō	adv	how, however
20.	开心	開心	kāixīn	adj	happy

REQUIRED VOCABULARY 10.2

SIMPLIFIED	TRADITIONAL	PINYIN	WORD CATEGORY	DEFINITION
MUSICAL INSTRUMENTS				
21. 乐器	樂器	yuèqì	*n*	musical instrument
22. 打鼓		dǎ gǔ	*vo*	to play the drums
23. 钢琴	鋼琴	gāngqín	*n*	piano
24. 大提琴		dàtíqín	*n*	cello
ADJECTIVES				
25. 快		kuài	*adj*	fast
26. 慢		màn	*adj*	slow

OPTIONAL VOCABULARY 10.2

SIMPLIFIED	TRADITIONAL	PINYIN	WORD CATEGORY	DEFINITION
MUSICAL GENRES				
27. 好听	好聽	hǎo tīng	*adj*	lovely; pleasant (to the ear)
28. 摇滚乐	摇滚樂	yáogǔnyuè	*n*	rock music
29. 古典音乐	古典音樂	gǔdiǎn yīnyuè	*n*	classical music
30. 流行音乐	流行音樂	liúxíng yīnyuè	*n*	pop music

 ONLINE RESOURCES
   Visit *http://college.betterchinese.com* for a list of other words related to music.

Verbs for Hobbies and Activities

In English, the verb "to play" is used with most hobbies (tennis, basketball, soccer, cards, video games, etc.). In Chinese, the verb 打 (dǎ: "to hit; to do; to play") covers much of the same ground. In particular, 打 is used when referring to sports played with the hands. However, there are some activities that require specific verbs. Below is a list of some of the common pairings.

The Verb 打

	篮球	lánqiú	basketball
	乒乓球	pīngpāngqiú	ping-pong
	高尔夫球	gāo'ěrfūqiú	golf
	羽毛球	yǔmáoqiú	badminton
	网球	wǎngqiú	tennis
打	排球	páiqiú	volleyball
	橄榄球	gǎnlǎnqiú	rugby; football (American)
	棒球	bàngqiú	baseball
	保龄球	bǎolíngqiú	bowling
	太极拳	tàijíquán	Tai Chi
	鼓	gǔ	drums

Other Activity Verbs

踢	tī	kick	足球、毽子	zúqiú, jiànzi	soccer, hacky sack
玩	wán	play	（电子）游戏	(diànzǐ) yóuxì	(video) games
看	kàn	watch, read	书、电影、电视	shū, diànyǐng, diànshì	books, movies, television
骑	qí	ride	马、自行车	mǎ, zìxíngchē	horses, bikes
弹	tán	play (lit. "pluck")	吉他、琴、钢琴	jítā, qín, gāngqín	guitar, harp, piano
拉	lā	play (lit. "pull")	小提琴、大提琴	xiǎotíqín, dàtíqín	violin, cello
唱	chàng	sing; recite	歌、诗	gē, shī	songs, poetry
画	huà	draw, paint	画儿	huàr	drawings, paintings
跑	pǎo	run	步、马拉松	bù, mǎlāsōng	jogging, marathons

STRUCTURE NOTE 10.9
Use 得 *to describe the manner of actions*

There are several patterns that can be used to describe the manner in which something is done. The most common wa~~y~~ to do this is to add 得 (de, pronounced the same as 的) to the verb followed by an adverb. Sentences that describe the manner of an action may contain modifiers such as 很 and 太 as well as comparative phrases, but they may not use 了. Note also that negation comes before the adverb and not the verb.

> Subject + Verb + 得 + Adverb

From the Lesson Text:

你们看，她笑得多开心。

Nǐmen kàn, tā xiào de duō kāixīn.
Look, she's smiling so happily.

大东拉得比我更好！

Dàdōng lā de bǐ wǒ hǎo!
Dadong plays better than I do!

Other examples:

他练习得不太认真。
Tā liànxí de bú tài rènzhēn.
He didn't practice that diligently.

说得好！
Shuō de hǎo!
Well said!

Most verbs phrases in Chinese consist of a verb-object pair. When an object is introduced into the equation, the basic rule is that 得 must directly follow the verb. This is achieved by using the whole verb-object phrase followed by a repetition of the verb. If the object in the verb-object pair is a noun that commonly appears on its own (e.g., 篮球), the verb can optionally be deleted before the object (他篮球打得很好). Some verb-object pairs are equivalen~~t~~ to intransitive verbs in English (e.g., 说话, "to talk words" – "to talk"), so it is important to remember which two-character verb phrases are verb-object pairs and which are two-character verbs.

> Subject (+ Verb) + Object + Verb + 得 + Adverb

From the Lesson Text:

念书念得好，网球打得好，画画儿也画得好，
还是个音乐家呀！

Niàn shū niàn de hǎo, wǎngqiú dǎ de hǎo, huà huàr yě huà de hǎo, hái shì gè yīnyuèjiā ya!
She studies well, plays tennis well, draws well, and she's a musician too!

Other examples:

他车开得很小心。
Tā chē kāi de hěn xiǎoxīn.
He drives very carefully.

她弹吉他弹得很好。
Tā tán jítā tán de hěn hǎo.
She plays the guitar very well.

Practice: Create statements with 得 that comment on the manner of an action using the information given below.

Example: 说中文 / 好 → 他说中文说得很好。

1. 写字 / 大 _____

2. 打球 / 不好 _____

3. 复习 / 认真 _____

4. 考试 / 差 _____

5. 做菜 / 好吃 _____

STRUCTURE NOTE 10.10

Use 每···都··· to express "every"

The 每···都··· *(měi…dōu…) pattern expresses that something is true for each item in a category. The* 每 *can be applied to the subject of the sentence, or to a unit of time to create a time expression. Place a measure word between* 每 *and nouns that normally use measure words; none is required for* 年, 天, *etc.*

> 每 (+ Measure Word) + Noun Phrase + 都 + Verb Phrase

From the Lesson Text: 她最近每天都练习五六个小时。
Tā zuìjìn měi tiān dōu liànxí wǔ liù gè xiǎoshí.
Recently, she's been practicing for five or six hours every day.

Other examples: 每个人都有一张纸。　　我每个星期三都去中国饭馆。
Měi gè rén dōu yǒu yì zhāng zhǐ.　Wǒ měi gè Xīngqī sān dōu qù Zhōngguó
Everyone has a sheet of paper.　　fànguǎn.
　　　　　　　　　　　　　　　I go to a Chinese restaurant every Wednesday.

Practice: Write the following sentences in Chinese using the 每···都··· pattern.

Example: He has a test every week. → 他每个星期都有考试。

1. Every year he goes back to China to see his family.

_____

2. Every student in the school likes Teacher Zhang.

_____

3. Every one of my classmates thinks that test was hard.

_____

4. I go to the gym every two days.

_____

5. Every item of clothing in this shop is really pretty.

_____

STRUCTURE NOTE 10.11
Use time periods to indicate duration

In expressions that indicate how long someone does something for, the duration follows the verb.

If the verb has an object, there are two methods that can be used. The first is to use the whole verb-object phrase

> Subject + Verb (+ 了) + Duration

and then repeat the verb. The second is to move the object to the end of the statement and attach it to the expression of duration with 的. 了 *can also be added after the verb in order to establish that the action took place in the past.*

> Subject + Verb + Object + Verb (+ 了) + Duration

> Subject + Verb (+ 了) + Duration + 的 + Object

From the Lesson Text: 她最近每天都练习五六个小时。
Tā zuìjìn měi tiān dōu liànxí wǔ liù gè xiǎoshí.
Recently she's been practicing for five or six hours every day.

Other examples: 她昨天跑步跑了两个小时。
Tā zuótiān pǎobù pǎo le liǎng gè xiǎoshí.
She went running for two hours yesterday.

我的同学上个星期学了十二个小时的中文。
Wǒ de tóngxué shàng ge xīngqī xué le shí èr gè xiǎoshí de Zhōngwén.
My classmate studied Chinese for twelve hours last week.

Practice: Create complete sentences with the following information. Use one of the three patterns given above, as appropriate.

Example: 我 / 写 / 汉字 / 一个小时
→ 我每天都写一个小时的汉字。

1.   妹妹 / 弹 / 钢琴 / 三个小时
_____

2.   我 / 睡 / 觉 / 六个小时
_____

3.   朋友 / 打 / 网球 / 四十分钟
_____

4.   同学 / 复习 / 一个小时
_____

5.   他 / 开 / 车 / 一天
_____

STRUCTURE NOTE 10.12
Use multiple numbers to estimate amounts

An estimate that lists two possible amounts, such as "three or four" in English, can be expressed in Chinese by simply listing two numbers consecutively. For estimates over 20, the first part of the number (the number 1 – 9)

> Number + Number + Measure Word + Noun

is repeated, but the unit (十, 百, 千, etc.) is not.

From the Lesson Text:

她最近每天都练习五六个小时。
Tā zuìjìn měi tiān dōu liànxí wǔ liù gè xiǎoshí.
Recently, she's been practicing for five or six hours a day.

Other examples:

我一共会写五六十个汉字。
Wǒ yígòng huì xiě wǔ liù shí gè Hànzì.
I can write fifty or sixty Chinese characters in total.

那个手机的价钱是四五百块。
Nèige shǒujī de jiàqián shì sì wǔ bǎi kuài.
The price of that cellphone is four or five hundred yuan.

Practice: Insert or substitute estimates that list two possible amounts into the appropriate places in the sentences below.

Example: 我昨天学了很多生词。
→ 我昨天学了五六十个生词。

1. 我今天晚上打算弹几个小时的吉他。

   _____

2. 学校要我选课。

   _____

3. 他在商店买了很多衣服。

   _____

4. 我的朋友每天都跑几个小时的步。

   _____

5. 我今天花了很多钱。

   _____

STRUCTURE NOTE 10.13
Use 不是……吗？ *to ask a rhetorical question*

In English, the question "Don't you know how to play the violin?" can imply that the speaker thinks that the listener does indeed know how to play the violin. In Chinese, the pattern 不是……吗？ is used in the same way in order to ask rhetorical questions.

Subject + 不是 + Verb Phrase + 吗 ？

From the Lesson Text:

你不是会拉小提琴吗？
Nǐ bú shì huì lā xiǎotíqín ma?
Don't you play the violin?

Other Examples:

你不是喜欢红色吗？
Nǐ bú shì xǐhuan hóngsè ma?
Don't you like the color red?

你不是说他西班牙语说得很好吗？
Nǐ bú shì shuō tā Xībānyáyǔ shuō de hěn hǎo ma?
Didn't you say that he speaks Spanish really well?

Practice: Turn the following statements into rhetorical questions using the 不是……吗？ pattern.

Example: 他说他没有钱了。→ 他不是说他没有钱了吗？

1. 她喜欢看电视。

   _____

2. 你说她是个天才。

   _____

3. 你哥哥弹吉他弹得很好。

   _____

4. 他觉得这门课很难。

   _____

5. 大东的朋友是个音乐家。

   _____

STRUCTURE NOTE 10.14
Use 对 *as the preposition "to, towards"*

对 (duì) *is a preposition meaning "towards" that is used in many common sentence patterns, as in the pattern* 对⋯⋯有兴趣. *Like most prepositional phrases in Chinese,* 对 *phrases are placed before the main verb phrase.*

Subject + 对 + Object + Verb Phrase

From the Lesson Text: 为什么小美只对你笑呢？
Wèishénme Xiǎoměi zhǐ duì nǐ xiào ne?
Why is Xiaomei only smiling at you?

Other examples: 你对我太好了。   他对我说生日快乐。
Nǐ duì wǒ tài hǎo le.   Tā duì wǒ shuō shēngrì kuàilè.
You are too good to me.   He said Happy Birthday to me.

Practice: Transform the following sentences into Chinese using 对 .

Example: You should say sorry to her. → 你应该对她说对不起。

1. She's very good to her friends.

_____

2. That student said thanks to the teacher.

_____

3. The teacher spoke to the boy.

_____

4. The girl is singing to me.

_____

5. He's very diligent when it comes to studying.

_____

练习 PRACTICE

PRACTICE 10.11

Write the appropriate noun and verb pairing next to the image to describe the activity depicted. Then, with a partner, practice the dialogue shown below.

弹钢琴

Example:
A: 他会做什么？
B: 他会弹钢琴。

PRACTICE 10.12

Working with a partner, ask and answer questions based on the activity schedule shown below.

Example:
A: 你什么时候练习钢琴？练习几个小时？
B: 我每个星期一和星期三练习五个小时的钢琴。

星期/时间	日	一	二	三	四	五	六
07:00 - 12:00		钢琴		钢琴	画画		画画
13:30 - 15:00			网球		网球		
16:00 - 20:00	大提琴					大提琴	
21:00 - 22:00	篮球	篮球	篮球	篮球	篮球	篮球	篮球

374 第十单元 ▪ 第二课 ▪ 娱

PRACTICE 10.13

Working in groups, ask your classmates what they can do well and what they cannot do well. Choose someone from your group to report your findings to your class.

Example: 李中平篮球打得好，可是钢琴弹得不好。

名字	什么活动做得好？	什么活动做得不好？

PRACTICE 10.14

Do a survey to determine which musical instrument most students play in the class. Record your findings below.

Musical Instrument	Number of Students

PRACTICE 10.15

Type the following sentences on your computer and provide answers to the questions.

1. 你明天晚上有空吗？
2. 我们一起去看小美的表演，好不好？
3. 他弟弟真是个天才！
4. 我最近每天练习四五个小时的钢琴。
5. 他弹吉他弹得比我好。

PRACTICE 10.16

Make an audio recording and send it to your teacher. In the recording, talk about any activities you participate in and how much time is required to be involved with it.

	Radical	Stroke Order
哪	口 kǒu mouth	丶 丨 冂 口 叮 叨 叼 明 哪 哪
特	牜(牛) niú cow	丿 ⺧ 牛 牛 牛 牲 牲 特 特
别	刂(刀) dāo knife	丶 口 口 弓 另 别 别
才	一 yī one	一 寸 才
表	一 yī one	一 二 キ 主 声 麦 表 表
演	氵(水) shuǐ water	丶 丶 氵 汁 浐 沪 沪 浐 浐 演 演 演 演
网	冂 jiōng down box	丨 冂 冂 网 网 网
近	辶 chuò walk	丿 厂 斤 斤 近 近 近
每	毋 wú not	丿 ⺈ 仁 勺 每 每 每
弹	弓 gōng bow	⁊ ⁊ 弓 弓 弜 弪 弹 弹 弹 弹
吉	口 kǒu mouth	一 十 士 吉 吉 吉
拉	扌(手) shǒu hand	一 十 扌 才 扩 扩 拉 拉
提	扌(手) shǒu hand	一 十 扌 扌 护 护 护 担 捏 提 提
琴	王 wáng king	一 二 千 王 玨 玨 玨 珏 珡 琴 琴 琴
笑	竹(竹) zhú bamboo	丿 ⺊ ⺊ ⺮ 竺 竺 竺 竺 笑 笑

PRACTICE 10.18

孙玛丽：你下个周末有空吗？

李中平：有。有什么特别的事吗？

孙玛丽：我会在学校的音乐会表演，你能来吗？

李中平：好啊！你会表演什么乐器？

孙玛丽：我会拉小提琴。最近我每天都练习六七个小时。

李中平：哇！你真认真！那我一定得去听听。

孙玛丽：太好了！音乐会是下星期六下午三点，不要忘哦！

李中平：行！

Read the dialogue and answer the following questions.
1. What musical instrument is Sun Mali going to play?
2. When is the performance?

PRACTICE 10.19

小美今天在学校打网球，她网球打得真不错！小美还会画画儿，弹吉他，拉小提琴，她真是个天才！小美说她常常练习，星期一和星期三练习两个小时的吉他，星期二和星期四练习一个小时的小提琴，星期五画画儿，周末就打网球。

Read Chen Dadong's diary and answer the following questions.
1. On what days does Xiaomei practice guitar? How long does she practice for?
2. What does she do on the weekend?

PRACTICE 10.20

Sender 祥安
Subject 音乐会

中平：你上个星期的西班牙文考试考得怎么样？明天晚上七点半有个音乐会，张安娜会拉大提琴，我们一起去听，好不好？

Read the e-mails and answer the following questions.
1. Who is performing in the concert?
2. Why doesn't Li Zhongping want to go to the concert?

Sender 中平
Subject re: 音乐会

祥安：我的西班牙文考试考得不好，明天早上要再考一次。晚上我要和我的同学打篮球。因为下个星期有篮球比赛，所以我们得多练习。我对音乐没什么兴趣，所以我不会去听音乐会了。

Peking Opera

Among the many of forms of opera that exist in China, 京剧 (Jīngjù: "Beijing Opera" or "Peking Opera") is undoubtedly the most well-known, both in China and abroad. Beijing Opera is a form of traditional Chinese theater that incorporates diverse elements of drama, music, vocal performance, costume, makeup, dance, and acrobatics. It presents dramatic plays and figures mainly by infusing four artistic methods: singing, dialogue, dancing, and martial arts.

At first, only men were permitted to perform in Beijing Opera. This trend slowly began to change towards the end of the nineteenth century. Today, many diverse roles of Beijing opera are played by both men and women. There are four main character types — 生 (shēng), 旦 (dàn), 净 (jìng), and 丑 (chǒu) — among these various roles.

生	leading male actors who might appear as decent, middle-aged men 老生 (lǎo shēng), acrobats who play military figures 武生 (wǔ shēng), young men 小生 (xiǎo shēng), or kids 娃娃生 (wáwa shēng).
旦	female characters comprising old ladies 老旦 (lǎo dàn), women skilled in martial arts 武旦 (wǔ dàn), strong-minded, middle-aged women of elegance 正旦 (zhèng dàn), and lively young girls from the lower class 花旦 (huā dàn).
净	males covered by elaborate face paint to depict the unique appearances or personalities of warriors, heroes, statesmen, adventurers, and demons.
丑	comical characters distinguished by a white patch on the nose. Most of the time, these clowns are witty characters who keep the audience laughing and the mood light.

Performers adhere to a variety of stylistic conventions and musical genres to help audiences navigate the plot. Certain costumes, makeup, and stage props help to identify roles within the opera. Beijing Opera is also famous for the many symbolic and suggestive gestures that are to be found in its performances. Simple footwork, hand gestures, and various kinds of body movements can all contribute to the portrayal of actions such as opening a door, climbing a hill, going upstairs, or rowing a boat.

Beijing Opera does not limit itself in space or time. The art allows audiences to enjoy vivid performances involving dynamic acrobatic fights, elaborate face paintings, and colorful costumes, all while peering into a narrative window of China's rich past.

孙玛丽：	大东，中平，你们下个周末有空吗？
李中平：	有什么特别的事吗？
孙玛丽：	星期六小美会在音乐会表演，我们一起去看，好不好？

陈大东：	哇，小美真是个天才！念书念得好，网球打得好，画画儿也画得好，还是个音乐家呀！
李中平：	她今天表演什么呢？
孙玛丽：	弹吉他。她最近每天都练习五六个小时，很认真！
李中平：	玛丽，你不是会拉小提琴吗？你也是个天才！
孙玛丽：	哪里，哪里！大东拉得比我好！
孙玛丽：	小美出来了！你们看，她笑得多开心。
李中平：	喂，大东，为什么小美只对你笑呢？

Dadong, Zhongping, are you free next weekend?

Is there something special going on?

Xiaomei is performing at a concert on Saturday. Let's go see her play, OK?

Wow, Xiaomei is so talented! She's good at her studies, tennis, and painting, and on top of that she's a musician!

What is she performing today?

She'll be playing the guitar. Recently, she's been practicing for five to six hours a day, she's very diligent!

Mali, don't you play the violin? You're talented too!

No, no, not at all! Dadong plays better than I do!

Xiaomei's coming on to the stage! Look, she's smiling so happily.

Hey, Dadong, why is Xiaomei only smiling at you?

What Can You Do?

INTERPRETIVE
- I can understand the terms for different kinds of musical instruments.
- I can understand terms for time periods and duration.

INTERPERSONAL
- I can discuss my musical preferences and abilities with others.
- I can invite people to attend concerts and understand their responses.

PRESENTATIONAL
- I can present information about the instruments I play and the kind of music I like.
- I can comment upon how well someone performs an action.

ACT IT OUT

Working in groups, compose an original three-minute skit that utilizes the vocabulary and structures introduced in Unit 10. Each of you should assume a role and have a roughly equal number of lines in the skit. Be prepared to perform your skit in class. You can either come up with your own story or choose from one of the following situations:

A) You are on vacation with some friends and cannot decide what to do.

B) You and your younger brother or sister went to see a movie and both have different opinions about it.

C) You go to a concert with a friend and discuss afterwards the performance of each of the musicians.

CHECK WHAT YOU CAN DO

RECOGNIZE

Adjectives
- 忙
- 行
- 特别
- 认真
- 开心
- 快
- 慢

Conjunction
- 一边

Adverbs
- 常常
- 很少
- 最近
- 多

Auxiliary Verb
- 能

Directional Complement
- 出来

Measure Words
- 些
- 部

Idiomatic Expressions
- 听起来
- 哪里哪里

Noun
- 活动
- 这些

- 兴趣
- 电影
- 电影院
- 功夫
- 门口
- 游戏
- 天才
- 网球
- 画儿
- 音乐家
- 吉他
- 小提琴
- 乐器
- 钢琴
- 大提琴

Particle
- 呀

Preposition
- 对

Pronoun
- 每

Verbs
- 有空
- 说话
- 打球
- 游泳
- 跑步
- 跳舞

- 唱歌
- 等
- 玩
- 表演
- 念书
- 画画(儿)
- 弹
- 拉
- 笑
- 打鼓

Onomatopoeia
- 哈哈

WRITE

- 说
- 打球
- 口
- 空
- 活动
- 些
- 常
- 部
- 夫
- 影
- 院
- 等

- 哪
- 特别
- 才
- 表演
- 网
- 近
- 每
- 弹
- 吉
- 拉
- 提琴
- 笑

USE

- 一边···一边··· to describe simultaneous actions.
- 什么 to mean "any."
- Topic-comment sentences.
- 有的 to mean "some."
- 对······有兴趣 to express interest in something.
- 常(常) to express "often."
- 能 to describe ability.
- Name + 他们 to refer to a group of people.

- 得 to describe the manner of actions.
- 每···都··· to express "every."
- Time periods to indicate duration.
- Multiple numbers to estimate amounts.
- 不是······吗？ to ask a rhetorical question.
- 对 as the preposition "to, towards."

情

Relationships & People

第十一单元
UNIT 11

Communication Goals

Lesson 1: 约会 **A Date**
- Arrange to go on a date with someone.
- Describe a person's qualities and attributes.

Lesson 2: 分手 **A Break Up**
- Discuss relationships, marriage, and break-ups.
- Describe your emotions.
- Refer to something using the passive voice.
- Talk about past experiences.

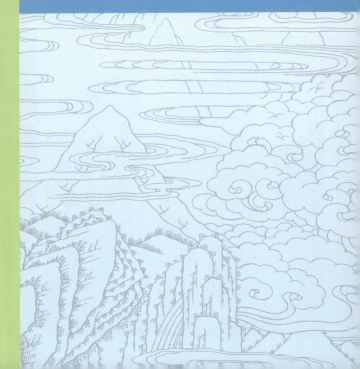

约会
A Date

小美，你的表演
bàng
真棒！我可以请
你吃晚饭吗？

好啊！玛丽、
中平他们也
一起去吗？

xiǎng yuē
我只想约你……

哦……好的！

wǎn diǎnr
我晚点儿跟你
jiàn miàn
说在哪儿见面。

好，你再打电
gào su
话告诉我吧！

jǐn zhāng   bù dé liǎo
我真的紧张得不得了。这是
cì   yuē huì
我第一次跟小美约会。

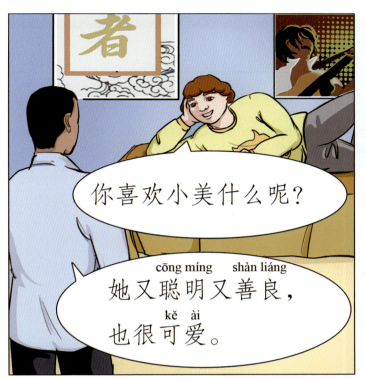

你喜欢小美什么呢？

cōng míng　shàn liáng
她又聪明又善良，
kě ài
也很可爱。

xī wàng
女孩子都希望
bié rén　　měi
听别人说她美。
diǎn　　wàng jì
这点你别忘记
ō
对她说喔。

jì bu zhù
什么，我记不住这么多！

ràng
你要让她
知道你对
她是很有
gǎn qíng
感情的！

祥安！别
kāi wán xiào
开玩笑了，
你还有什么
jiàn yì
建议吗？

吃完饭，
你可以跟她
gōng yuán sàn san bù
去公园散散步，
yuē　　　xià cì chū
再约她下次出
qu wán
去玩。

嗨！

你今天真
漂亮……

LESSON TEXT 11.1

A Date 约会

A couple of days after the concert, Chen Dadong asks Wang Xiaomei to dinner. The day of the date, Chen Dadong confesses to Huang Xiang'an that he is extremely nervous, and Huang Xiang'an offers him some advice.

陈大东:	小美，你的表演真棒！我可以请你吃晚饭吗？	Xiǎoměi, nǐ de biǎoyǎn zhēn bàng! Wǒ kěyǐ qǐng nǐ chī wǎnfàn ma?
王小美:	好啊！玛丽、中平他们也一起去吗？	Hǎo a! Mǎlì, Zhōngpíng tāmen yě yìqǐ qù ma?
陈大东:	我只想约你……	Wǒ zhǐ xiǎng yuē nǐ……
王小美:	哦……好的！	Ò……hǎo de!
陈大东:	我晚点儿跟你说在哪儿见面。	Wǒ wǎndiǎnr gēn nǐ shuō zài nǎr jiàn miàn.
王小美:	好，你再打电话告诉我吧！	Hǎo, nǐ zài dǎ diànhuà gàosu wǒ ba!

陈大东:	我真的紧张得不得了。这是我第一次跟小美约会。	Wǒ zhēnde jǐnzhāng de bùdéliǎo. Zhè shì wǒ dì-yī cì gēn Xiǎoměi yuēhuì.
黄祥安:	你喜欢小美什么呢？	Nǐ xǐhuan Xiǎoměi shénme ne?
陈大东:	她又聪明又善良，也很可爱。	Tā yòu cōngmíng yòu shànliáng, yě hěn kěài.
黄祥安:	女孩子都希望听别人说她美。这点你别忘记对她说喔。	Nǚháizi dōu xīwàng tīng biérén shuō tā měi. Zhèi diǎn nǐ bié wàngjì duì tā shuō ō.
陈大东:	什么！我记不住这么多！	Shénme, wǒ jì bu zhù zhème duō!
黄祥安:	你要让她知道你对她是很有感情的！	Nǐ yào ràng tā zhīdào nǐ duì tā shì hěn yǒu gǎnqíng de!
陈大东:	祥安！别开玩笑了，你还有什么建议吗？	Xiáng'ān! Bié kāiwánxiào le, nǐ hái yǒu shénme jiànyì ma?

黄祥安：　吃完饭，你可以跟她去公园散散步，再约她下次出去玩。

Chī wán fàn, nǐ kěyǐ gēn tā qù gōngyuán sànsan bù, zài yuē tā xià cì chūqu wán.

王小美：　嗨！

Hēi!

陈大东：　你今天真漂亮……

Nǐ jīntiān zhēn piàoliang……

LESSON VOCABULARY 11.1

	SIMPLIFIED	TRADITIONAL	PINYIN	WORD CATEGORY	DEFINITION
1.	棒		bàng	*adj*	great; wonderful
2.	想		xiǎng	*v*	to think
3.	约	約	yuē	*v*	to arrange; to make an appointment
4.	晚点(儿)	晚點(兒)	wǎndiǎnr	*adv*	(a bit) later
5.	见面	見面	jiànmiàn	*vo*	to meet
6.	告诉	告訴	gàosu	*v*	to tell
7.	紧张	緊張	jǐnzhāng	*adj*	nervous
8.	不得了		bùdéliǎo	*adv*	(to an extreme degree)
9.	次		cì	*mw*	(used to describe the frequency of an action)
10.	约会	約會	yuēhuì	*vo, n*	to go on a date; date
11.	聪明	聰明	cōngmíng	*adj*	smart, intelligent
12.	善良		shànliáng	*adj*	nice, kind, kind-hearted
13.	可爱	可愛	kě'ài	*adj*	cute
14.	希望		xīwàng	*v, n*	to hope; hope
15.	别人	別人	biérén	*n*	other people
16.	美		měi	*adj*	beautiful
17.	点	點	diǎn	*n*	point, characteristic
18.	忘记	忘記	wàngjì	*rv*	to forget

	SIMPLIFIED	TRADITIONAL	PINYIN	WORD CATEGORY	DEFINITION
19.	喔		ō	*interj*	(used to indicate a reminder, admonition, or warning)
20.	记不住	記不住	jì bu zhù	*rv*	to be unable to remember
21.	让	讓	ràng	*v*	to allow or cause (somebody to do something)
22.	感情		gǎnqíng	*n*	feeling, emotion
23.	开玩笑	開玩笑	kāi wánxiào	*v*	to joke
	玩笑		wánxiào	*n*	joke
24.	建议	建議	jiànyì	*v, n*	to suggest; suggestion, advice
25.	公园	公園	gōngyuán	*n*	park
26.	散步		sàn bù	*vo*	to go for a stroll
27.	下次		xià cì	*n*	next time
28.	出去玩(儿)	出去玩(兒)	chūqu wán(r)	*ie*	to go out and play, have a good time
	出去		chūqu	*dc*	to go outside

REQUIRED VOCABULARY 11.1

ADJECTIVES

29.	好看		hǎokàn	*adj*	pretty; good-looking
30.	帅	帥	shuài	*adj*	handsome
31.	不要闹了	不要鬧了	bú yào nào le	*ie*	stop it! (used when others are not being serious, poking fun at someone)
	闹	鬧	nào	*v*	to stir up trouble; to make noise

OPTIONAL VOCABULARY 11.1

RELATED TO RELATIONSHIPS

32.	玫瑰花		méiguīhuā	*n*	rose
33.	送花		sòng huā	*vo*	to give flowers
34.	吻		wěn	*v, n*	to kiss; kiss

OTHER

35.	上次		shàng cì	*n*	last time

Loan Words

A loan word is a word that one language borrows from another. English has an abundance of such words; from French phrases like "déjà vu," "faux pas," and "souvenir," to "kindergarten" from German and "guerilla" from Spanish.

As China's contact with the world has increased, so too has the amount of loan words in the Chinese language. Chinese has taken many loan words from English, but there are also a number from other languages. In Taiwan, a common example is 便当 (biàndāng), meaning "boxed meal," which is taken from the Japanese "bento," while both Taiwan and Mainland China use 榻榻米 (tàtàmǐ) as the word for "tatami."

Loan words in Chinese are absorbed in two primary ways. Some words are translated in conceptual terms, for example 电脑 (diànnǎo: "electric brain" – "computer"), while others are simply a phonetic representation of the original word. The following is a list of the main phonetic loan words that have been introduced so far. Note that some of the words combine phonetic components with existing Chinese terms.

Term	Pinyin	Meaning
咖啡	kāfēi	coffee
派对	pàiduì	party
沙发	shāfā	sofa
摩托车	mótuōchē	motorcycle

Term	Pinyin	Meaning
T-恤衫	T-xùshān	T-Shirt
酷	kù	cool
高尔夫球	gāo'ěrfūqiú	golf
吉他	jítā	guitar

English is not without its share of words borrowed from Chinese, either. "Kung Fu" 功夫 (gōngfu), "feng shui" 风水 (fēngshuǐ), "typhoon" 台风 (táifēng), and "gung-ho" 工合 (gōnghé) are just some of the diverse words and phrases that have been adapted into the English vocabulary.

Online Resources

Visit *http://college.betterchinese.com* for a list of other loan words.

Associative Compounds

As has been seen in previous lessons, Chinese characters can be classified as phono-semantic compounds, pictographs, and ideographs. Another classification that is relatively common is the associative compound (会意: huìyì). With associative compounds, different elements are joined into a single character, the meaning of which is suggested by the combination of its components. Below are some examples of associative compounds.

Compound	Components
好 (hǎo: "good")	女 (nǚ: "woman")
	子 (zǐ: "son")
男 (nán: "male")	田 (tián: "field")
	力 (lì: "strength")
明 (míng: "bright")	日 (rì: "sun")
	月 (yuè: "moon")

Compound	Components
安 (ān: "peaceful; safe")	女 (nǚ: "woman")
	宀 (mián: "roof")
家 (jiā: "home; family")	豕 (shǐ: "pig")
	宀 (mián: "roof")

STRUCTURE NOTE 11.1
Use 得 to indicate degree or result

In Structure Note 10.9, 得 was used to describe the manner in which something is done. With this pattern, it is also possible to place a complement of degree after the adjective instead of using the standard adverbial modifiers before it. 很 and 不得了 (bùdéliǎo) are the most common of these, both of which mean "very" or "extremely" in English. However, when a whole phrase follows 得, it is equivalent to "so much that . . ." or "to the extent that . . ." in English.

> Subject + Adjective + 得 + 很

> Subject + Adjective + 得 + 不得了

> Subject + Adjective + 得 + Clause

From the Lesson Text:

我真的紧张得不得了。
Wǒ zhēnde jǐnzhāng de bùdéliǎo.
I'm so nervous.

Other examples:

他的女儿聪明得很。
Tā de nǚér cōngmíng de hěn.
His daughter is really smart.

我高兴得想跳舞了！
Wǒ gāoxìng de xiǎng tiàowǔ le!
I'm so happy that I want to dance!

Practice: Transform the following sentences into Chinese using 得 and a complement of degree.

Example: Their kids are really cute. → 他们的小孩子可爱得很。

1. This park is really beautiful.

   _____

2. I'm so tired that I can't get out of bed.

   _____

3. After he finished the test, he was incredibly happy.

   _____

4. It's extremely quiet in this library.

   _____

5. He's so busy that he doesn't have time to meet his friends.

   _____

STRUCTURE NOTE 11.2
Use 次 to express number of times

次 (cì) *is a special type of measure word called a verbal measure word that measure events. 次 is used similarly to the English word "times," as in "I have been to China three times." To express that something has happened a certain number of times, the 次 phrase is usually placed between the verb and the object, but may also appear after the object. To talk about a particular time, such as the first time, the 次 phrase is placed before the event, as in* 我第一次跟小美约会 *("The first time I had a date with Xiaomei") or* 我上次去商店，买了一本书 *("The last time I went to the store, I bought a book").*

Subject + Verb + Number + 次 (+ Object)

Subject + Verb (+ Object) + Number + 次

Subject + 次 Phrase + Verb Phrase

From the Lesson Text:　这是我第一次跟小美约会。
Zhè shì wǒ dì-yī cì gēn Xiǎoměi yuē huì.
This is my first date with Xiaomei.

Other examples:

我去了两次北京。
Wǒ qù le liǎng cì Běijīng.
I went to Beijing twice.

我去了北京两次。
Wǒ qù le Běijīng liǎng cì.
I went to Beijing twice.

你这个星期给爸爸妈妈打了几次电话？
Nǐ zhèige xīngqī gěi bàba māma dǎ le jǐ cì diànhuà?
How many times did you call your parents this week?

Practice: Form complete sentences using the information below, following the example given.

Example:　二〇〇八年 / 波士顿 (三次)
→ 二〇〇八年，我去了三次波士顿。

1. 昨天 / 打 / 网球 (第一次)

   _____

2. 今天 / 看 / 课文 (两次)

   _____

3. 昨天 / 去 / 图书馆 (三次)

   _____

4. 今天 / 拉 / 小提琴 (一次)

   _____

5. 最近 / 回 / 家 (几次)

   _____

STRUCTURE NOTE 11.3

Use 让 to express to "let" or "make" someone do something

The verb 让 *(ràng) has several distinct meanings. It can mean, among other things, to allow someone to do something or to make someone do something. These meanings are expressed using the same sentence structure, so be careful to check the context of the statement to figure out the specific meaning of* 让 *in each instance.*

Subject + 让 + Someone + Verb Phrase

From the Lesson Text:

你要让她知道你对她是很有感情的！
Nǐ yào ràng tā zhīdào nǐ duì tā shì hěn yǒu gǎnqíng de!
You also have to let her know that you have a lot of feelings for her!

Other examples:

我哥哥常常让我送他
去看他的女朋友。
Wǒ gēge chángcháng ràng wǒ
sòng tā qù kàn tā de nǚ péngyou.
My older brother often makes me
take him to see his girlfriend.

她爸爸妈妈不会让她来
我们的派对。
Tā bàba māma bú huì ràng tā lái
wǒmen de pàiduì.
Her parents aren't going to let her
come to our party.

Practice: Change the following Chinese sentences into English. Remember to pay attention to the meaning of 让 in different contexts.

Example: 她不喜欢让别人弹她爸爸的吉他。
→ She doesn't like to let other people play her dad's guitar.

1. 妈妈让我给弟弟做晚饭。

   _____

2. 他不让我开他新买的车子。

   _____

3. 老师让同学帮我做作业。

   _____

4. 这家商店不让客人刷卡，你得付现金。

   _____

5. 你应该让她知道你对她有感情。

   _____

STRUCTURE NOTE 11.4
Use 记住 *to describe keeping something in mind*

The character 记 *(jì) on its own means "to remember," but in Chinese this meaning is usually expressed with one of several two-character expressions. In this lesson,* 记 *is combined with the resultative complement* 住 *(zhù) to describe keeping something in mind. As with all resultative complement patterns,* 得 *or* 不 *can be inserted between the verb and its complement to express that someone is or is not able to keep something in mind.*

> Subject + 记 + (得 / 不) + 住

From the Lesson Text:
我记不住这么多！
Wǒ jì bu zhù zhème duō!
I can't remember all this!

Other examples:
记住，明天要给我
打电话！
Jìzhù, míngtiān yào gěi wǒ
dǎ diànhuà!
Remember, you must call me
tomorrow!

这么难的生词，你记得
住吗？
Zhème nán de shēngcí, nǐ jì de zhù
ma?
Will you be able to remember such difficult vocabulary?

Practice: Turn the following fragments into complete sentences using 记住, 记得住, or 记不住 as directed.

Example:　明天有考试
→ 同学们，你们明天有考试，你们要记住啊！

1.　这么容易的语法 (记住)

　　_____

2.　到图书馆怎么走 (记不住)

　　_____

3.　老师给你的建议 (记得住)

　　_____

4.　给他生日礼物 (记住)

　　_____

5.　小美星期六要表演 (记住)

　　_____

PRACTICE 11.1

Working with a partner, use the images and numbers below to act out dialogues in which you ask each other how many times you have done the activities shown before.

Example:

A: 这是你第几次去北京？
B: 这是我第三次去北京。

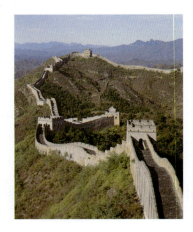

PRACTICE 11.2

With a partner, create a short dialogue based on the following scenario.
1. You want to ask someone to go out.
2. You try to coordinate schedules to meet, but his or her schedule keeps conflicting.
3. Discuss where to go, where to meet, and what to do.
4. After a date is settled, write the final decision in the table.

Where are you going?	What are you doing?	Where are you meeting?	When are you going?

✏ PRACTICE 11.3

Write a letter to someone you like using the vocabulary and sentence patterns that you have learned. An example is given for you.

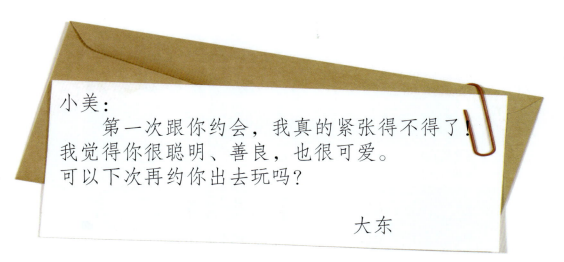

小美：

　　第一次跟你约会，我真的紧张得不得了！
我觉得你很聪明、善良，也很可爱。
可以下次再约你出去玩吗？

大东

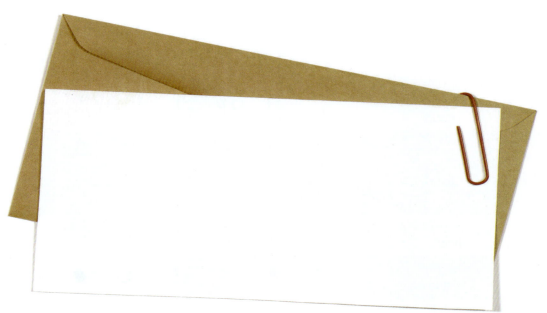

💬 PRACTICE 11.4

Make an audio recording and send it to your teacher. In the recording, describe some of the positive or admirable qualities of someone you know.

	Radical	Stroke Order
美	羊 yáng sheep	丶 丷 丷 丷 丷 羊 羊 美 美
告	口 kǒu mouth	丿 丿 屮 牛 牛 告 告
诉	讠(言) yán speech	丶 讠 讠 讠 诉 诉 诉
紧	纟(丝) sī silk	丨 刂 刂 刞 坚 竖 竖 紧 紧
约	纟(丝) sī silk	乙 纟 纟 纟 约 约
聪	耳 ěr ear	一 丆 厅 厅 月 耳 耵 耵 聍 耴 耴 聪 聪 聪
希	巾 jīn cloth	丿 乄 兰 产 矛 希 希
望	月 yuè moon	丶 亠 亡 切 切 胡 胡 望 望 望
让	讠(言) yán speech	丶 讠 讠 让 让
感	心 xīn heart	一 厂 厂 厅 后 咸 咸 咸 咸 感 感 感
情	忄(心) xīn heart	丶 丷 忄 忄 忄 忄 情 情 情 情
建	廴 yǐn stride	乛 彐 彐 彐 聿 聿 建 建
议	讠(言) yán speech	丶 讠 讠 议 议
公	八 bā eight	丿 八 公 公
散	攵(攴) pū knock	一 十 サ 昔 昔 昔 肯 肯 肯 散 散

PRACTICE 11.6

Type the following sentences on your computer and provide an answer to the question.

1. 你今晚的表演真棒！
2. 我晚点儿再打电话告诉你在哪儿见面。
3. 这是我第一次约会，真的紧张得不得了。
4. 我的女朋友又聪明又善良。
5. 你对我的感情是真的吗？

PRACTICE 11.7

明天我要跟小美约会。因为这是我第一次约会，所以我紧张得不得了！我不知道应该对她说什么。祥安说我要对小美说她很漂亮，也很可爱。还要让她知道，我很喜欢她，我对她的感情是真的。祥安还建议吃完晚饭以后带小美去公园散散步，再约她下次见面。

Read Chen Dadong's diary and answer the following questions.
1. How does Chen Dadong feel about his upcoming date?
2. What does Huang Xiang'an suggest that Chen Dadong do after dinner?

PRACTICE 11.8

黄祥安：我可以请你吃晚饭吗？
张安娜：好啊！你还请了哪些人？
黄祥安：我只请你一个人。
张安娜：哦……好的！我们在哪儿见面？
黄祥安：我五点半在你宿舍的门口等你。
张安娜：行，我们去哪儿吃饭？
黄祥安：你喜欢吃法国菜吗？
张安娜：法国菜太贵了，我们还是吃便宜一点儿的吧！
黄祥安：你真好！

Read the dialogue and answer the following questions.
1. Where are Huang Xiang'an and Zhang Anna going to meet?
2. Are they going to have French food? Why?

Sender	玛丽
Subject	约会

大东：

　　你跟小美的第一次约会怎么样？小美约会回来以后高兴得不得了！你们去哪儿玩了？她喜欢吃中国菜，你跟她去中国饭馆吃晚饭了吗？

Sender	大东
Subject	re: 约会

玛丽：

　　上个星期六我跟小美约会了，很开心。我跟她去听钢琴音乐会，然后我们去中国饭馆吃她喜欢的烧鸡。我下个月要回加拿大，我打算问小美要不要跟我一起去那儿玩。

Read the e-mails and answer the following questions.
1. Where did Chen Dadong take Wang Xiaomei for their date?
2. What does he plan to ask her to do next?

Chinese Valentine's Day: The Story of the Cowherd and Weaver Girl

The story of the cowherd and the weaver girl is a well-known romantic folk tale in China. Although there are many versions of the tale, the basic story goes something like this:

One day, 牛郎 (niúláng: "the cowherd") encountered seven immortal fairy sisters. The cowherd fell in love with the youngest fairy, 织女 (zhīnǚ: "the weaver girl"), the most beautiful of the sisters and a skilled seamstress. The pair was soon happily wed with two children. Everything was going well until the Goddess of Heaven found out about the forbidden marriage between the mortal and the fairy. Enraged, she forced the weaver girl to return to the heavens.

One of the cowherd's oxen saw how distraught his master was and suddenly began to speak. The ox told the cowherd that if he killed him and put on his hide, the cowherd would be able to ascend to Heaven in search of his wife. The cowherd followed the ox's instructions and rose to the sky carrying his two children. After discovering this, the wrathful Goddess of Heaven used her hairpin to create a wide river in the sky separating the two lovers forever. From then on, the weaver girl lived on one side of the river crafting embroidery, while the cowherd lived on the other side taking care of their two children. But, once every year, magpies take to the sky to form a bridge across the river so that the cowherd and the weaver girl can be together again for one night.

On 七夕 (Qīxī: "the seventh night of the seventh lunar month"), the stars which represent the cowherd and the weaver girl appear to be moving closer together, and thus this day became the Qixi Festival, a time to celebrate romance and relationships.

China's Tallest Couple

At 7'6" and 6'3", 姚明 (Yáo Míng) and 叶莉 (Yè Lì) are certainly the tallest celebrity couple in China! Yao Ming, an international basketball superstar who has played for the NBA's Houston Rockets, is a huge source of national pride in China. Arguably the most influential athlete in Chinese history, Yao Ming was the number one NBA draft pick in 2002 and made the All-Star team in his rookie year. But he is not the first in his family to excel at the sport — Yao Ming's father was a professional basketball player, and his mother a captain of the women's Chinese national team.

His wife, the only woman he has ever dated, is also a former basketball player. She played professionally in China and was also a captain of the national team. Initially, Ye Li was not interested in dating Yao Ming. However, she began to reconsider after Yao Ming gave her the team pins he had collected during the Olympic Games in Sydney. After eight years of dating, Yao Ming and Ye Li married in Shanghai in August 2007. The couple is praised not only for their athletic talent, but also for their numerous contributions to charity. Yao Ming has been active in environmental protection campaigns and has served as a global ambassador for the Special Olympics. In addition, he created the Yao Ming Foundation, an organization dedicated to rebuilding schools destroyed by the 2008 earthquake in Sichuan and helping those affected by Hurricane Ike in Houston.

陈大东：小美，你的表演真棒！我可以请你吃晚饭吗？

Xiaomei, your performance was great! May I treat you to dinner?

王小美：好啊！玛丽、中平他们也一起去吗？

Sure! Will Mali, Zhongping and the others be going too?

陈大东：我只想约你……

I was just thinking it would be just you and me . . .

王小美：哦……好的！

Oh . . . OK!

陈大东：我晚点儿跟你说在哪儿见面。

I'll tell you later where we should meet.

王小美：好，你再打电话告诉我吧！

Sure, just call me.

陈大东：我真的紧张得不得了。这是我第一次跟小美约会。

I'm so nervous. This is my first date with Xiaomei.

黄祥安：你喜欢小美什么呢？

What do you like about Xiaomei?

陈大东：她又聪明又善良，也很可爱。

She's both smart and kind-hearted, and also very cute.

黄祥安：女孩子都希望听别人说她美。这点你别忘记对她说喔。

Girls all want to be told that they're beautiful. Don't forget to tell her, OK?

陈大东：什么！我记不住这么多！

What? I can't remember all this!

黄祥安：你要让她知道你对她是很有感情的！

You also have to let her know that you have a lot of feelings for her!

黄祥安：祥安！别开玩笑了，你还有什么建议吗？

Stop joking around Xiang'an! Do you have any other suggestions?

王小美：吃完饭，你可以跟她去公园散散步，再约她下次出去玩。

After dinner, you can take her for a stroll in the park, and then ask her out on another date.

王小美：嗨！

Hi!

陈大东：你今天真漂亮……

You look so pretty today . . .

398 第十一单元 • 第一课 • 情

What Can You Do?

INTERPRETIVE
- I can understand different terms for personal characteristics and features.

INTERPERSONAL
- I can arrange to go on a date with someone.
- I can offer suggestions to someone and receive them in return.

PRESENTATIONAL
- I can give a basic presentation about a person's qualities and attributes.

分手
A Break Up

安娜，你 zěn me le 怎么了？ fā shēng 发生什么事了？可以跟我说说吗？

我······跟我男 nán péng you fēn 朋友分 shǒu 手了。

nán guò 哦，别难过了！

nán guò 我不是难过，我是 fēi cháng shēng qì 非常生气。

他做什么了？

bèi piàn 我被他骗了。他跟我 jiāo wǎng 交往的时候，还一直跟他在俄罗斯 nǚ péng you 的女朋友有 lián xì 联系。

LESSON TEXT 11.2

A Break Up 分手

Sun Mali sees that Zhang Anna is upset and asks her what is wrong. Zhang Anna reveals that she has broken up with her boyfriend.

孙玛丽:	安娜，你怎么了？发生什么事了？可以跟我说说吗？	Ānnà, nǐ zěnme le? Fāshēng shénme shì le? Kěyǐ gēn wǒ shuōshuo ma?
张安娜:	我……跟我男朋友分手了。	Wǒ……gēn wǒ nán péngyou fēnshǒu le.
孙玛丽:	哦，别难过了！	Ò, bié nánguò le!
张安娜:	我不是难过，我是非常生气。	Wǒ bú shì nánguò, wǒ shì fēicháng shēngqì.
孙玛丽:	他做什么了？	Tā zuò shénme le?
张安娜:	我被他骗了。他跟我交往的时候，还一直跟他在俄罗斯的女朋友有联系。	Wǒ bèi tā piàn le. Tā gēn wǒ jiāowǎng de shíhou, hái yìzhí gēn tā zài Éluósī de nǚ péngyou yǒu liánxì.

孙玛丽:	真的吗？怎么会这样？	Zhēnde ma? Zěnme huì zhèyàng?
张安娜:	我们还谈过结婚的事，可是现在……	Wǒmen hái tán guo jiéhūn de shì, kěshì xiànzài……
孙玛丽:	唉，别哭了。忘了他吧。	Ài, bié kū le. Wàngle tā ba.
张安娜:	可是我做不到，我从来没有这么爱过一个人。	Kěshì wǒ zuò bu dào, wǒ cónglái méiyǒu zhème ài guo yí gè rén.
孙玛丽:	你会找到一个更好的男朋友。	Nǐ huì zhǎo dào yí gè gèng hǎo de nán péngyou.

LESSON VOCABULARY 11.2

	SIMPLIFIED	TRADITIONAL	PINYIN	WORD CATEGORY	DEFINITION
1.	怎么了	怎麼了	zěnme le	qph	what's wrong; what's the matter
2.	发生	發生	fāshēng	v	to happen
3.	男朋友		nán péngyou	n	boyfriend
4.	分手		fēnshǒu	vo	to break up
5.	难过	難過	nánguò	adj	sad
6.	非常		fēicháng	adv	very, extremely
7.	生气	生氣	shēngqì	adj	mad, angry
8.	被		bèi	prep	by (passive)
9.	骗	騙	piàn	v	to cheat, to trick, to fool
10.	交往		jiāowǎng	v	to be in a relationship; to associate (with); to contact
11.	俄罗斯	俄羅斯	Éluósī	n	Russia
12.	女朋友		nǚ péngyou	n	girlfriend
13.	联系	聯繫	liánxì	v	to contact, to get in touch with
14.	谈	談	tán	v	to talk, discuss
15.	过	過	guo	p	(used after a verb to indicate a past experience)
16.	结婚	結婚	jiéhūn	vo	to get married
17.	唉		ài	interj	(expresses sadness, sympathy, disappointment etc.)
18.	哭		kū	v	to cry
19.	从来	從來	cónglái	adv	always, all along; never (when used in the negative)
20.	爱	愛	ài	v	to love

REQUIRED VOCABULARY 11.2

SIMPLIFIED	TRADITIONAL	PINYIN	WORD CATEGORY	DEFINITION
RELATED TO RELATIONSHIPS				
21. 相信		xiāngxìn	*v*	to believe
22. 心		xīn	*n*	heart
OTHER				
23. 联络	聯絡	liánluò	*v*	to contact; to have contact

OPTIONAL VOCABULARY 11.2

SIMPLIFIED	TRADITIONAL	PINYIN	WORD CATEGORY	DEFINITION
RELATED TO RELATIONSHIPS				
24. 眼泪	眼淚	yǎnlèi	*n*	tears
25. 情人		qíngrén	*n*	lover; sweetheart
26. 离婚	離婚	líhūn	*vo*	to divorce
27. 坏	壞	huài	*adj*	bad
28. 吵架		chǎojià	*vo*	to quarrel; to fight

Relationship Terms

Just as in other languages, terms for relationships and dating change in Chinese as customs change and trends come and go. Below are some common relationship terms that one may come across.

Term	Pinyin	Meaning	Example	Meaning
交往	jiāowǎng	to date	我在跟他交往。	I am dating him.
分手	fēn shǒu	to break up	我跟他分手了。	I broke up with him.
吹	chuī	to break up (slang)	我跟他吹了。	I broke up with him.
对象	duìxiàng	boyfriend or girlfriend; partner	她有没有对象？	Does she have a partner?
男朋友	nán péngyou	boyfriend	她有没有男朋友？	Does she have a boyfriend?
宝贝	bǎobèi	treasure, darling, baby	宝贝，我爱你。	Baby, I love you.

Chinese Punctuation

By now, you may have noticed that Chinese punctuation is not always identical to punctuation in English. While Chinese has borrowed the question mark, exclamation mark, and comma, among other things, it also has a number of punctuation marks of its own. We have already encountered one of these in the form of the enumeration comma (、). The following are some of the other punctuation marks used in modern Chinese.

Punctuation Mark	Name	Usage
。	句号 jùhào	Period – used in the same way as its English equivalent.
《 》	双书名号 shuāng shūmínghào	Title marks – used for the title of a book or film, e.g., 《三国演义》.
·	间隔号 jiàngéhào	Middle dot – sometimes used to separate foreign names, e.g., 文森特·梵·高 (Wénsēntè·Fàn·Gāo: Vincent Van Gogh).
" "	引号 yǐnhào	Quotation marks – Simplified Chinese uses the same quotation marks as English when written horizontally. Traditional Chinese indicates single quotation marks with 「…」 and double quotation marks with 『…』.
——	破折号 pòzhéhào	Dash – The dash in Chinese is longer than its English counterpart in order to distinguish it from the character 一.
＿＿	专名号 zhuānmínghào	In some texts, proper nouns are underscored with a straight line, e.g., <u>陈大东</u>.
˙˙˙	着重号 zhuózhònghào	Chinese does not commonly use italics. Instead, a single dot is written underneath every character that one wishes to emphasize.
⋯⋯	省略号 shěnglüèhào	The Chinese ellipsis consists of six dots, unlike the English equivalent which is made up of three (. . .).

STRUCTURE NOTE 11.5
Use 被 to form the passive voice

The passive voice is used when the subject is acted upon by something else. In English, "he was hit" and "he was hit by a car" are both examples of passive statements. The first example is called an "agentless passive," because the person or thing responsible for the action is not specified, while in the second statement the agent is clearly specified. In Chinese, there are similar patterns for passive statements with and without agents. One way to form these is with the passive marker 被 (bèi). As is the case with 把, sentences with passive markers require that the verb take a suffix or complement.

In general, Chinese uses the passive voice less frequently than English. It is usually used in situations where something unpleasant has happened, such as getting hit by a car or being tricked. In neutral or positive situations, one should therefore avoid using 被.

Subject + 被 + Agent + Verb Phrase

Subject + 被 + Verb Phrase

From the Lesson Text:
我被他骗了。
Wǒ bèi tā piàn le.
He cheated on me.

Other examples:

不好意思，那本书被人借走了。
Bù hǎo yìsi, nà běn shū bèi rén jiè zǒu le.
I'm sorry, that book has been checked out by someone.

真的，我的作业被狗吃了！
Zhēn de, wǒ de zuòyè bèi gǒu chī le!
Honestly, my homework was eaten by the dog!

NOTE: 被 *is the most frequent passive marker in the written language, but* 让, 给, *and* 叫 *can also be used for the same purpose.* 叫 *and* 让 *are not used without an agent.*

Practice: Use 被 to rewrite the following statements as passive expressions.

Example: 他打了我三次。→ 我被他打了三次。

1.   哎呀！那个售货员骗了我。

_____

2.   哥哥吃我们的米饭了。

_____

3.   玛丽买了那件红色的毛衣。

_____

4.   我要一双新的筷子，妹妹用过这双筷子了。

_____

5.   小狗把我做的蛋糕都吃了！

_____

STRUCTURE NOTE 11.6
Use 一直 *to express "constantly"*

There are a few ways in Chinese to express that something has repeatedly or continuously been going on over a period of time. The term 一直 *(yìzhí) literally means "straight," but it is also used figuratively to mean "always" or "the whole time." This is appropriate to use for a state or situation that has been consistent over a given period. In this pattern,* 都 *can also be added after* 一直 *for emphasis.*

Subject + 一直 (+ 都) + Verb Phrase

From the Lesson Text:

他跟我交往的时候，还一直跟他在俄罗斯的女朋友有联系。

Tā gēn wǒ jiāowǎng de shíhou, hái yìzhí gēn tā zài Éluósī de nǚ péngyou yǒu liánxì.

While we were dating, he was still in contact with his girlfriend in Russia.

Other examples:

我在他家的时候，他一直都在看功夫片。

Wǒ zài tā jiā de shíhou, tā yìzhí dōu zài kàn gōngfu piàn.

When I was at his house, he was watching kung fu movies the whole time.

我一直都希望可以找到一个爱我的人。

Wǒ yìzhí dōu xīwàng kěyǐ zhǎo dào yí gè ài wǒ de rén.

I have always hoped to be able to find a person to love me.

Practice: Use 一直 to change the following sentences into Chinese, following the example provided.

Example: I've always liked that teacher. → 我一直都喜欢那位老师。

1.   She has always been good to her friends.

_____

2.   My girlfriend has always been a vegetarian.

_____

3.   Last Saturday he was watching TV all day long.

_____

4.   Those two girls are always singing and dancing at parties.

_____

5.   When we had exams, he was always in the library reading.

_____

STRUCTURE NOTE 11.7
Use Verb + 过 *to express a past experience*

To express that one has done something before, as in "I have been to Beijing before," the suffix 过 *(guo) is used. This is distinct from the* 了 *described in Structure Notes 5.11 and 6.11, which marks an action that was completed at a certain point in the past. As opposed to the relative specificity of* 了, *the* 过 *suffix refers to a more general or undefined time period and is often used to ask people about things they have or have not done in their lifetime.* 过 *must always immediately follow the verb; any object, including in a verb-object construction, comes afterwards.*

> Subject + Verb + 过 (+ Object)

From the Lesson Text:

我们还谈过结婚的事，可是现在⋯⋯
Wǒmen hái tán guo jiéhūn de shì, kěshì xiànzài……
We even talked about getting married, but now . . .

Other examples:

他去过加州。
Tā qù guo Jiāzhōu.
He has been to California.

我哥哥吃过烧鸡。
Wǒ gēge chī guo shāojī.
My older brother has eaten roast chicken before.

Like 了, *the suffix* 过 *is negated by* 没(有). *Unlike* 了, *however,* 过 *is preserved in negative sentences rather than omitted. To give added emphasis to a negative* 过 *sentence,* 从来 *(cónglái) may be added in front of* 没有 *to express "never (before)."*

> Subject + 从来没(有) + Verb + 过 (+ Object)

From the Lesson Text:

我从来没有这么爱过一个人。
Wǒ cónglái méiyǒu zhème ài guo yí gè rén.
I never loved anyone this much.

Other examples:

我从来没有去过日本。
Wǒ cónglái méiyǒu qù guo Rìběn.
I've never been to Japan in my life.

烧鸡，我没吃过。
Shāojī, wǒ méi chī guo.
I've never had Roast Chicken before.

Practice: Create affirmative or negative sentences using 过 or (从来)没(有)⋯⋯过 in conjunction with the verbs, objects, and verb-object pairs given below.

Example: 我 / 去 / 北京 → 我从来没有去过北京。

1. 我们 / 打 / 网球 _____
2. 他 / 看 / 功夫片 _____
3. 我哥哥 / 结婚 _____
4. 我朋友 / 表演 _____
5. 她 / 学 / 中文 _____

PRACTICE 11.10

Working with a partner, use the passive voice to ask and answer questions about the situations below.

Example:
A: 你被谁骗了？
B: 我被男朋友骗了。

PRACTICE 11.11

Working with a partner, use the information below to ask each other what you have and have not done before.

钢琴

Example:
A: 我学过钢琴，你学过钢琴吗？
B: 我也学过。/ 我从来没有学过。

英国

宿舍

车

筷子

PRACTICE 11.12

Using the words in the box, write the correct emotion or feeling for each picture in the space provided.

难过　紧张　高兴　累　生气

	Radical	Stroke Order
男	田 tián field	丶 冂 冂 冂 田 田 毗 男
女	女 nǚ woman	乚 乆 女
朋	月 yuè moon	丿 刀 月 月 朋 朋 朋 朋
友	又 yòu again	一 ナ 方 友
难	又 yòu again	乛 又 刄 对 邓 矿 邓 难 难
过	辶 chuò walk	一 寸 寸 寸 讨 过
分	刀 dāo knife	丶 八 分 分
非	非 fēi wrong	丨 刂 扌 扌 非 非 非 非
被	衤(衣) yī clothes	丶 衤 衤 衤 衤 衬 衬 袘 被 被
交	亠 tóu lid	丶 亠 六 六 六 交
络	纟(丝) sī silk	乚 纟 纟 纟 纱 纹 终 络 络
联	耳 ěr ear	一 丆 丌 丌 丌 耳 耳 耵 耴 联 联 联
谈	讠(言) yán speech	丶 讠 讠 讠 谈 谈 谈 谈 谈 谈
结	纟(丝) sī silk	乚 纟 纟 纟 纠 纣 结 结 结
婚	女 nǚ woman	乚 乆 女 女 妒 妒 婚 婚 婚 婚 婚

Make an audio recording and send it to your teacher. In the recording, use the Verb + 过 pattern to describe places that you have been to and experiences that you have had.

Type the following sentences on your computer and provide an answer to the question.

1. 发生了什么事？可以告诉我吗？
2. 我跟我的女朋友分手了。
3. 我不是生气，我是非常难过。
4. 我从来没有这么爱过一个人。
5. 他跟我交往的时候，还跟别的女孩约会。

PRACTICE 11.16

Sender　祥安

Subject　女朋友

大东：

　　我昨天听到我的女朋友在房间里打电话，我问她打电话给谁，她说她跟她以前的男朋友一直还有联系。现在我应该怎么办呢？我也不知道我是生气还是难过。你觉得我应该怎么办？

Sender　大东

Subject　re: 女朋友

祥安：

　　我觉得她没有骗你啊！她是个好女孩吧！你应该找时间跟她谈谈，多跟她约会，这样你们的感情才会好。

Read the e-mails and answer the following questions.
1. Is Huang Xiang'an angry or sad?
2. What does Chen Dadong say that Huang Xiang'an should do?

国粹传情

PRACTICE 11.17

王小美：喂，安娜，你在做什么？
张安娜：没做什么，你有什么特别的事吗？
王小美：我想找你去看电影。
张安娜：对不起，我不想去。
王小美：你不是最爱看电影的吗？你怎么了？
张安娜：我很难过，昨天跟男朋友分手了。
王小美：别难过了！那我们去喝杯咖啡，谈一谈！
张安娜：好吧，我也希望听听你的建议。

Read the dialogue and answer the following questions.
1. Why doesn't Zhang Anna want to go to see a movie?
2. What do they decide to do instead?

PRACTICE 11.18

昨天我跟大东去看电影的时候很紧张，因为我很喜欢他，想跟他交往。可是他一直没有问我是不是可以做他的女朋友。我不想跟大东只做好朋友，我想做他的女朋友。我应该告诉他我的这些想法吗？他会怎么想呢？我们会怎么样呢？

Read Wang Xiaomei's diary and answer the following questions.
1. What is Wang Xiaomei waiting for Chen Dadong to ask her?
2. What does Wang Xiaomei think about Chen Dadong?

Chinese Wedding Traditions

Historically, Chinese marriages were arranged by the couple's parents and matchmakers. The couple would also consult a Chinese fortune-teller who would examine their birth dates and determine their compatibility. Many Chinese couples continue to follow a belief in lucky calendar dates today to pick the most auspicious day to wed.

Modern-day Chinese weddings have many unique conventions that are based on old customs and many that were created in the present era. Below are some of the typical features of a Chinese wedding.

Wedding Portraits

Many couples take their formal wedding portraits well before the ceremony itself; sometimes so early that they are even included with the invitations. These photo shoots are often very elaborate and expensive. The bride and groom will model different outfits and take pictures in a variety of fairytale studio backgrounds, as well as idyllic natural settings and famous locations.

Fetching the Bride

Another unique element of a Chinese wedding is a playful game where the bride's parents and friends officially "give away" the bride to the groom. Nowadays, this game is usually held at the bride's family home, where the bride is hidden inside a room. The groom, accompanied by his best man, attempts to coax the bride out by persuading her friends that he is worthy of her. To test his sincerity, he may have to answer questions about his bride, sing love songs, recite poetry, or even demonstrate his physical strength. Finally, after the groom has satisfied the demands of the bride's friends, the bride emerges and her friends and family wish the couple well as they depart.

Lavish Ceremonies

As a result of many Chinese families having only one child, the parents will often pay for a highly lavish ceremony. Wealthier families typically rent luxury cars adorned with special decorations for the couple and their motorcade. Chinese brides usually wear at least three dresses: a white, western style gown during the wedding ceremony; an elegant, traditional red cheongsam for the reception; and another ballroom dress to be worn at the end of the reception as guests leave.

Wedding Banquet

Wedding ceremonies are typically followed by a large banquet where guests enjoy food and entertainment. Following the Chinese belief that red is a lucky color, foods such as lobster, Peking duck, and red bean soup are served. It is common to serve a total of eight courses, with eight being a lucky number in Chinese culture. However, the couple does not typically eat with everyone else — instead, they visit each table, toasting their guests and thanking them for attending.

孙玛丽：	安娜，你怎么了？发生什么事了？可以跟我说说吗？	Anna, what's wrong? What happened? Do you want to talk about it?
张安娜：	我……跟我男朋友分手了。	I . . . broke up with my boyfriend.
孙玛丽：	哦，别难过了！	Oh, don't be sad!
张安娜：	我不是难过，我是非常生气。	I'm not sad, I'm extremely angry.
孙玛丽：	他做什么了？	What did he do?
张安娜：	我被他骗了。他跟我交往的时候，还一直跟他在俄罗斯的女朋友有联系。	He cheated on me. While we were dating, he was still in contact with his girlfriend in Russia.

孙玛丽：	真的吗？怎么会这样？	Really? How can that be?
张安娜：	我们还谈过结婚的事，可是现在……	We even talked about getting married, but now . . .
孙玛丽：	唉，别哭了。忘了他吧。	There there, don't cry. Forget about him.
张安娜：	可是我做不到，我从来没有这么爱过一个人。	But I can't. I never loved anyone this much.
孙玛丽：	你会找到一个更好的男朋友。	You will find a much better boyfriend.

What Can You Do?

INTERPRETIVE
- I can understand expressions in the passive voice.
- I can understand when someone is referring to a past experience.

INTERPERSONAL
- I can discuss issues relating to interpersonal relationships.
- I can talk about my emotions with someone.

PRESENTATIONAL
- I can give an account of a relationship between two people.
- I can give a description of how someone is feeling.

ACT IT OUT

Working in groups, compose an original three-minute skit that utilizes the vocabulary and structures introduced in Unit 11. Each of you should assume a role and have a roughly equal number of lines in the skit. Be prepared to perform your skit in class. You can either come up with your own story or choose from one of the following situations:

A) Your friend is planning a date with his new girlfriend and asks you for suggestions on what to do.

B) You come across two of your close friends arguing, and you help resolve the conflict.

C) Your friend is thinking of breaking up with her boyfriend. She explains to you why and you offer advice.

CHECK WHAT YOU CAN DO

RECOGNIZE

Adjectives
- □ 棒
- □ 紧张
- □ 聪明
- □ 善良
- □ 可爱
- □ 美
- □ 好看
- □ 帅
- □ 难过
- □ 生气

Adverbs
- □ 晚点
- □ 不得了
- □ 非常
- □ 从来

Idiomatic Expressions
- □ 不要闹了
- □ 出去玩（儿）

Interjections
- □ 喔
- □ 唉

Measure Word
- □ 次

Nouns
- □ 别人
- □ 点
- □ 感情
- □ 玩笑
- □ 公园
- □ 下次
- □ 玫瑰花
- □ 男朋友
- □ 俄罗斯
- □ 女朋友
- □ 心

Particle
- □ 过

Preposition
- □ 被

Question Phrases
- □ 怎么了

Verbs
- □ 想
- □ 约
- □ 见面
- □ 告诉
- □ 约会
- □ 希望
- □ 忘记
- □ 记不住
- □ 让
- □ 开玩笑

- □ 建议
- □ 散步
- □ 发生
- □ 分手
- □ 骗
- □ 交往
- □ 联系
- □ 谈
- □ 结婚
- □ 哭
- □ 爱
- □ 相信
- □ 联络

WRITE

- □ 美
- □ 告诉
- □ 紧约
- □ 聪希
- □ 望让
- □ 感情
- □ 建议
- □ 公散

- □ 男女朋友
- □ 难过
- □ 分非
- □ 被交
- □ 络联
- □ 谈结婚

USE

- □ 得 to indicate degree or result.
- □ 次 to express number of times.
- □ 让 to express to "let" or "make" someone do something.
- □ 记住 to describe keeping something in mind.

- □ 被 to form the passive voice.
- □ 一直 to express "constantly."
- □ Verb + 过 to express a past experience.

Medicine

医

Communication Goals

Lesson 1: 生病了 **Getting Sick**
- Inquire after a person's health.
- Describe the symptoms of an illness.
- Talk about the weather and the seasons.

Lesson 2: 看病 **At the Doctor's**
- Name illnesses and afflictions.
- Refer to different parts of the body.
- Describe some of the differences between Chinese and Western medicine.

第十二单元
UNIT 12

生病了
Getting Sick

安娜，你看起来不太
shū fu
舒服，是不是生病了？
shēng bìng

可能是吧。我跟男朋友分
tiān tiān shuì bu zháo
手以后，天天睡不着。

现在身体很不舒服，
dù zi téng tóu téng
肚子疼，头也很疼。

tiān qì lěng
最近天气冷得很，你要
bǎo zhòng shēn tǐ yǎn jing bí zi
保重身体啊！你的眼睛和鼻子都
zuì hǎo kàn bìng
红了，你最好去看病。

xià
可是现在下
yǔ
雨了，我不
想出去……

我可以送你去啊！你在这儿等我，我马上回来。

好吧，谢谢！

我认识一个很好的中医。我带你去他那儿看看，好不好？

中医？为什么不去看西医？

这位中医很不错。

好，试试吧。

LESSON TEXT 12.1

Getting Sick 生病了

Huang Xiang'an visits Zhang Anna and finds out that she is not feeling well. They decide to see a doctor of Traditional Chinese Medicine.

黄祥安：	安娜，你看起来不太舒服，是不是生病了？	Ānnà, nǐ kànqilai bú tài shūfu, shì bu shì shēngbìng le?
张安娜：	可能是吧。我跟男朋友分手以后，天天睡不着。现在身体很不舒服，肚子疼，头也很疼。	Kěnéng shì ba. Wǒ gēn nán péngyou fēn-shǒu yǐhòu, tiāntiān shuìbuzhao. Xiànzài shēntǐ hěn bù shūfu, dùzi téng, tóu yě hěn téng.
黄祥安：	最近天气冷得很，你要保重身体啊！你的眼睛和鼻子都红了，你最好去看病。	Zuìjìn tiānqì lěng de hěn, nǐ yào bǎozhòng shēntǐ a! Nǐ de yǎnjing hé bízi dōu hóng le, nǐ zuìhǎo qù kànbìng.
张安娜：	可是现在下雨了，我不想出去……	Kěshì xiànzài xià yǔ le, wǒ bù xiǎng chūqu……
黄祥安：	我可以送你去啊！你在这儿等我，我马上回来。	Wǒ kěyǐ sòng nǐ qù a! Nǐ zài zhèr děng wǒ, wǒ mǎshàng huílai.
张安娜：	好吧，谢谢！	Hǎo ba, xièxie!

黄祥安：	我认识一个很好的中医。我带你去他那儿看看，好不好？	Wǒ rènshi yí gè hěn hǎo de zhōngyī. Wǒ dài nǐ qù tā nàr kànkan, hǎo bu hǎo?
张安娜：	中医？为什么不去看西医？	Zhōngyī? Wèishénme bú qù kàn xīyī?
黄祥安：	这位中医很不错。	Zhèi wèi zhōngyī hěn búcuò.
张安娜：	好，试试吧。	Hǎo, shìshi ba.

字 词 VOCABULARY

LESSON VOCABULARY 12.1

	SIMPLIFIED	TRADITIONAL	PINYIN	WORD CATEGORY	DEFINITION
1.	舒服		shūfu	*adj*	comfortable; feeling well
2.	生病		shēngbìng	*vo*	to get sick
3.	天天		tiāntiān	*adv*	every day
4.	睡不着		shuìbuzháo	*rv*	to be unable to sleep
5.	肚子		dùzi	*n*	stomach
6.	疼		téng	*adj*	painful; sore
7.	头	頭	tóu	*n*	head
8.	天气	天氣	tiānqì	*n*	weather
9.	冷		lěng	*adj*	cold
10.	保重		bǎozhòng	*v*	to take care (of oneself)
11.	身体	身體	shēntǐ	*n*	body
12.	眼睛		yǎnjing	*n*	eyes
13.	鼻子		bízi	*n*	nose
14.	最好		zuìhǎo	*adv*	had better
15.	看病		kànbìng	*vo*	to see a doctor
16.	下雨		xià yǔ	*vo*	to rain
17.	中医	中醫	zhōngyī	*n*	(doctor of) Traditional Chinese Medicine
18.	西医	西醫	xīyī	*n*	(doctor of) Western medicine

REQUIRED VOCABULARY 12.1

	SIMPLIFIED	TRADITIONAL	PINYIN	WORD CATEGORY	DEFINITION
BODY PARTS					
19.	手		shǒu	*n*	hand
20.	脚	腳	jiǎo	*n*	foot
SEASONS					
21.	春天		chūntiān	*n*	spring
22.	夏天		xiàtiān	*n*	summer
23.	秋天		qiūtiān	*n*	autumn
24.	冬天		dōngtiān	*n*	winter
OTHER					
25.	痛		tòng	*adj*	painful
26.	还好	還好	hái hǎo	*adj*	not bad; OK; so-so
27.	下雪		xià xuě	*vo*	to snow
28.	热	熱	rè	*adj*	hot (as in temperature)

OPTIONAL VOCABULARY 12.1

	SIMPLIFIED	TRADITIONAL	PINYIN	WORD CATEGORY	DEFINITION
WEATHER					
29.	晴天		qíngtiān	*n*	clear day, sunny day
30.	阴天	陰天	yīntiān	*n*	cloudy day

Review of Intensifiers

Chinese includes a wide variety of intensifiers (adverbs that increase the degree of an adjective). Here are the intensifiers that have appeared in the lessons so far.

Intensifier	Meaning
还 + ADJ	Quite
很 + ADJ	Very
好 + ADJ	Very
真的 + ADV + ADJ	Really (真的 is usually followed by another intensifier, such as "真的很漂亮")
太 + ADJ + 了	So very
非常 + ADJ	Extremely
ADJ + 得很	Extremely
ADJ + 得不得了	Extremely

Weather Vocabulary

There are innumerable set expressions regarding weather and the seasons in Chinese. Many of these are four-character phrases that have their origins in classical poetry or fiction. Some are used in everyday speech and some have a more ornate feel, but it is nevertheless common to send poetic seasonal greetings to friends, particularly in the spring. Below are some examples of set expressions relating to different types of weather.

Expressions	Pinyin	Literal Meaning	Describes
滴水成冰	dīshuǐchéngbīng	dripping water becomes ice	freezing weather
骄阳似火	jiāoyángsìhuǒ	a harsh sun is like fire	very hot weather
风和日丽	fēnghérìlì	wind gentle, sun beautiful	warm and sunny weather
万里无云	wànlǐwúyún	10,000 *li,* no clouds	clear and sunny weather

STRUCTURE NOTE 12.1
Use 最好 to make suggestions

The expression 最好 (zuìhǎo) is similar to 只好, which was introduced in Structure Note 8.3 as a means to express "the only thing to do is . . ." 最好 is likewise used to suggest the best course of action in a given situation and is similar in meaning to "it would be best to . . ." It differs slightly in emphasis from 只好, which lays stress on the fact that one is being somewhat forced to do something.

Subject + 最好 + Verb Phrase

From the Lesson Text:

你最好去看病。
Nǐ zuìhǎo qù kànbìng.
You'd better go see a doctor.

Other examples:

你最好少玩游戏。
Nǐ zuìhǎo shǎo wán yóuxì.
You should play games less.

下次他最好跑得快一点儿。
Xiàcì tā zuìhǎo pǎo de kuài yìdiǎnr.
Next time, he should run a bit faster.

Practice: Using 最好, suggest a course of action that could be taken in the following situations, following the example provided.

Example: 大东生病了。→ 你最好送他去看病。

1. 你看，外面下雨了。

_____

2. 西医我已经看了，还是不舒服。

_____

3. 他说他昨天晚上睡不着。

_____

4. 我真爱他！

_____

5. 我不爱他了。

_____

STRUCTURE NOTE 12.2
Use 带 to express bringing objects or people

带 (dài) means "to bring/take an item/person to a destination." In some cases, 带 is equivalent to 送. However, while 送 means to escort or transport someone somewhere, 带 is more frequently employed when taking someone along to a shared destination, or to a destination where the subject was heading anyway.

Subject + 带 + Something / Someone (+ Verb Phrase)

From the Lesson Text:	我带你去他那儿看看好不好？
	Wǒ dài nǐ qù tā nàr kànkan hǎo bu hǎo?
	I'll take you to go see him, okay?

Other examples:

我忘了带我的本子。	他没有带他妹妹去看医生。
Wǒ wàngle dài wǒ de běnzi.	Tā méiyǒu dài tā mèimei qù kàn yīshēng.
I forgot to bring my notebook.	He didn't take his younger sister to see the doctor.

Practice: Complete the sentences below using expressions containing 带, as in the example given.

Example:　去上课的时候······　→ 不应该带手机。

1. 明天是她的生日······　　_____
2. 我们明天在音乐会表演······　_____
3. 去商店买东西的时候······　_____
4. 学校离这里不远······　_____
5. 外面冷了······　_____

STRUCTURE NOTE 12.3
Use noun or measure word reduplication to express "every"

When nouns and measure words are reduplicated, it creates the meaning "every," as in "every book." Only certain words are capable of reduplication. Among these, 人, 天, 年, 个, and 本 are some of the most common. Such expressions are often augmented with the use of 都, which follows the reduplicated noun or measure word.

> Noun + Noun (+ 都) + Verb Phrase/Adjective

> Measure Word + Measure Word (+ 都) + Verb Phrase/Adjective

From the Lesson Text:	我跟男朋友分手以后，天天睡不着。
	Wǒ gēn nán péngyou fēnshǒu yǐhòu, tiāntiān shuì bu zháo.
	After I broke up with my boyfriend, I haven't been sleeping well.

Other examples:

人人都会生病。	他写的书本本都很有意思。
Rénrén dōu huì shēng bìng.	Tā xiě de shū běnběn dōu hěn yǒu yìsi.
Everyone gets sick.	All of the books that he writes are interesting.

Practice: Change the following sentences into "every" sentences using noun or measure word reduplication.

Example: 这里的天气 / 天 / 热 → 这里的天气天天都很热。

1. 不是 / 家 / 有宠物 _____
2. 这本课本 / 课 / 难 _____
3. 小朋友 / 个 / 可爱 _____
4. 最近 / 天 / 做功课 _____
5. 这些菜 / 盘 / 好吃 _____

STRUCTURE NOTE 12.4
Use name/pronoun + 那儿 to talk about someone's location or home

Adding 那儿 after someone's name or a pronoun can either refer to someone's home, as in "his place," or simply to their location. As is the case with the term "his place" in English, this expression has a colloquial feel in Chinese.

Noun / Pronoun + 那儿

From the Lesson Text: 我带你去他那儿看看，好不好？
Wǒ dài nǐ qù tā nàr kànkan, hǎo bu hǎo?
I'll take you to see him, OK?

Other examples:
大东那儿有很多书。
Dàdōng nàr yǒu hěn duō shū.
There are a lot of books at Dadong's place.

你那儿有笔吗？
Nǐ nàr yǒu bǐ ma?
Do you have a pen over there?

Practice: Change the following sentences into Chinese, using the Name/Pronoun + 那儿 pattern.

Example: Have you ever been to his place? → 你去过他那儿吗？

1. Do they have a television at their place?

   _____

2. She has a cat at her place.

   _____

3. His place is huge; he has five bedrooms and three bathrooms!

   _____

4. Do you have a notebook over there?

   _____

5. My cellphone is over there with him.

   _____

练习 PRACTICE

PRACTICE 12.1

Working with a partner, practice the following dialogue. You see that your friend is not feeling well and you ask what is wrong with him or her. Your friend responds by describing his or her symptoms.

Example:

A: 你还好吗？你看起来不舒服，你生病了吗？

B: 我想是吧。我头很疼，晚上都睡不着，觉得很累。

PRACTICE 12.2

Take a survey of the class to find out whether students would go to see a doctor of Traditional Chinese Medicine or a doctor of Western medicine if they were sick. Record the most popular answer choice below.

Kind of Doctor	Number of Students

PRACTICE 12.3

In the spaces provided, write down an appropriate description of how you think the person in the picture feels.

  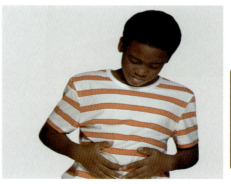 

💬 PRACTICE 12.4

Look at the pictures below and suggest what each person should do using 最好.

Example:
A: 现在下雨了。
B: 你最好别出去。

现在下雨了。

我妹妹看起来生病了。

明天有考试。

今天天气冷得很。

我忘了带作业。

💻 PRACTICE 12.5

Type the following sentences on your computer.

1. 我跟男朋友分手以后，天天都睡不着。
2. 我肚子疼，头也很疼。
3. 你看起来很不舒服，眼睛和鼻子都红了。
4. 你最好去看中医。
5. 最近天气冷得很，你要多保重身体。

PRACTICE 12.6

	Radical	Stroke Order
服	月 yuè moon	丿 刀 月 月 肝 那 服 服
身	身 shēn body	丶 亻 勺 身 身 身
体	亻(人) rén person	丿 亻 仁 什 付 休 体
头	大 dà big	丶 丷 二 头 头
疼	疒 chuáng sick	丶 二 广 广 疒 疒 疒 疼 疼 疼
睡	目 mù eye	丨 冂 冂 月 目 目 目 睡 睡 睡 睡 睡
舒	人 rén person	丿 亽 片 长 伞 令 舍 舍 舒 舒 舒 舒
病	疒 chuáng sick	丶 二 广 广 疒 疒 疒 病 病 病
着	目 mù eye	丶 二 兰 兰 羊 羊 并 着 着 着
冷	冫(冰) bīng ice	丶 冫 冫 汁 冷 冷 冷
保	亻(人) rén person	丿 亻 亻 仁 伫 俨 伴 保 保
眼	目 mù eye	丨 冂 冂 月 目 目 眇 眇 眼 眼
睛	目 mù eye	丨 冂 冂 月 目 目 目 睛 睛 睛 睛 睛
医	匚 xì box	一 丆 匚 匚 医 医 医
带	巾 jīn cloth	一 十 卅 卅 卅 卅 带 带 带

PRACTICE 12.7

Make an audio recording and send it to your teacher. In the recording, describe what the weather in your hometown is like. Is it very hot in the summer? Does it snow in winter?

PRACTICE 12.8

李中平：大东，要不要一起去健身房运动？

陈大东：对不起，我不太舒服。我现在要去看病。

李中平：你还好吧？身体哪儿不舒服？

陈大东：从昨天晚上开始我的肚子就很痛，可能昨天在派对吃了太多东西。

李中平：你下次还是少吃点东西吧。

陈大东：我知道了……

李中平：我开车送你去看医生吧。

Read the dialogue and answer the following questions.
1. Where is Chen Dadong going?
2. Why is he feeling sick?

PRACTICE 12.9

安娜：

　　我今天有点不舒服，眼睛和鼻子都红红的，头也很疼。可能是最近天气冷了，昨晚又睡不着，所以生病了。大东昨天约了我今天下午五点半去看电影，可是我现在要去看医生。如果他来宿舍找我的话，你跟他说我生病了，不能跟他一起去看电影，好吗？还有，可不可以帮我买晚饭回来？谢谢。晚上见。

小美

Read Wang Xiaomei's note and answer the following questions.
1. What symptoms does Wang Xiaomei describe in the note?
2. What does she ask Zhang Anna to tell Chen Dadong?

Sender	妈妈
Subject	注意身体

小美：

　　你们那儿天气怎么样？你要多穿点儿衣服，别太晚睡觉。还有，要是身体不舒服，你要去看中医。你要保重身体啊！

Sender	小美
Subject	re: 注意身体

妈妈：

　　最近天气冷得很，昨晚还下雪了。你们那儿呢？妈妈，我不是小孩子了，生病的话我当然会去看医生啊！可是我们这儿找不到中医，只有西医。妈妈，你也要多保重身体啊！

Read the e-mails and answer the following questions.
1. What is Wang Xiaomei's mother's advice to her daughter?
2. What kind of doctor is Wang Xiaomei able to go see?

Massages

Chinese massages have a long history of providing health benefits. In the West, a massage would likely be had for recreation and relaxation. For the Chinese, however, massages not only relieve stress, they are also believed to affect organ, muscle, and mental performance. The traditional 按摩 (ànmó: "massage") employs a mixture of herbal remedies and massage to improve various facets of one's health. Compared to other methods, this type of massage is relatively pain-free and is popular for improving circulation and relieving muscle pain. Another common type of massage is 推拿 (tuīná: "press and rub"). This method stimulates the body's circulation of 气 (qì: "life force"), helping to boost energy flow and treat minor ailments such as insomnia, headaches, and hormonal imbalance.

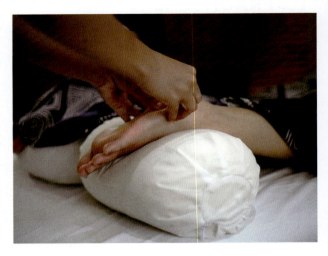

For those brave enough to try a more intense treatment, the famous 足疗 (zúliáo: "foot massage") is performed by highly trained masseurs who, with great dexterity, apply heavy pressure to unique points in the foot which correspond to the sensory nerves of each of the body's internal organs. By manipulating these nerves, the procedure is thought to assist the function and operation of organs in a non-invasive manner.

Morning Exercises

Any visitor to China will likely notice the large numbers of people exercising in public squares, parks, and gardens in the early morning. Exercises like 太极拳 (tàijíquán: "Supreme Ultimate Fist"; known in the West as "Tai Chi") and 气功 (qìgōng: "qigong") are all popular methods of staying healthy and fit, particularly among older generations. Some of these habits also have more recent origins. During the Mao era, Chinese citizens regularly gathered for loudspeaker-regulated mass calisthenics. Perhaps one of the more curious exercises prescribed by the Chairman was eye rubbing, which he believed improved eyesight and averted the need for glasses.

Nowadays, China's public spaces play host to a broad range of different fitness activities. Many people are content to undertake exercises as simple as hand clapping or walking on cobbled roads, which is thought to stimulate acupuncture points in the palms and feet, and thus the organs they correspond to. Tai Chi is one of China's most popular forms of traditional exercise and its practitioners can be seen all over the country. It is based on the controlled movement of *qi*, which is achieved by orchestrated movements and careful concentration. Tai Chi is in fact so popular that one can even witness this early morning ritual in the populous cities of Europe and America.

黄祥安：	安娜，你看起来不太舒服，是不是生病了？	Anna, you don't look so well. Are you sick?
张安娜：	可能是吧。我跟男朋友分手以后，天天睡不着。现在身体很不舒服，肚子疼，头也很疼。	Probably. After I broke up with my boyfriend, I haven't been sleeping well. I don't feel so well right now. My stomach hurts and my head hurts too.
黄祥安：	最近天气冷得很，你要保重身体啊！你的眼睛和鼻子都红了，你最好去看病。	The weather has been very cold lately; you need to take care of yourself! Your eyes and nose are both red. You'd better go see a doctor.
张安娜：	可是现在下雨了，我不想出去……	But it's raining now, I don't feel like going outside . . .
黄祥安：	我可以送你去啊！你在这儿等我，我马上回来。	I can take you. Wait here, I'll be right back.
张安娜：	好吧，谢谢！	OK, thanks!
黄祥安：	我认识一个很好的中医。我带你去他那儿看看，好不好？	I know of a really good Traditional Chinese Medicine doctor. I'll take you to see him, OK?
张安娜：	中医？为什么不去看西医？	A Chinese Medicine doctor? Why not a Western medicine doctor?
黄祥安：	这位中医很不错。	This Chinese Medicine doctor is really good, honest.
张安娜：	好，试试吧。	OK, let's try it.

What Can You Do?

INTERPRETIVE
- I can understand terms for weather and the seasons.
- I can understand descriptions of illnesses.

INTERPERSONAL
- I can discuss someone's wellbeing with him or her.

PRESENTATIONAL
- I can describe the weather.
- I can talk about the state of someone's health and symptoms of illness.

Unit 12 ▪ Lesson 1 ▪ Medicine **433**

看病
At the Doctor's

来，请坐。你哪儿不舒服？

我有点发烧，头疼……
fā shāo　　tóu téng
而且肚子也不舒服。
ér qiě

我帮你看看。请你
张开嘴巴，让我看看
zhāng kāi zuǐ ba
你的舌头。
shé tou

你的感冒不
gǎn mào
是很严重。
yán zhòng

需要打针吗？
dǎ zhēn

中医不用打针。
dǎ zhēn
我给你开一周的药，
kāi　　zhōu　　yào
吃完就没事了。
méi shì

中药怎么吃？
zhōng yào
会不会很苦？

有一点儿苦，别担心。
护士一会儿会告诉你怎么吃。
（dān xīn）
（hù shi yí huìr）

记住，你要多喝水，好好儿地休息。
（de xiū xi）

谢谢医生，我一定会记住。
（yī shēng）
（yí dìng jì zhù）

医生说什么了？
（yī shēng）

还好，他说我感冒了。
（gǎn mào）

这是你的药，一天两次，吃七天。
（yào）

穿好大衣，外面又下雨了。
（dà yī）（wài mian yòu）

你男朋友对你真好。

我们……只是好朋友！

LESSON TEXT 12.2

At the Doctor's 看病

At the doctor's office, Zhang Anna and the doctor discuss her symptoms and appropriate treatments while Huang Xiang'an waits outside.

医生：	来，请坐。你哪儿不舒服？	Lái, qǐng zuò. Nǐ nǎr bù shūfu?
张安娜：	我有点发烧，头疼…… 而且肚子也不舒服.	Wǒ yǒu diǎn fāshāo, tóuténg……érqiě dùzi yě bù shūfu.
医生：	我帮你看看。请你张开嘴巴，让我看看你的舌头。	Wǒ bāng nǐ kànkan. Qǐng nǐ zhāngkāi zuǐba, ràng wǒ kànkan nǐde shétou.
医生：	你的感冒不是很严重。	Nǐ de gǎnmào bú shì hěn yánzhòng.
张安娜：	需要打针吗？	Xūyào dǎ zhēn ma?
医生：	中医不用打针。 我给你开一周的药，吃完就没事了。	Zhōngyī bú yòng dǎzhēn. Wǒ gěi nǐ kāi yì zhōu de yào, chī wán jiù méi shì le.
张安娜：	中药怎么吃？会不会很苦？	Zhōngyào zěnme chī? Huì bu huì hěn kǔ?
医生：	有一点儿苦，别担心。护士一会儿会告诉你怎么吃。记住，你要多喝水，好好儿地休息。	Yǒu yìdiǎnr kǔ, bié dānxīn. Hùshi yíhuìr huì gàosu nǐ zěnme chī. Jìzhù, nǐ yào duō hēshuǐ, hǎohǎor de xiūxi.
张安娜：	谢谢医生，我一定会记住。	Xièxie yīshēng, wǒ yídìng huì jìzhù.

黄祥安：	医生说什么了？	Yīshēng shuō shénme le?
张安娜：	还好，他说我感冒了。	Hái hǎo, tā shuō wǒ gǎnmào le.
护士：	这是你的药， 一天两次，吃七天。	Zhè shì nǐ de yào, yì tiān liǎng cì, chī qī tiān.
黄祥安：	穿好大衣，外面又下雨了。	Chuān hǎo dàyī, wàimiàn yòu xià yǔ le.

护士：　　　你男朋友对你真好。　　　　　Nǐ nán péngyou duì nǐ zhēn hǎo.

张安娜：　我们……只是好朋友。　　　　Wǒmen……zhǐ shì hǎo péngyou.

LESSON VOCABULARY 12.2

	SIMPLIFIED	TRADITIONAL	PINYIN	WORD CATEGORY	DEFINITION
1.	发烧	發燒	fā shāo	vo	to have a fever
2.	头疼	頭疼	tóuténg	adj, n	to have a headache; headache
3.	而且		érqiě	cj	furthermore; and also
4.	张开	張開	zhāngkāi	rv	to open
5.	嘴巴		zuǐba	n	mouth
6.	舌头	舌頭	shétou	n	tongue
7.	感冒		gǎnmào	v, n	to catch or have a cold; a cold
8.	严重	嚴重	yánzhòng	adj	serious
9.	打针	打針	dǎzhēn	vo	to give or have an injection
10.	开药	開藥	kāi yào	vo	to prescribe medicine
11.	周	週	zhōu	n	week
12.	没事	沒事	méi shì	vo	it doesn't matter; it's not a problem
13.	中药	中藥	zhōngyào	n	Chinese herbal medicine
14.	担心	擔心	dānxīn	adj, vo	anxious; to worry
15.	护士	護士	hùshi	n	nurse
16.	一会儿	一會兒	yí huìr	adv	in a while, in a moment
17.	地		de	p	(used to express the manner in which an action is performed)
18.	休息		xiūxi	v	to rest
19.	医生	醫生	yīshēng	n	doctor
20.	一定		yídìng	adj, adv	certain(ly), definite(ly)
21.	记住	記住	jìzhù	v	to remember, to bear in mind
22.	大衣		dàyī	n	overcoat
23.	外面		wàimiàn	n	outside

LESSON VOCABULARY 12.2 (continued)

SIMPLIFIED	TRADITIONAL	PINYIN	WORD CATEGORY	DEFINITION
24. 又		yòu	*adv*	again; moreover

REQUIRED VOCABULARY 12.2

RELATED TO MEDICINE

25. 医院	醫院	yīyuàn	*n*	hospital
26. 吃药	吃藥	chī yào	*vo*	to take medicine

OPTIONAL VOCABULARY 12.2

RELATED TO MEDICINE

27. 开刀	開刀	kāidāo	*vo*	to perform or have an operation
28. 血		xiě, xuè	*n*	blood

Body Parts

头
tóu
head

头发
tóufa
hair

耳朵
ěrduo
ear

脖子
bózi
neck

眼睛
yǎnjing
eye

鼻子
bízi
nose

嘴巴
zuǐba
mouth

手臂
shǒubì
arm

手
shǒu
hand

腿
tuǐ
leg

脚
jiǎo
foot

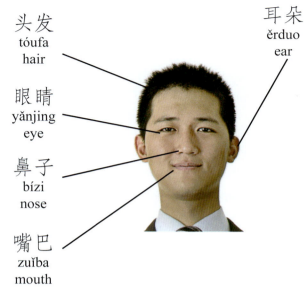

Online Resources
Visit *http://college.betterchinese.com* for a list of other body parts.

The Difference between 一会儿 and 一下

一会儿 means "a short while," and 一下 means "a moment." The two expressions differ very slightly in that 一下 emphasizes the action and 一会儿 stresses the duration. For example, 坐一下 means "have a seat" (emphasis on the action), while 坐一会儿 means "sit down for a while" (emphasis on the duration).

Different Ways to Talk about Weeks

There are several ways in Chinese to refer to weeks. The most common term is 星期, as in 星期一. The character 周 is sometimes used to refer to weeks, mainly in writing and formal speech. 周 can be used on its own to mean week, combined with other characters to create compound words (e.g., 周末, weekend), and also combined with numbers to create days of the week, as in 周一 (Monday). 礼拜 is another alternative way of saying week in Chinese, mostly used in informal speech. It originally meant "worship" but evolved over time to also mean "week." Like 周, 礼拜 can also be combined with numbers to indicate different days of the week, such as 礼拜二 (Tuesday).

STRUCTURE NOTE 12.5
Use 地 to express the manner in which an action is performed

In Structure Note 10.9, it was shown that the particle 得 is used to add modifying expressions after verbs. 地 (de, pronounced the same as 的) is also used to link modifying phrases to verbs, but in this case the modifier precedes the verb. In general, 得 tends to be used to describe how people perform actions on the whole (e.g., "he writes quickly"), while 地 is more often used for how an action is performed in a specific instance (e.g., "he quickly wrote something down").

The adjective in this pattern must be at least two characters long, one-character adjectives are therefore reduplicated. In many cases, the second character in these reduplicated adjectives switches to first tone. In northern China, it is also common to add 儿 after the second character, as in 好好儿. When disyllabic adjectives are reduplicated, they follow the AABB pattern covered in Structure Note 9.10.

Subject + Adjective + 地 + Verb

From the Lesson Text:

记住，你要多喝水，好好儿地休息。
Jìzhù, nǐ yào duō hē shuǐ, hǎohāor de xiūxi.
Remember, drink a lot of water and rest well.

Other examples:

她认真地听。
Tā rènzhēn de tīng.
She listened attentively.

孩子们高高兴兴地出去玩儿。
Háizimen gāogāoxìngxìng de chūqu wánr.
The children happily went out to play.

Practice: Create complete sentences using 地 and the information provided.

Example:　他/看课文/认真 → 他在认真地看课文。

1. 同学们/准备考试/紧张

   _____

2. 弟弟/做功课/安静

   _____

3. 她/唱歌/大声

   _____

4. 他们/开车/小心

   _____

5. 他/问/担心：/"你怎么这么累？"

   _____

STRUCTURE NOTE 12.6
Use 帮 to mean "for"

帮 (bāng) *has already been introduced as a verb meaning "to help." In some cases, however, a phrase which on the surface expresses "to help someone to do something" in fact means "to do something for someone." One can usually work this out from context.*

Subject + 帮 + Someone + Verb Phrase

From the Lesson Text:

我帮你看看。
Wǒ bāng nǐ kànkan.
Let me take a look.

Other examples:

你可以帮我还那本书吗？
Nǐ kěyǐ bāng wǒ huán nèi běn shū ma?
Could you return that book for me?

我生病了，你可以帮我买药吗？
Wǒ shēngbìng le, nǐ kěyǐ bāng wǒ mǎi yào ma?
I'm sick, can you buy some medicine for me?

NOTE: *There are a few other verbs which can also act in the same way as* 帮 *to mean "for" or "on behalf of," one such example being* 给. *Once again, attention must be given to the context to distinguish this* 给 *from the preposition introduced in Structure Note 6.3, which means "to." Sometimes, however, the meaning may remain ambiguous.*

Practice: Respond to the following prompts using the verb provided and 帮 to mean "for."

Example:

我忘了带我的钱包，怎么办？（付钱）
→ 没问题，我帮你付钱。

1. 米饭做好了没有？（看看）

   _____

2. 我借的书太多了。（还）

   _____

3. 我吃饱了，这盘菜吃不完。（吃）

   _____

4. 那个字我忘了怎么写。（写）

   _____

5. 这里的菜看起来都很好吃，不知道选哪一个好！（选）

   _____

STRUCTURE NOTE 12.7

Use 好 as a resultative complement to describe a properly completed action

好 *can be used as a resultative complement with a very similar meaning to* 完, *"to finish." In some cases, the resultative complement* 好 *indicates that a certain action is being performed correctly or properly, for example* 坐好, *"to sit properly."*

> Subject + Verb + 好

From the Lesson Text:

穿好大衣。
Chuān hǎo dàyī.
Put your coat on.

Other examples:

同学们坐好!
Tóngxuémen zuò hǎo!
Students, sit properly!

书看好了没有?
Shū kàn hǎo le méiyǒu?
Did you finish reading the book?

Practice: Complete these fragments to create questions containing the resultative complement 好.

Example: 今天的作业…… → 今天的作业你已经做好了吗?

1. 那本课本…… _____
2. 下个星期的考试…… _____
3. 今天的晚饭…… _____
4. 明天的作业…… _____
5. 那张画…… _____

STRUCTURE NOTE 12.8

Use 又……了 to say "again"

In Structure Note 6.7, 再 *was introduced as a way to mark recurring actions.* 再 *is typically used to talk about future repetitions that have not yet occurred. To describe a recurring event that took place in the past, or an event that has just reoccurred in the present, the adverb* 又 *is used. The sentence-final particle* 了 *is often used with this pattern.*

> Subject + 又 + Verb Phrase + 了

From the Lesson Text:

外面又下雨了。
Wàimiàn yòu xià yǔ le.
It's started to rain again.

Other examples:

你又来了!
Nǐ yòu lái le!
You again!

她昨天又打网球了。
Tā zuótiān yòu dǎ wǎngqiú le.
She played tennis again yesterday.

Practice: Change the following sentences into Chinese using the 又 ······ 了 pattern.

Example: How did you forget your homework again!

→ 你的作业怎么又忘了！

1. Dad, are we lost again?

   _____

2. Yesterday, he went to see that kung fu movie again.

   _____

3. My older brother borrowed my car again.

   _____

4. How come you are reading that book again?

   _____

5. I went to the bank again this morning.

   _____

PRACTICE 12.11

Using the information given below, enact a roleplay with a partner in which one person plays the doctor and the other the patient.

Example:

A: 你哪儿不舒服？

B: 我头疼，觉得很冷。

A: 你感冒了，我给你开感冒药。

Name:	张安娜
Symptoms:	眼睛和鼻子红红的，觉得很冷
Diagnosis:	感冒
Prescription:	感冒药

Name:	李中平
Symptoms:	头疼，觉得很累
Diagnosis:	发烧
Prescription:	打针

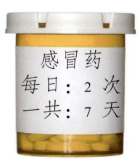

Name:	陈大东
Symptoms:	肚子疼
Diagnosis:	东西吃得太多了
Prescription:	中药

Name:	王小美
Symptoms:	头疼，睡不着
Diagnosis:	感冒
Prescription:	头痛药

PRACTICE 12.12

Working with a partner, take turns giving each other instructions about taking the medicine below.

Example: 这是你的感冒药，一天两次，吃七天。

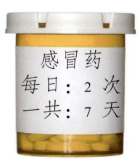

感冒药
每日：2 次
一共：7 天

感冒药
每日：3 次
一共：4 天

感冒药
每日：4 次
一共：5 天

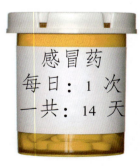

感冒药
每日：1 次
一共：14 天

PRACTICE 12.13

Working with a partner, look at the information below and take turns describing the problems (indicated by the text box), followed by an appropriate solution (indicated by the picture).

Example:
A: 我感冒了。
B: 我可以帮你买感冒药。

我感冒了。

我累了。

我很冷。

我饿了。

我发烧了。

PRACTICE 12.14

In the spaces provided, write the names for the body parts indicated.

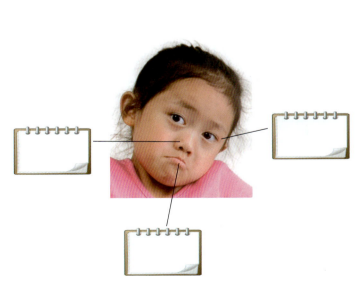

	Radical	Stroke Order
而	而 ér and	一 ア ブ 丙 而 而
儿	儿 rén person	ノ 儿
周	口 kǒu mouth	ノ 刀 月 用 用 周 周 周
烧	火 huǒ fire	丶 丷 少 火 灯 炒 烘 烊 烤 烧
嘴	口 kǒu mouth	丨 口 口 叮 叶 呰 啙 啙 啙 啙 嘴 嘴 嘴 嘴 嘴 嘴 嘴
巴	乙 yǐ second heavenly stem	フ コ 凸 巴
冒	日 yuē say	丨 冂 冂 曰 冃 冒 冒 冒 冒
严	一 yī one	一 丆 严 严 亚 亚 严
药	艹(草) cǎo grass	一 十 艹 艻 芍 芍 药 药 药
且	一 yī one	丨 冂 月 月 且
担	扌(手) shǒu hand	一 扌 扌 扫 扣 扣 担
记	讠(言) yán speech	丶 讠 记 记 记
休	亻(人) rén person	ノ 亻 仁 什 休 休
息	心 xīn heart	丶 亻 白 白 自 自 息 息 息
外	夕 xī evening	ノ 夕 夕 列 外

PRACTICE 12.16

Type the following sentences on your computer and provide an answer to the question.

1. 请你张开嘴巴，让我看看你的舌头。
2. 我的病是不是很严重？
3. 我给你开一周的中药。
4. 感冒的时候要多喝水。
5. 你的眼睛红红的，而且还有点发烧。

PRACTICE 12.17

Make an audio recording and send it to your teacher. In the recording, describe a time that you went to see the doctor. Talk about how you were feeling and what the doctor recommended that you do.

PRACTICE 12.18

护士：　　张安娜，请跟我来。
张安娜：好的。
医生：　　你哪儿不舒服？
张安娜：我常常头疼，晚上也睡不着。
医生：　　让我先看看你的眼睛。
医生：　　请你张开嘴巴，我看看你的舌头。
张安娜：我的病严重吗？
医生：　　别担心，我给你开三天的药，好好儿地休息，吃完药就没事了。
张安娜：谢谢医生。

Read the dialogue and answer the following questions.
1. What symptoms does Zhang Anna describe to the doctor?
2. What does the doctor tell Zhang Anna to do?

PRACTICE 12.19

安娜：
　　这是你的药。这是三天的感冒药，每六个小时吃一次，一天四次，最好饭后吃。护士说，如果三天以后你觉得还没好，你要再来看医生。还有，记住要多喝水，多休息。
　　　　　　　　祥安

Read Huang Xiang'an's note and answer the following questions.
1. What are the instructions for taking the medicine?
2. What does the nurse remind Zhang Anna to do?

PRACTICE 12.20

　　我最近常常头疼，所以上个星期我去看西医了。医生说要给我打针，可是我不想打，医生只好开三天的药给我。我吃完以后还觉得不舒服，小美说我应该去试试看中医，但是我担心中药会很苦，所以我还是去看西医了。

Read Zhang Anna's diary and answer the following questions.
1. Did Zhang Anna get an injection?
2. Why didn't Zhang Anna go see a Traditional Chinese Medicine doctor?

Traditional Chinese Medicine

Contrary to the Western philosophy of treating illnesses on a case-by-case basis, Traditional Chinese Medicine (TCM) takes a holistic approach that aims to help the body heal itself. According to this system, the body may better equip itself to handle adverse symptoms by reconciling the opposing forces of 阴 (yīn) and 阳 (yáng). TCM makes use of a number of herbal concoctions and animal products that are largely alien to modern Western medicine. Many of these ingredients and combinations were developed by Daoists who coincidentally discovered cures to various common ailments by seeking to create elixirs of immortality.

Processes such as acupuncture, moxibustion, and cupping are also common aspects of TCM. Acupuncture is a treatment method consisting of the insertion of stainless steel needles into the body at various *qi* points. The intention of the process is to reduce pain and alleviate various bodily afflictions. Moxibustion, a procedure which often accompanies acupuncture, involves burning certain herbs on or near the body. Cupping is a form of reverse-pressure massage. The practitioner will take a glass cup, light a match to heat the air inside, and then press the cup against the patient's back, creating a suction effect.

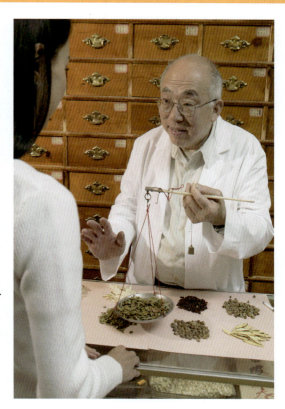

Hot and Cold Foods

食疗 (shíliáo: "food therapy") is a medical system which espouses the healing properties of certain foodstuffs. Medicine itself is in fact only one aspect of conventional Chinese beliefs regarding health and the body. In the Chinese medical tradition, all forms of consumption are believed to have different medicinal effects, both positive and negative. Medicine can be taken for ailments, but it does not necessarily take precedence over everyday food and drink. This close association of medicine and food is even reflected in the Chinese language itself. In English, one "takes" medicine. In Chinese, on the other hand, one "eats" it (吃药: chī yào).

Nutritional therapy relies on a systematic balancing of "hot" and "cold" foods, a dichotomy that also originates with the concept of 阴阳 (yīnyáng: "yin and yang"). Foodstuffs are not categorized by temperature, but rather by their associated benefits or the alterations to the body they may cause. *Yin* foods, such as carrots and crab, are considered "cold" foods that decrease the body's temperature, thus lowering metabolism. Conversely, *yang* foods, such as beef and mushrooms, are thought to be "hot" foods that increase the body's temperature and metabolism. The philosophy extends beyond substance to the method of preparation. For example, cooking by boiling, steaming, and poaching is associated with *yin*, while deep-frying, stir-frying, and roasting are all associated with *yang*.

医生:	来，请坐。你哪儿不舒服？	Here, please have a seat. What seems to be the problem?
张安娜:	我有点发烧，头疼······而且肚子也不舒服。	I have a slight fever, a headache . . . and my stomach doesn't feel good either.
医生:	我帮你看看。请你张开嘴巴，让我看看你的舌头。	Let me take a look. Please open your mouth and let me see your tongue.
医生:	你的感冒不是很严重。	Your cold is not that serious.
张安娜:	需要打针吗？	Do I need to get a shot?
医生:	中医不用打针。我给你开一周的药，吃完就没事了。	You don't need to get shots with Chinese medicine. Let me give you a week's worth of medicine. After you take it, you'll be fine.
张安娜:	中药怎么吃？会不会很苦？	How do you take Chinese medicine? Is it bitter?
医生:	有一点儿苦，别担心。护士一会儿会告诉你怎么吃。记住，你要多喝水，好好儿地休息。	It's a little bitter, but don't worry. The nurse will tell you how to take it in a moment. Remember, drink lots of water and rest well.
张安娜:	谢谢医生，我一定会记住。	Thanks, doctor. I'll remember.

黄祥安:	医生说什么了？	What did the doctor say?
张安娜:	还好，他说我感冒了。	It's fine, he said I have a cold.
护士:	这是你的药，一天两次，吃七天。	This is your medicine. Take it twice a day for seven days.
黄祥安:	穿好大衣，外面又下雨了。	Put your coat on. It's started to rain again.
护士:	你男朋友对你真好。	Your boyfriend is so good to you.

张安娜： 我们……只是好朋友。

We're . . . just good friends.

What Can You Do?

INTERPRETIVE

- I can understand the names of different ailments.
- I can understand the names for different parts of the body.
- I can understand doctors' advice and prescriptions.

INTERPERSONAL

- I can have a discussion with the doctor about how I am feeling.
- I can discuss treatments with the doctor or nurse.

PRESENTATIONAL

- I can give a presentation on some of the basic features of Chinese and Western medicine.
- I can give a presentation on a visit to a practitioner of Chinese medicine.

ACT IT OUT

Working in groups, compose an original three-minute skit that utilizes the vocabulary and structures introduced in Unit 12. Each of you should assume a role and have a roughly equal number of lines in the skit. Be prepared to perform your skit in class. You can either come up with your own story or choose from one of the following situations:

a) You are starting to feel sick so you discuss your symptoms with a friend.

b) You interview a doctor about what he does on the job.

c) It is starting to snow and your mother has some warnings and advice about the cold.

CHECK WHAT YOU CAN DO

RECOGNIZE

Adjectives
- □ 还好
- □ 舒服
- □ 疼
- □ 冷
- □ 痛
- □ 热
- □ 头疼
- □ 严重
- □ 担心

Adverbs
- □ 天天
- □ 最好
- □ 一会儿

- □ 一定
- □ 又

Conjunction
- □ 而且

Nouns
- □ 肚子
- □ 头
- □ 天气
- □ 身体
- □ 眼睛
- □ 鼻子
- □ 中西医
- □ 手

- □ 脚
- □ 春天
- □ 夏天
- □ 秋天
- □ 冬天
- □ 嘴巴
- □ 舌头
- □ 周
- □ 中药
- □ 医院
- □ 护士
- □ 医生
- □ 大衣
- □ 外面

Particle
- □ 地

Verbs
- □ 生病
- □ 睡不着
- □ 注意
- □ 看病
- □ 下雨
- □ 下雪
- □ 发烧
- □ 张开
- □ 感冒
- □ 打针
- □ 打开药

- □ 没事
- □ 休息
- □ 记住
- □ 吃药

WRITE

- □ 服
- □ 身体
- □ 头疼
- □ 睡
- □ 舒服
- □ 病
- □ 着
- □ 冷
- □ 保
- □ 眼睛
- □ 医
- □ 带

- □ 而儿
- □ 周
- □ 烧
- □ 嘴巴
- □ 冒
- □ 严
- □ 药
- □ 且
- □ 担
- □ 记
- □ 休息
- □ 外

USE

- □ 最好 to make suggestions.
- □ 带 to express bringing objects or people.
- □ Noun or measure word reduplication to express "every."
- □ Name/pronoun + 那儿 to talk about someone's location or home.

- □ 地 to express the manner in which an action is performed.
- □ 帮 to mean "for."
- □ 好 as a resultative complement to describe a properly completed action.
- □ 又……了 to say "again."

商

Business

Communication Goals

Lesson 1: 打工 **Part-Time Job**
- Talk about your full- or part-time job.
- Offer words of encouragement.
- Indicate that something is unexpected.

Lesson 2: 去中国实习 **Internship in China**
- Discuss internships and working in China.
- Talk about your employment experience and résumé.
- Discuss your post-graduation plans.
- Learn about the importance of guanxi or "connections."

打工
Part-Time Job

小美！
méi xiǎng dào
没想到你会来这儿！

dǎ gōng
我想看看你打工的地方。

huán jìng
这儿环境真不错，你每天在这儿工作几小时？

四个小时，我每天晚上从八点到十二点在这
shàng bān
儿上班。

xià bān   nán guài
你十二点才下班，难怪
hěn shǎo
晚上很少见到你。

你在这儿都做些什么样的事？

我要泡咖啡、收银、还要打扫厨房。

你要做的事真不少！

我以前只管打扫，后来老板看我很努力，慢慢地就让我管更多的事了。

你不但要上学，而且还要工作。这样一天到晚都很忙，不会太累吗？

虽然累一点，但是我想赚点儿钱，这样的话，今年暑假就可以出国旅行了。

听起来不错。加油！

LESSON TEXT 13.1

Part-Time Job 打工

Wang Xiaomei visits Chen Dadong at the coffee shop where he works and the two chat about his job.

陈大东： 小美！没想到你会来这儿！

Xiǎoměi! Méi xiǎng dào nǐ huì lái zhèr!

王小美： 我想看看你打工的地方。这儿环境真不错，你每天在这儿工作几小时？

Wǒ xiǎng kànkan nǐ dǎ gōng de dìfang. Zhèr huánjìng zhēn bú cuò, nǐ měi tiān zài zhèr gōngzuò jǐ xiǎoshí?

陈大东： 四个小时，我每天晚上从八点到十二点在这儿上班。

Sì gè xiǎoshí, wǒ měi tiān wǎnshang cóng bā diǎn dào shí èr diǎn zài zhèr shàngbān.

王小美： 你十二点才下班，难怪晚上很少见到你。

Nǐ shí èr diǎn cái xià bān, nánguài wǎnshang hěn shǎo jiàn dào nǐ.

王小美： 你在这儿都做些什么样的事？

Nǐ zài zhèr dōu zuò xiē shénme yàng de shì?

陈大东： 我要泡咖啡、收银、还要打扫厨房。

Wǒ yào pào kāfēi, shōuyín, hái yào dǎsǎo chúfáng.

王小美： 你要做的事真不少！

Nǐ yào zuò de shì zhēn bù shǎo!

陈大东： 我以前只管打扫，后来老板看我很努力，慢慢地就让我管更多的事了。

Wǒ yǐqián zhǐ guǎn dǎsǎo, hòulái lǎobǎn kàn wǒ hěn nǔlì, mànmàn de jiù ràng wǒ guǎn gèng duō de shì le.

王小美： 你不但要上学，而且还要工作。这样一天到晚都很忙，不会太累吗？

Nǐ búdàn yào shàngxué, érqiě hái yào gōngzuò. Zhèiyàng yìtiān-dàowǎn dōu hěn máng, bú huì tài lèi ma?

陈大东： 虽然累一点，但是我想赚点儿钱，这样的话，今年暑假就可以出国旅行了。

Suīrán lèi yì diǎn, dànshì wǒ xiǎng zhuàn diǎnr qián, zhèi yàng de huà, jīnnián shǔjià jiù kěyǐ chūguó lǚxíng le.

王小美： 听起来不错。加油！

Tīngqilai bú cuò. Jiāyóu!

字 词 VOCABULARY

LESSON VOCABULARY 13.1

	SIMPLIFIED	TRADITIONAL	PINYIN	WORD CATEGORY	DEFINITION
1.	没想到	沒想到	méi xiǎng dào	*ie*	to not have expected or thought of
2.	打工		dǎgōng	*vo*	to work part-time, to temp
3.	环境	環境	huánjìng	*n*	environment
4.	上班		shàngbān	*vo*	to go to work
5.	下班		xiàbān	*vo*	to get off work
6.	难怪	難怪	nánguài	*adv*	no wonder
7.	很少		hěn shǎo	*adv*	very infrequently; rarely
8.	做事		zuò shì	*vo*	to work; to handle matters
9.	什么样	甚麼樣	shénme yàng	*pr*	what kind/sort
10.	泡		pào	*v*	to make (coffee or tea); to steep
11.	收银	收銀	shōuyín	*vo*	to collect money
12.	打扫	打掃	dǎsǎo	*v*	to clean up; to sweep
13.	厨房	廚房	chúfáng	*n*	kitchen
14.	以前		yǐqián	*prep*	before
15.	管		guǎn	*v*	to be in charge of
16.	后来	後來	hòulái	*adv*	afterwards
17.	老板		lǎobǎn	*n*	boss
18.	努力		nǔlì	*adj, v*	diligent; to work hard
19.	慢慢		mànmàn	*adv*	slowly; gradually
20.	不但		búdàn	*cj*	not only
21.	上学	上學	shàngxué	*vo*	to attend school
22.	一天到晚		yìtiān-dàowǎn	*adv*	from morning until night; all day long
23.	虽然	雖然	suīrán	*cj*	even though
24.	赚钱	賺錢	zhuàn qián	*vo*	to earn money
25.	暑假		shǔjià	*n*	summer vacation
26.	出国	出國	chūguó	*vo*	to leave the country

LESSON VOCABULARY 13.1 (continued)

	SIMPLIFIED	TRADITIONAL	PINYIN	WORD CATEGORY	DEFINITION
27.	加油		jiāyóu	*ie*	you can do it! (literally "add oil"; used when offering words of encouragement)

REQUIRED VOCABULARY 13.1

RELATED TO WORK

	SIMPLIFIED	TRADITIONAL	PINYIN	WORD CATEGORY	DEFINITION
28.	整理		zhěnglǐ	*v*	to sort out; to put in order; to arrange
29.	干净	乾淨	gānjìng	*adj*	clean
30.	接待		jiēdài	*v*	to receive (guests)
31.	客人		kèrén	*n*	guests; customers

OPTIONAL VOCABULARY 13.1

OTHER PROFESSIONS

	SIMPLIFIED	TRADITIONAL	PINYIN	WORD CATEGORY	DEFINITION
32.	家教		jiājiào	*n*	tutor
33.	助教		zhùjiào	*n*	teaching assistant
34.	厨师	廚師	chúshī	*n*	cook, chef

Work Titles

While in the past, co-workers at a 单位 (dānwèi: "work unit") would most likely call each other 同志 (tóngzhì: "comrade"), these days people simply use the term 同事 (tóngshì: "colleague"). Other titles used in the workplace generally correspond to those used in English, but there are some notable exceptions. Below are some examples of common forms of address for professionals. Remember that as with other professional titles covered so far, a person's surname precedes the title.

Corporate titles

Title	Pinyin	Meaning
总经理	zǒngjīnglǐ	general manager
经理	jīnglǐ	manager
主席	zhǔxí	chairman
主任	zhǔrèn	director
董事长	dǒngshìzhǎng	president; chairman of the board

Other titles

Title	Pinyin	Use
师傅	shīfu	The term 师傅 literally means "master." While this term would indeed be employed for a master of a skill such as martial arts, it is also widely used to refer to any skilled worker. Taxi drivers, for example, are referred to as 师傅.
阿姨	āyí	阿姨 means "aunt." When used in a professional context, it is a generic form of address for females employed in such roles as maids, babysitters, or care takers.
服务员	fúwùyuán	Literally "attendant" or "service person," this is the most common form of address for a male or female working in the service industry, from a humble tea house all the way to a high class restaurant.
老板	lǎobǎn	This term, akin to "boss" and mostly used in the same way, is also the common term for any shopkeeper or proprietor of a business. One may also hear 老板娘 (lǎobǎnniáng), the female equivalent, meaning "proprietress."
老(姓)	lǎo (xìng)	Calling someone old may seem a little offensive in the West, but in China, where Confucian principles have instilled veneration for older generations, addressing someone with the prefix 老 is both a marker of familiarity and respect.
小(姓)	xiǎo (xìng)	The opposite of 老, 小 is a prefix that would be given to a younger member of a working or social group.

STRUCTURE NOTE 13.1
Use 没想到 *to introduce an unexpected event*

The phrase 没想到 *(méi xiǎng dào) literally means "didn't think of." Its usage is similar to "didn't expect" or "who'd have thought" in English.*

(Subject +) 没想到 + Sentence

From the Lesson Text:

小美！没想到你会来这儿！
Xiǎoměi! Méi xiǎng dào nǐ huì lái zhèr!
Xiaomei, I didn't expect you to come here!

Other examples:

真的没想到我们学校会有这么漂亮的学生。
Zhēnde méi xiǎng dào wǒmen xuéxiào huì yǒu zhème piàoliang de xuéshēng.
I really didn't think our school would have students who were this pretty.

我没想到你们都会骗我。
Wǒ méi xiǎng dào nǐmen dōu huì piàn wǒ.
I didn't expect you all to cheat me.

Practice: Change the following statements into Chinese expressions containing the 没想到 pattern.

Example: I didn't think he'd go to bed that late.
→ 没想到他那么晚才去睡觉。

1.   I didn't expect that she would break up with her boyfriend.

    _____

2.   I didn't think the test would be that easy.

    _____

3.   Who would have thought that he plays the guitar so well.

    _____

4.   We didn't expect that leaving the country to go traveling would be so expensive.

    _____

5.   I didn't expect that she planned to go to Russia to find a job.

    _____

STRUCTURE NOTE 13.2
Use 难怪 *to express "no wonder"*

难怪 *(nánguài) expresses the equivalent of "no wonder."* 难怪 *is placed before the subject at the beginning of the phrase.*

难怪 + Subject + Verb Phrase

From the Lesson Text:

难怪晚上很少见到你。
Nánguài wǎnshang hěn shǎo jiàn dào nǐ.
No wonder I rarely see you at night.

Other examples:

难怪你找不到女朋友，
你一直都在工作啊！
Nánguài nǐ zhǎo bu dào nǚ péngyou,
nǐ yìzhí dōu zài gōngzuò a!
No wonder you can't find a girlfriend,
you're always working!

他从来没打扫过房
间，难怪你不喜欢住
在那儿。
Tā cónglái méi dǎsǎo guo fángjiān,
nánguài nǐ bù xǐhuan zhù zài nàr.
He's never cleaned him room; no
wonder you don't like to live there.

Practice: Match a phrase from one box with an appropriate phrase from the other to make a complete sentence.

这家饭馆的饺子真好吃，	难怪外面没有人。
她一天到晚都上班，	难怪客人这么多。
天气冷得很，	难怪肚子饿。
他感冒了，	难怪鼻子那么红。
你今天没吃早饭 ，	难怪那么累。

STRUCTURE NOTE 13.3
Use 什么样的 *to ask "what kind?"*

什么样的 (shénme yàng de) *can be added to nouns in order to elicit a more specific response. It is equivalent to "what kind of?" or "what sort of?" in English.*

Subject + Verb + 什么样 + 的 + Noun Phrase

From the Lesson Text:

你在这儿都做些什么样的事？
Nǐ zài zhèr dōu zuò xiē shénme yàng de shì?
What kind of work do you do here?

Other examples:

你喜欢什么样的菜？
Nǐ xǐhuan shénme yàng de cài?
What kind of food do you like?

那是什么样的手机？
Nà shì shénme yàng de shǒujī?
What kind of cellphone is that?

NOTE: *In the example from the Lesson Text,* 都 *is added to the question to imply that a response containing more than one thing is expected (i.e., Xiaomei anticipates that Dadong does more than one thing at the coffee shop).* 什么样的 *pairs quite naturally with this use of* 都 *as it is a question that usually anticipates a multiple response.*

Practice: For each of the following statements, provide a question containing 什么样的 that could elicit such a response, following the example shown below.

Example: 我喜欢吃中国菜。 → 你喜欢吃什么样的菜？

1. 我的老板是个很认真的人。

_____

2. 我觉得她应该买一条短一点儿的牛仔裤。

_____

3. 我想找个很聪明的女朋友。

_____

4. 我今年想选一门考试少的课。

_____

5. 那儿的天气冷，你应该带一件毛衣。

_____

STRUCTURE NOTE 13.4

Use 不但…而且… to express "not only . . . but also . . ."

There are a number of two-part sentence patterns in Chinese. In this particular pattern, the initial part, 不但 (búdàn), means "not only." It pairs with 而且 (érqiě), meaning "moreover." As in other structures of this type, if the subject of the two clauses remains the same, the subject can precede 不但.

Subject + 不但 + Verb Phrase A + , + 而且 + Verb Phrase B

不但 + Clause A + , + 而且 + Clause B

From the Lesson Text: 你不但要上学，而且还要工作。
Nǐ búdàn yào shàngxué, érqiě hái yào gōngzuò.
Not only do you have to go to school, you also have to work.

Other examples:

不但中平知道了，
而且别的同学也知道
了！
Búdàn Zhōngpíng zhīdào le, érqiě
bié de tóngxué yě zhīdào le!
Not only did Zhongping know it, but
the other classmates also knew it!

他不但会接待客人，
而且会泡咖啡。
Tā búdàn huì jiēdài kèrén, érqiě huì
pào kāfēi.
Not only does he know how to
serve customers, but he also knows
how to brew coffee.

Practice: Create complete sentences using 不但···而且··· and the word pairs provided below.

Example: 这个孩子 / 会说汉语 / 会写汉字
→ 这个孩子不但会说汉语，而且会写汉字。

1. 安娜 / 唱歌 / 拉小提琴
   _____

2. 饺子 / 好吃 / 便宜
   _____

3. 大东 / 准备考试 / 上班
   _____

4. 小美 / 聪明 / 漂亮
   _____

5. 她 / 会说中文 / 会说法语
   _____

STRUCTURE NOTE 13.5

Use 虽然···但是··· *to express "although . . . however . . ."*

In English, it would sound strange to say both "although" and "however" in the same sentence — usually we pick one or the other. In Chinese, however, these sayings appear together as a set pattern. The second clause is generally introduced by 但是 *or* 可是*. As in Structure Note 13.4, if the subject remains the same for both clauses, it can precede* 虽然 (suīrán).

> Subject + 虽然 + Verb Phrase A + , + 但是 / 可是 + Verb Phrase B

> 虽然 + Subject + Verb Phrase A + , + 但是 / 可是 + Verb Phrase B

From the Lesson Text: 虽然累一点，但是我想赚点儿钱。
Suīrán lèi yì diǎn, dànshì wǒ xiǎng zhuàn diǎnr qián.
Although it's a bit tiring, I want to make money.

Other examples:

虽然他才学了一年的中文，但是他说得很好。
Suīrán tā cái xuéle yì nián de Zhōngwén, dànshì tā shuō de hěn hǎo.
Although he has only studied Chinese for a year, he speaks Chinese well.

虽然我很忙，但是我很高兴。
Suīrán wǒ hěn máng, dànshì wǒ hěn gāoxìng.
Although I'm busy, I'm very happy.

Practice: Create complete sentences using the following word pairs with the 虽然⋯但是⋯ construction.

Example: 这家饭馆 / 青菜 / 有点咸 / 味道还不错
→ 这家饭馆的青菜虽然有点咸，但是味道还不错。

1. 这家饭馆 / 不便宜 / 客人还很多

   _____

2. 教室 / 打扫过 / 看起来还是不干净

   _____

3. 课文 / 有点难 / 很有意思

   _____

4. 我 / 生病了 / 不想看病

   _____

5. 我和她 / 分手了 / 还是好朋友

   _____

STRUCTURE NOTE 13.6

Use 从⋯到⋯ to express length of time

In Structure Note 7.7, 从 A 到 B was used to express "from location A to location B." As well as distance in space, this pattern can also be used to express distance between two points in time. As with the pattern introduced previously the main verb of the sentence follows the 从⋯到⋯ construction.

> Subject + 从 + Time A + 到 + Time B + Verb Phrase

From the Lesson Text:　我每天晚上从八点到十二点在这儿上班。
Wǒ měi tiān wǎnshang cóng bā diǎn dào shí èr diǎn zàizhèr shàngbān.
I work every evening from 8 p.m. to 12 a.m.

Other examples:

她从早上十点到下午两点都有课。
Tā cóng zǎoshang shí diǎn dào xiàwǔ liǎng diǎn dōu yǒu kè.
She has classes from 10 a.m. to 2 a.m.

他从下午到晚上都要学习。
Tā cóng xiàwǔ dào wǎnshang dōu yào xuéxí.
He has to study from the afternoon through to the evening.

Practice: Use 从…到… to create sentences with the times given below and the activity in parentheses.

Example:　　　从 7:30 p.m. ／ 到　9:00 p.m.

→ 我昨天晚上从七点半到九点都在看电视。

1.　从　9:00 a.m. ／ 到　1:00 p.m.（上课）

_____

2.　从　2:30 p.m. ／ 到　3:30 p.m.（打球）

_____

3.　从　4:00 p.m. ／ 到　6:00 p.m.（看电影）

_____

4.　从　6:10 p.m. ／ 到　7:20 p.m.（跟朋友吃饭）

_____

5.　从　8:00 p.m. ／ 到　9:30 p.m.（做作业）

_____

PRACTICE 13.1

Working with a partner, write profiles for the pictured characters using the words provided, then ask and answer questions about their work schedules and duties.

Work place: 咖啡店
Work time:
每天晚上从八点
到十二点
Duties:
泡咖啡，收银

Example:

A: 你每天在这儿工作几个小时？

B: 我每天晚上从八点到十二点上班。

A: 你在这儿都做些什么样的事？

B: 我要泡咖啡、收银。

Work places: 餐厅 医院 饭馆 商店
Duties: 打扫厨房 卖衣服 表演 开药 接待客人 开刀 收银

Work place:

Work time:

Duties:

Work place:

Work time:

Duties:

```
┌─────────────────────────────┐
│  Work place:                │
│                             │
│  Work time:                 │
│                             │
│                             │
│  Duties:                    │
│                             │
└─────────────────────────────┘
```

```
┌─────────────────────────────┐
│  Work place:                │
│                             │
│  Work time:                 │
│                             │
│                             │
│  Duties:                    │
│                             │
└─────────────────────────────┘
```

PRACTICE 13.2

Working with a partner, first change the responses of the characters on the right into 虽然……但是 sentences, then practice the dialogues using the new sentences that you have made.

你打了一天篮球，不会累吗？

我玩得很高兴。

Example:
虽然有点累，但是我玩得很高兴。

你第一次表演，不会紧张吗？

我会好好地表演。

你跟男朋友分手了，不会难过吗？

我会找到一个更好的男朋友。

这条项链卖一百块，不会太贵吗？

我要把它送给玛丽。

	Radical	Stroke Order
工	工 gōng work	一 丁 工
房	户 hù door	丶 亠 亐 户 户 庐 房 房
银	钅(金) jīn gold	丿 𠂉 𠂉 钅 钅 钊 钊 钊 钅 银 银
假	亻(人) rén person	丿 亻 亻 亻 作 作 作 假 假 假
班	王 wáng king	一 二 干 王 玉 玌 玒 珏 班 班
板	木 mù wood	一 十 才 木 朼 朾 杤 板
环	王 wáng king	一 二 干 王 玉 玗 玶 环
境	土 tǔ earth	一 十 土 圵 圹 圹 圹 垃 垃 培 培 培 埣 境
怪	忄(心) xīn heart	丶 丷 忄 忆 怀 怪 怪 怪
前	刂(刀) dāo knife	丶 丷 䒑 广 前 前 前 前 前
管	竹(竹) zhú bamboo	丿 𠂊 𠂉 竻 竻 竻 竻 筲 筲 竻 管 管 管
但	亻(人) rén person	丿 亻 亻 佃 佃 但 但
泡	氵(水) shuǐ water	丶 冫 氵 氵 沟 沟 沟 泡
慢	忄(心) xīn heart	丶 丷 忄 忄 忙 忙 忸 悍 悍 悍 慢 慢 慢
虽	虫 chóng insect	丶 口 口 巴 吕 吕 吊 虽 虽

Make an audio recording and send it to your teacher. In the recording, describe a part time job that you have had. What were the hours like? What kind of responsibilities did you have?

PRACTICE 13.5

Type the following sentences on your computer.

1. 这里环境真不错，我也想在这儿打工。
2. 没想到你每天晚上十二点才下班！
3. 你这么努力工作，难怪老板让你管更多的事。
4. 他不但要泡咖啡、收银，而且要打扫厨房。
5. 虽然工作累一点，但是赚了钱就可以出国旅行了。

PRACTICE 13.6

Sender	祥安
Subject	音乐会

大东：

　　最近晚上很少见到你，你在忙什么？安娜说上个星期在医院里看到你了，你怎么了？下个周末你有空吗？我们一起去听小美的音乐会吧！

Sender	大东
Subject	re: 音乐会

祥安：

　　我上个星期身体不舒服，所以去看病了。医生说可能是因为我太累了。最近不但要上学，而且还要上班，真是太忙了！我也想去听小美的音乐会，可是我得问问我的老板，看看可不可以早一点下班。

Read the e-mails and answer the following questions.
1. What does the doctor suggest is the reason for Chen Dadong not feeling well?
2. Will Chen Dadong go to Wang Xiaomei's concert?

PRACTICE 13.7

陈大东：你每天打几个小时的工？

孙玛丽：差不多三个小时，从下午三点到六点。

陈大东：你都做些什么？

孙玛丽：卖衣服、收银，还要打扫。

陈大东：你喜欢你的工作吗？

孙玛丽：这里环境不错，可是我有点忙。

陈大东：你不但要上学，而且还要打工，会不会太累？

孙玛丽：还好，我会找时间做作业、准备考试。

陈大东：你要多注意身体！

Read the dialogue and answer the following questions.
1. How many hours does Sun Mali work each day?
2. What are her duties at work?

PRACTICE 13.8

中平：

我找到了一份新的工作，在学校餐厅后面的咖啡店打工。星期一到星期五从晚上八点到十点，每天工作两个小时。周末的工作时间比较长，从下午五点到晚上十点，所以以后晚上不能跟你们去看足球比赛了。

Read Huang Xiang'an's note and answer the following questions.
1. Where does Huang Xiang'an work?
2. What are his working hours?

Guanxi

关系 (guānxi) is a powerful force in Chinese business culture. The closest English rendering of the term would be "connections" or "networking," but its actual usage refers to a complex cultural system of personal relationships and moral obligations.

Implications of the Term

Although *guanxi* is considered a vital aspect of conducting business in China, it has also acquired a slightly unethical reputation over the years. In terms of its implications, the concept of guanxi is to some extent comparable to the English saying "if you scratch my back, I'll scratch yours." So, it is perhaps unsurprising that for some people there is a fine line between *guanxi* and corruption. While this negative view may be accurate in some instances, *guanxi* has also been used to gain valid favors, such as helping one's company win a contract, negotiate better rates, or secure better quality products.

Chinese and Western Business Culture

There are a number of ways in which the system of *guanxi* has made Chinese business culture different from Western business culture. *Guanxi* does not always signify a straightforward exchange between companies. Instead, it tends to involve a further connection between representatives from the organizations at a personal level. For instance, it is common for individuals to visit the residences of their business acquaintances bearing gifts such as alcohol, cigarettes, and sports accessories. Furthermore, it is perfectly appropriate to inquire about a client's family and other matters that may seem overly personal to a Western businessperson.

Though *guanxi* is in some ways a trait unique to Chinese business culture, in other ways it is not so different to how trade is conducted in the West. As the saying goes, "it's not about what you know, it's about who you know." Networking and connections are just as essential in the Western business environment as they are in China, and while gift-giving may not be so common in the West, wining and dining is an integral part of wooing potential clients in any business culture.

Above all, when conducting business in China, one must bear in mind the phrase 入境随俗 (rùjìngsuísú): "When you enter a place, follow its customs," equivalent to the English "When in Rome, do as the Romans do." Undoubtedly the most effective way to avert undesired strife is to gain a thorough understanding of modern business practices in China and to adapt oneself to them accordingly.

陈大东： 小美！没想到你会来这儿！！

Xiaomei! I didn't expect you to come here!

王小美： 我想看看你打工的地方。这里环境真不错，你每天在这儿工作几小时？

I wanted to see your workplace. This place isn't bad at all. How many hours do you work a day here?

陈大东： 四个小时，我每天晚上从八点到十二点在这儿上班。

Four hours. I work every evening from 8 p.m. to 12 a.m.

王小美： 你十二点才下班，难怪晚上很少见到你。

You don't get off work until 12 a.m.; no wonder I rarely see you at night.

———

王小美： 你在这儿都做些什么样的事？

What kind of work do you do here?

陈大东： 我要泡咖啡、收银、还要打扫厨房。

I make coffee, man the register, and also clean the kitchen.

王小美： 你要做的事真不少！

Sounds like you're really busy!

陈大东： 我以前只管打扫，后来老板看我很努力，慢慢地就让我管更多的事了。

I used to only be responsible for cleaning. After seeing how hard I work, the boss gradually started giving me more to do.

王小美： 你不但要上学，而且还要工作。这样一天到晚都很忙，不会太累吗？

Not only do you have to go to school, you also have to work. You're so busy all day long. Isn't it tiring?

陈大东： 虽然累一点，但是我想赚点儿钱，这样的话，今年暑假就可以出国旅行了。

Although it is a little tiring, I want to earn some money. That way I can travel abroad during summer vacation.

王小美： 听起来不错。加油！

Sounds great. You can do it!

What Can You Do?

INTERPRETIVE
- I can understand instructions regarding the tasks involved in doing a job.
- I can distinguish different professional titles and use them in the correct context.

INTERPERSONAL
- I can have a discussion about employment with someone.
- I can ask and answer questions about lengths of time.

PRESENTATIONAL
- I can present information about a job and what it entails.
- I can give a more formal presentation by using structures like "not only . . . but also . . . " and "although . . . however . . ."

去中国实习
Internship in China

刘老师，我打算今年夏天去中国，在中国 gōng sī shí xí 公司实习。您有什么建议吗？

我已经准备了 jiǎn lì 一份简历，介绍了 bèi jǐng xué lì 我的背景、学历 jīng lì 和工作经历。

jí le 好极了！ xiǎng yào 你想要找什么样的工作？在中国有 jī huì 很多工作机会。

bì yè 我毕业后 shāng 想做跟商 wù yǒu guān 务有关 的事。

在中国做商务，关系很重要。

你可以先问问你的中国朋友。

他们可以帮你问一下他们认识的人，有很多外国公司和中国公司都需要你这样的人才。

谢谢老师！

祝你今年夏天实习成功！

LESSON TEXT 13.2

Internship in China 去中国实习

Sun Mali wants to find a summer internship in China and asks Teacher Liu for advice. Teacher Liu gives her some tips.

孙玛丽： 刘老师，我打算今年夏天去中国，在中国公司实习。您有什么建议吗？

Liú lǎoshī, wǒ dǎsuan jīnnián xiàtiān qù Zhōngguó, zài Zhōngguó gōngsī shíxí. Nín yǒu shénme jiànyì ma?

我已经准备了一份简历，介绍了我的背景、学历和工作经历。

Wǒ yǐjīng zhǔnbèi le yí fèn jiǎnlì, jièshào le wǒ de bèijǐng, xuélì hé gōngzuò jīnglì.

刘老师： 好极了！你想要找什么样的工作？在中国有很多工作机会。

Hǎo jí le! Nǐ xiǎngyào zhǎo shénme yàng de gōngzuò? Zài Zhōngguó yǒu hěn duō gōngzuò jīhuì.

孙玛丽： 我毕业后想做跟商务有关的事。

Wǒ bìyè hòu xiǎng zuò gēn shāngwù yǒuguān de shì.

刘老师： 在中国做商务，关系很重要。你可以先问问你的中国朋友。

Zài Zhōngguó zuò shāngwù, guānxi hěn zhòngyào. Nǐ kěyǐ xiān wènwen nǐde Zhōngguó péngyou.

他们可以帮你问一下他们认识的人，有很多外国公司和中国公司都需要你这样的人才。

Tāmen kěyǐ bāng nǐ wèn yí xià tāmen rènshi de rén, yǒu hěn duō wàiguó gōngsī hé Zhōngguó gōngsī dōu xūyào nǐ zhèiyàng de réncái.

孙玛丽： 谢谢老师！

Xièxie lǎoshī!

刘老师： 祝你今年夏天实习成功！

Zhù nǐ jīnnián xiàtiān shíxí chénggōng!

字 词 VOCABULARY

LESSON VOCABULARY 13.2

	SIMPLIFIED	TRADITIONAL	PINYIN	WORD CATEGORY	DEFINITION
1.	公司		gōngsī	*n*	company
2.	实习	實習	shíxí	*v*	to intern; to have an internship
3.	简历	簡歷	jiǎnlì	*n*	résumé; curriculum vitae
4.	背景		bèijǐng	*n*	background
5.	学历	學歷	xuélì	*n*	educational background
6.	经历	經歷	jīnglì	*n*	experience
7.	极了	極了	jíle	*adv*	extremely
8.	想要		xiǎngyào	*av*	want; wish; would like
9.	机会	機會	jīhuì	*n*	opportunity
10.	毕业	畢業	bìyè	*vo*	to graduate
11.	商务	商務	shāngwù	*n*	business
12.	有关	有關	yǒuguān	*vo*	to be relevant; to be about; to do with
13.	关系	關係	guānxi	*n*	relation; relationship; connections
14.	外国	外國	wàiguó	*adj, n*	foreign; foreign country
15.	人才		réncái	*n*	a person of ability or talent
16.	成功		chénggōng	*v, n*	to succeed; success

REQUIRED VOCABULARY 13.2

	SIMPLIFIED	TRADITIONAL	PINYIN	WORD CATEGORY	DEFINITION
RELATED TO PROFESSIONS					
17.	当	當	dāng	*v*	to serve as, to be (a profession)
18.	经验	經驗	jīngyàn	*n*	experience
RELATED TO RESUMES					
19.	求职意向	求職意向	qiúzhí yìxiàng	*n*	work objective
20.	专业技能	專業技能	zhuānyè jìnéng	*n*	professional skills
	技能		jìnéng	*n*	skill

OPTIONAL VOCABULARY 13.2

	SIMPLIFIED	TRADITIONAL	PINYIN	WORD CATEGORY	DEFINITION
BUSINESS					
21.	做生意		zuò shēngyì	*vo*	to do business
22.	官员	官員	guānyuán	*n*	official
23.	翻译	翻譯	fānyì	*v, n*	to translate; translation; translator
OTHER PROFESSIONS					
24.	家庭主妇	家庭主婦	jiātíng zhǔfù	*n*	homemaker
25.	工程师	工程師	gōngchéngshī	*n*	engineer
26.	作家		zuòjiā	*n*	writer, author
27.	画家	畫家	huàjiā	*n*	artist

Review of Professions

Profession	Pinyin	Meaning	Profession	Pinyin	Meaning
老师	lǎoshī	teacher	商人	shāngrén	businessman
医生	yīshēng	doctor	家教	jiājiào	tutor
护士	hùshi	nurse	助教	zhùjiào	teaching assistant
服务员	fúwùyuán	waiter, waitress	厨师	chúshī	chef
教授	jiàoshòu	professor	家庭主妇	jiātíngzhǔfù	homemaker
律师	lǜshī	lawyer	工程师	gōngchéngshī	engineer

Online Resources

Visit *http://college.betterchinese.com* for a list of other professions.

Chinese Resumes

Résumé in Mainland China and Taiwan look similar to English resumes, but there are a few different conventions. In Mainland China, for example, it is common to include one's birthdate, ethnicity, and health status on a résumé. Here are some common terms used in Chinese résumé:

Term	Pinyin	Meaning
个人简历	gèrén jiǎnlì	résumé, c.v.
性别	xìngbié	gender
年龄	niánlíng	age
教育	jiàoyù	education
工作经历	gōngzuò jīnglì	work experience
推荐	tuījiàn	recommendation or reference

STRUCTURE NOTE 13.7
Use 想要 to express a desire
Individually, 想 *and* 要 *can both be used to express "to want to do something." Together, they form a two-character word that is a more polite, formal way of expressing the same meaning.*

> Subject + 想要 + Verb Phrase

From the Lesson Text:

你想要找什么样的工作？
Nǐ xiǎngyào zhǎo shénmeyàng de gōngzuò?
What kind of job do you want?

Other examples:

您想要吃什么样的菜？
Nín xiǎngyào chī shénme yàng de cài?
What type of food would you like to eat?

我不想要这件衣服了。
Wǒ bù xiǎngyào zhèi jiàn yīfu le.
I don't want this skirt anymore.

Practice: Change the following English sentences into Chinese sentences containing the verb 想要.

Example: Tonight, I would like to go to a restaurant.
→ 今天晚上我想要去饭馆吃饭。

1. If you wish to go to China to attend university, you must study diligently.
   _____

2. This summer, he wants to do an internship at a company in California.
   _____

3. She has always wanted to go traveling abroad.
   _____

4. If you want to find a job, you should prepare a résumé first.
   _____

5. She doesn't want to go to piano lessons anymore.
   _____

STRUCTURE NOTE 13.8
Use 极了 as an intensifier
Structure Note 11.1 discussed complements of degree that may follow an adjective when used with the particle 得. 极了 *(jíle), meaning "to a great extent" or "extremely," is another such intensifier that is placed after an adjective. Its meaning is similar to* 得很 *or* 得不得了 *, but, unlike these complements,* 极了 *follows on directly from an adjective, without the connecting* 得.

> Subject + Adjective + 极了

From the Lesson Text:

好极了！
Hǎo jíle!
That's great!

Other examples:

我最近忙极了。
Wǒ zuìjìn máng jíle.
Recently, I've been extremely busy.

今天冷极了。
Jīntiān lěng jíle.
It's extremely cold today.

Practice: Modify the following sentences so that they express the same meaning but with the intensifier 极了 instead of the existing intensifiers.

Example:　昨天天气非常冷。→ 昨天天气冷极了。

1. 你拉小提琴拉得很好。

_____

2. 他的卧室干净得很。

_____

3. 夏天出国旅行非常贵。

_____

4. 你的中文太好了。

_____

5. 她画的画儿漂亮得不得了。

_____

STRUCTURE NOTE 13.9

Use 跟……有关 to express relevance to a subject

跟……有关 (gēn……yǒuguān) *indicates that a noun is related to a particular topic, as in "books about China." 有关 is a contraction of 有关系, which can also be used in the same structure.*

> 跟 + Topic + 有关 (+ 的 + Noun)

From the Lesson Text:

我毕业后想做跟商务有关的事。
Wǒ bì yè hòu xiǎng zuò gēn shāngwù yǒuguān de shì.
After I graduate, I would like to do something related to business.

Other examples:

我想找几本跟中国有关的书。
Wǒ xiǎng zhǎo jǐ běn gēn Zhōngguó yǒuguān de shū.
I want to find a few books about China.

你有没有什么跟买手机有关的建议？
Nǐ yǒu méiyǒu shénme gēn mǎi shǒujī yǒu guān de jiànyì?
Do you have any advice about buying a cellphone?

Practice: Complete the following sentences using 跟······有关.

Example: 我买几本书······(历史)→我买了几本跟历史有关的书。

1. 我想看电影······(功夫) _____
2. 他要找工作······(教中文) _____
3. 她唱的歌······(感情) _____
4. 老师的话······(考试) _____
5. 他写的信······(商务) _____

STRUCTURE NOTE 13.10
Use Noun + 这样/那样 to say "this/that type of . . ."

Adding 这样 *or* 那样 *after a noun conveys the meaning "things like this" or "things like that." A greater degree of specificity is introduced to the structure by adding* 的 *and a noun after the expression, which indicates the type of "thing" one is referring to. For example: "this type of book" or "that type of teacher."*

Noun + 这样 / 那样 + 的 + Noun

From the Lesson Text: 有很多外国公司和中国公司都需要你这样的人才。
Yǒu hěn duō wàiguó gōngsī hé Zhōngguó gōngsī dōu xūyào nǐ zhèyàng de réncái.
Many foreign and Chinese companies need talent like yours.

Other examples:

我很喜欢吃饺子那样的东西。
Wǒ hěn xǐhuan chī jiǎozi nàyàng de dōngxi.
I really like to eat things like dumplings.

你应该找他那样的老师。
Nǐ yīnggāi zhǎo tā nàyàng de lǎoshī.
You should look for teachers like him.

Practice: Insert 这样 or 那样 and a 'type' category of noun to the sentences below, following the pattern in the example given.

    Example: 吃素的人当然不吃烧鸡。(菜)
                  → 吃素的人当然不吃烧鸡那样的菜。

1.   她对数学没有兴趣。(课)

      _____

2.   去上课不应该忘记带笔。(文具)

      _____

3.   他喜欢跳舞、唱歌。(活动)

      _____

4.   故宫、长城我都去过。(地方)

      _____

5.   这家商店卖小提琴。(乐器)

      _____

PRACTICE 13.9

Interview five of your classmates about what they are planning to do during the summer vacation, during the winter vacation, and after graduation.

Example:

A: 你暑假 / 寒假打算做什么？
你毕业后打算做什么工作？

B: 我暑假打算出国旅行。
我毕业后打算当老师。

名字	暑假 / 寒假	毕业后

PRACTICE 13.10

Have a discussion with a partner in which you cover the following:
1. Where do you want to go for an internship and why?
2. What kind of internship do you want to do?
3. Tell your partner what to prepare and what is important.

PRACTICE 13.11

Take a survey of the class to find out which of the following factors people think is most important in finding a job: 工作经验 (gōngzuò jīngyàn: "work experience"), 关系 (guānxi: "connections"), or 教育 (jiàoyù: "education"). Record the most popular answer choice below.

Most Important Factor	Number of Students

PRACTICE 13.12

Make an audio recording and send it to your teacher. In the recording, talk about what some of your plans are after graduation.

PRACTICE 13.13

Working with a partner, practice asking each other the questions shown and respond on the basis of the information in the pictures.

Example:

A: 你想做什么样的实习？
B: 我想做跟商务有关的实习。

你想做什么样的实习？

你想做什么样的工作？

你想选什么样的课？

你想找什么样的书？

你想做什么样的活动？

PRACTICE 13.14

Read the passage and help Sun Mali write her résumé in Chinese. Refer to the Language Notes for vocabulary relating to résumés.

我是孙玛丽，今年十九岁。我是成功大学一年级的学生。我当过售货员，也当过服务员。毕业后我想做跟商务有关的工作。我认识这家公司的老板陈先生。

简历

姓名：
年龄：
性别：
教育：
工作经验：
推荐人：

PRACTICE 13.15

	Radical	Stroke Order
务	力 lì power	丿 夕 冬 冬 务
关	⌄ (八) bā eight	丶 丷 丷 关 关
系	纟(丝) sī silk	一 幺 幺 玄 乏 系 系
简	竹 (竹) zhú bamboo	丿 ⺮ ⺮ 𥫗 竹 竹 竹 笡 笡 简 简 简 简
商	口 kǒu mouth	丶 亠 产 产 产 产 产 商 商 商
毕	比 bǐ compare	一 匕 比 比 比 毕
实	宀 mián roof	丶 宀 宀 宀 宊 实 实
习	乙 yǐ second heavenly stem	丁 习 习
司	口 kǒu mouth	丁 刁 刁 司 司
背	月 (肉) ròu meat	丨 十 非 非 北 背 背 背
景	日 rì sun	丶 口 日 日 旦 旦 昇 昌 昌 景 景 景
验	马 mǎ horse	丁 马 马 马 驱 验 验 验 验
极	木 mù wood	一 十 才 木 杦 极 极
求	一 yī one	一 寸 寸 寸 求 求 求
成	戈 gē spear	一 厂 万 成 成 成

PRACTICE 13.16

Type the following sentences on your computer and provide answers to the questions.

1. 我打算今年夏天去中国实习。

2. 你大学毕业以后想做什么样的工作？

3. 我想做跟商务有关的工作。

4. 很多外国公司都需要这样的人才。

5. 你可以帮我跟你认识的公司联络一下吗？

PRACTICE 13.17

因为我毕业以后想要做跟商务有关的工作，所以今年暑假我想找一个实习的机会。朋友都说现在中国有很多工作机会，可是我不知道怎样去找。老师建议我先准备一份简历，她可以帮我问一下她的朋友。

Read Sun Mali's diary and answer the following questions.
1. What does Sun Mali want to do this summer?
2. What does the teacher suggest?

PRACTICE 13.18

Sender　玛丽

Subject　工作

爸爸：
听说现在中国有很多工作机会，所以我打算毕业后去中国工作。可是，老师说在中国关系很重要。爸爸，你在中国有没有朋友？可以帮我问一下吗？谢谢！

Sender　爸爸

Subject　re: 工作

玛丽：
我有个老同学是一个公司的老板，我可以问一下他。我想他的公司会很需要你这样的人才。

Read the e-mails and answer the following questions.
1. What does the teacher say is important for finding a job in China?
2. How does Sun Mali's dad offer to help her?

PRACTICE 13.19

孙玛丽：您好，这是我的简历。

陈先生：你有跟商务有关的工作经验吗？

孙玛丽：有，去年夏天我在中国实习了两个月。

陈先生：你学中文学了多长时间？

孙玛丽：我在大学学了两年中文，中文读写都不错。

陈先生：你还会说哪些语言？

孙玛丽：我会说英语，也会说一点法语和西班牙语。

陈先生：好极了！我们很需要这样的人才。

Read the dialogue and answer the following questions.
1. Does Sun Mali have any experience in business?
2. What skill does Mr. Chen emphasize the most?

China's Special Economic Zones

Since their inception in the late 1970s, Special Economic Zones (SEZs) have been a cornerstone of China's economic reforms. Initially, five coastal locations were classified as SEZs: Shenzhen, Zhuhai, Shantou, Xiamen, and Hainan. These regions enjoyed preferential economic policies and relaxed governmental regulations exclusively designed to bring about greater international exchange. The intention of the plan was to create powerful models of economic progress that could eventually be emulated by other cities and districts across the country. The project was indeed a great success. Since the 1980s, numerous other regions have been granted SEZ status.

The favorable policies offered to these zones included assistance in establishing new infrastructure, upgrading of industries, and cultivating science and technology. The policies were largely based around five points:

1. Special tax incentives for foreign investment in the SEZ
2. Greater independence for international trade activities
3. Export oriented production of goods
4. Market driven economic activity
5. Attraction and utilization of foreign capital for local development

These policies have not only brought colossal amounts of money into the Chinese market, but they have also increased China's exposure to foreign expertise. This has in turn helped China build toward establishing its own companies and presence in the global market.

Breaking the Iron Rice Bowl

Before the economic reforms toward a market economy that began in 1979, work in China was state-run and collectivized. Many people worked for large factories that also provided social benefits, including education, pensions, housing, and healthcare. With many thousands of people working and living in a factory complex and organized by work unit (单位: dānwèi), they resembled small villages: there were schools, clinics, and even theatres.

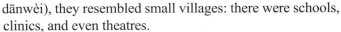

People working in the factories also enjoyed what was called the 'iron rice bowl' (铁饭碗: tiěfànwǎn) — their jobs were secure from cradle to grave.

With reforms, the nature of work in China changed significantly. Instead of being tied to the factory town and to one area, workers were able to choose between jobs in both the public and private sectors all across China. However, their jobs are no longer guaranteed for life, and companies no longer provide social benefits. Some parts of the system do remain, depending on the company — some may offer housing, and others may offer a company lunch.

While the iron rice bowl may be a thing of the past, new and varied opportunities have risen in its place. Undoubtedly, changes will lead to the country continuing its rapid development.

孙玛丽：	刘老师，我打算今年夏天去中国，在中国公司实习。您有什么建议吗？	Teacher Liu, I plan to go to China this summer and do an internship at a Chinese company. Do you have any advice?
	我已经准备了一份简历，介绍了我的背景、学历和工作经历。	I already prepared a résumé detailing my background, educational background, and work experience.
刘老师：	好极了！你想要找什么样的工作？在中国有很多工作机会。	That's great! What kind of job do you want? There are many opportunities in China.
孙玛丽：	我毕业后想做跟商务有关的事。	After I graduate, I would like to do something related to business.

刘老师：	在中国做商务，关系很重要。你可以先问问你的中国朋友。	Networking is very important for doing business in China. You can start by asking your Chinese friends.
	他们可以帮你问一下他们认识的人，有很多外国公司和中国公司都需要你这样的人才。	They can also help by asking people they know. Many foreign and Chinese companies need talent like yours.
孙玛丽：	谢谢老师！	Thank you, Teacher Liu!
刘老师：	祝你今年夏天实习成功！	Hope you have a successful internship this summer!

What Can You Do?

INTERPRETIVE
- I can understand terms related to employment experiences.
- I can understand advice about employment.

INTERPERSONAL
- I can discuss plans for after graduation with others.
- I can attend a job interview in China.

PRESENTATIONAL
- I can give a presentation about my future plans and the kind of employment I am seeking.
- I can describe my employment history.

ACT IT OUT

Working in groups, compose an original three-minute skit that utilizes the vocabulary and structures introduced in Unit 13. Each of you should assume a role and have a roughly equal number of lines in the skit. Be prepared to perform your skit in class. You can either come up with your own story or choose from one of the following situations:

A) You are at a job interview and discuss the details of the job with the interviewer, such as hours, location, your job interests, previous experience, etc.

B) You and a friend are discussing what types of professions you are considering after graduation and share your interests.

C) Your friend has a new job and you ask him or her for details about it.

CHECK WHAT YOU CAN DO

RECOGNIZE

Adjectives
- □ 努力
- □ 干净
- □ 外国

Adverbs
- □ 难怪
- □ 很少
- □ 后来
- □ 慢慢
- □ 一天到晚
- □ 极了

Auxiliary Verb
- □ 想要

Conjunctions
- □ 不但
- □ 虽然

Idiomatic Expressions
- □ 没想到
- □ 加油

Nouns
- □ 环境
- □ 厨房
- □ 老板
- □ 暑假
- □ 客人
- □ 公司
- □ 简历
- □ 背景
- □ 学历
- □ 经历
- □ 机会
- □ 商务

- □ 关系
- □ 人才
- □ 经验
- □ 求职意向
- □ 专业技能

Preposition
- □ 以前

Pronoun
- □ 什么样

Verb
- □ 打工

- □ 上班
- □ 下班
- □ 做事
- □ 泡
- □ 收银
- □ 打扫
- □ 管
- □ 上学
- □ 赚钱
- □ 出国
- □ 整理
- □ 接待
- □ 实习
- □ 毕业

- □ 有关
- □ 成功
- □ 当

WRITE

- □ 工
- □ 房
- □ 银
- □ 假
- □ 班
- □ 板
- □ 环
- □ 境
- □ 怪
- □ 前
- □ 管
- □ 但
- □ 泡
- □ 慢
- □ 虽

- □ 务
- □ 关
- □ 系
- □ 简
- □ 商
- □ 毕
- □ 实
- □ 习
- □ 司
- □ 背
- □ 景
- □ 验
- □ 极
- □ 求
- □ 成

USE

- □ 没想到 to introduce an unexpected event.
- □ 难怪 to express "no wonder."
- □ 什么样的 to ask "what kind?"
- □ 不但···而且··· to express "not only ... but also ..."
- □ 虽然···但是··· to express "although ... however ..."

- □ 从···到··· to express length of time
- □ 想要 to express a desire.
- □ 极了 as an intensifier.
- □ 跟······有关 to express relevance to a subject.
- □ Noun + 这样/那样 to say "this/that type of ..."

节

Festivals

第十四单元
UNIT 14

新年快乐!
Happy Chinese New Year!

小美，你家真漂亮，有这么多红色的装饰。
zhuāng shì

中国人过春节喜欢用红色来装饰，这是传统习惯。
guò chūn jié
zhuāng shì chuán tǒng xí guàn

难怪你要我们今天穿红色的衣服。你看，我戴着红帽子。
zhe mào zi

祥安，你呢?

我穿着红袜子!
zhe

你们见到我爸妈的时候，要说"恭喜发财"!
gōng xǐ fā cái

LESSON TEXT 14.1

Happy Chinese New Year! 新年快乐！

Sun Mali, Chen Dadong, Li Zhongping, Zhang Anna, and Huang Xiang'an visit Wang Xiaomei's house to celebrate Chinese New Year with her and her parents.

孙玛丽：	小美，你家真漂亮，有这么多红色的装饰。	Xiǎoměi, nǐ jiā zhēn piàoliang, yǒu zhème duō hóngsè de zhuāngshì.
王小美：	中国人过春节喜欢用红色来装饰，这是传统习惯。	Zhōngguó rén guò Chūnjié xǐhuan yòng hóngsè lái zhuāngshì, zhè shì chuántǒng xíguàn.
张安娜：	难怪你要我们今天穿红色的衣服。你看，我戴着红帽子。祥安，你呢？	Nánguài nǐ yào wǒmen jīntiān chuān hóngsè de yīfu. Nǐ kàn, wǒ dàizhe hóng màozi. Xiáng'ān, nǐ ne?
黄祥安：	我穿着红袜子！	Wǒ chuānzhe hóng wàzi!
王小美：	你们见到我爸妈的时候，要说"恭喜发财"！	Nǐmen jiàn dào wǒ bàmā de shíhou, yào shuō "gōngxǐfācái"!

———————————

大家：	伯父伯母，恭喜发财！	Bófù bómǔ, gōngxǐfācái!
小美妈：	新年快乐！	Xīnnián kuàilè!
小美爸：	来来来，每个人都有一个红包，祝你们学业进步，万事如意。	Lái lái lái, měi gè rén dōu yǒu yí gè hóngbāo, zhù nǐmen xuéyè jìnbù, wànshì rúyì.
孙玛丽：	谢谢！祝伯父伯母身体健康。	Xièxie! Zhù bófù bómǔ shēntǐ jiànkāng.
小美妈：	请坐，先吃些糖果，我去拿年糕和瓜子。	Qǐng zuò, xiān chī xiē tángguǒ, wǒ qù ná niángāo hé guāzǐ.
李中平：	伯父，您这儿有那么多的花灯啊！	Bófù, nín zhèr yǒu nàme duō de huādēng a!

字 词 VOCABULARY

小美爸： 是啊，元宵节快要到了，我
们会挂花灯，放烟火，那一
天会非常热闹。到时候欢迎
你们再来玩儿！

Shì a, Yuánxiāojié kuài yào dào le, wǒmen
huì guà huādēng, fàng yānhuǒ, nà yì tiān
huì fēicháng rènao. Dào shíhou huānyíng
nǐmen zài lái wánr!

LESSON VOCABULARY 14.1

	SIMPLIFIED	TRADITIONAL	PINYIN	WORD CATEGORY	DEFINITION
1.	装饰	裝飾	zhuāngshì	*v, n*	to decorate; decoration
2.	过	過	guò	*v*	to spend (the holiday, an occasion)
3.	春节	春節	Chūnjié	*n*	Spring Festival
4.	传统	傳統	chuántǒng	*adj, n*	traditional; tradition
5.	习惯	習慣	xíguàn	*n, v*	habit; to be used to
6.	着		zhe	*p*	(added to verb or adjective to indicate a continued action or state)
7.	恭喜发财	恭喜發財	gōngxǐfācái	*ie*	wishing you happiness and prosperity (greeting used during the New Year)
	恭喜		gōngxǐ	*v*	to congratulate
8.	伯父		bófù	*n*	uncle (polite term of address for a man of one's parents' generation)
9.	伯母		bómǔ	*n*	aunt (polite term of address for a woman of one's parents' generation)
10.	新年		xīnnián	*n*	new year
11.	红包	红包	hóngbāo	*n*	red envelope
12.	学业	學業	xuéyè	*n*	studies; academics
13.	万事如意	萬事如意	wànshìrúyì	*ie*	(wishing you) all the best (greeting used during the New Year)
14.	健康		jiànkāng	*adj, n*	healthy; health
15.	糖果		tángguǒ	*n*	candy
16.	年糕		niángāo	*n*	New Year's rice cake
17.	瓜子		guāzǐ	*n*	melon seeds, dried seeds
18.	花灯	花燈	huādēng	*n*	festive or decorative lantern

LESSON VOCABULARY 14.1 (continued)

	SIMPLIFIED	TRADITIONAL	PINYIN	WORD CATEGORY	DEFINITION
19.	元宵节	元宵節	Yuánxiāojié	*n*	Lantern Festival
20.	挂	掛	guà	*v*	to hang
21.	放		fàng	*v*	to put; to set off
22.	烟火	煙火	yānhuǒ	*n*	fireworks
23.	热闹	熱鬧	rènao	*adj*	lively

OPTIONAL VOCABULARY 14.1

RELATED TO FESTIVALS

	SIMPLIFIED	TRADITIONAL	PINYIN	WORD CATEGORY	DEFINITION
24.	猜谜	猜謎	cāi mí	*vo*	to guess a riddle
25.	除夕		Chúxī	*n*	(Chinese) New Year's Eve
26.	正月		zhēngyuè	*n*	first month of the lunar year
27.	锣鼓	鑼鼓	luó gǔ	*n*	gong and drum
28.	舞龙舞狮	舞龍舞獅	wǔlóngwǔshī	*n*	dragon and lion dance

Spring Festival Greetings

An important part of celebrating the Spring Festival is visiting family and friends. People often greet each other with traditional phrases, generally containing good wishes for the new year. Children often request 红包 from adults with the joking phrase, 恭喜发财，红包拿来! (gōngxǐ fācái, hóngbāo nálái!: "Happy New Year, bring out my red envelope!"). Below are a few common greetings used at the Spring Festival.

Phrase	Pinyin	Meaning	Usage
恭喜发财	gōngxǐfācái	congratulations and be prosperous	equivalent to "Happy New Year!"
万事如意	wànshìrúyì	all things as you wish	general greeting
心想事成	xīnxiǎng shìchéng	your wishes come true	general greeting
学业进步	xuéyè jìnbù	progress in your studies	for students
身体健康	shēntǐ jiànkāng	healthy body	for the elderly

Idioms

Idioms are a challenging and fascinating feature of any language, and Chinese is no exception. In Chinese, the majority of idioms come in the form of phrases that consist of four characters, known as 成语 (chéngyǔ).

成语 are not to be confused with what this book terms "idiomatic expressions," which covers phrases like 你好，对不起, and 欢迎光临. Although it can sometimes be hard to differentiate, a 成语 is also distinct from a 四个字的结构 (sì ge zì de jiégòu: "four-character expression"). The New Year's greetings listed above, for example, do not fall under the category of 成语 because the characters directly express the meaning of the phrase. 成语, on the other hand, are idiomatic — that is, their intended meaning is different than its literal meaning.

As a general rule, a four-character expression is only a 成语 if it has a story attached to it. Most of these stories derive from historical and literary sources; novels like *Romance of the Three Kingdoms* and *Dream of the Red Chamber* alone contain scores of idioms.

There are countless 成语 in Chinese; even a highly literate person may find the need to consult a dictionary when faced with a more obscure one. Nevertheless, they are a significant feature of the written language, and often come in handy in everyday speech. Some examples of 成语 are provided below.

Idiom	Pinyin	Meaning
对牛弹琴	duì niú tánqín	Literally "playing the zither to an ox," this is equivalent to the English idiom "casting pearls before swine" and means to give something valuable to someone who cannot appreciate it.
井底之蛙	jǐng dǐ zhī wā	Literally "a frog at the bottom of a well," this idiom describes a person with limited outlook and experience.
一箭双雕	yíjiàn shuāngdiāo	Literally "one arrow, two vultures," this idiom is the same as the English "to kill two birds with one stone."
如鱼得水	rú yú dé shuǐ	Literally "like a fish that gets water," this describes someone who is very happy or in their element, like the English idiom "like a duck to water."

STRUCTURE NOTE 14.1

Use 用…(来)… *to describe the means of doing something*

用 (yòng) *is used with a noun phrase and a verb phrase to express "use A to do B." The noun phrase follows* 用*, and the verb phrase is placed after the noun phrase. In this pattern,* 来 *can be added before the verb phrase for emphasis.*

Subject + 用 + Noun Phrase +（来）+ Verb Phrase

From the Lesson Text:

中国人过春节喜欢用红色来装饰，这是传统习惯。

Zhōngguó rén guò Chūnjié xǐhuan yòng hóngsè lái zhuāngshì, zhè shì chuántǒng xíguàn.

During Spring Festival, Chinese people like to decorate with the color red. This has been a long-standing tradition.

Other examples:

请你用铅笔来写作业。

Qǐng nǐ yòng qiānbǐ lái xiě zuòyè.

Please use a pencil to write your homework.

他要用爸爸妈妈给他的钱买车。

Tā yào yòng bàba māma gěi tā de qián mǎi chē.

They are going to use their parents' money to buy a car.

Practice: Use the following noun/verb pairs to form complete sentences.

Example: 红色的毛衣 / 配黑色的裤子
　　　　　→ 小美用红色的毛衣来配黑色的裤子。

1.　筷子 / 吃米饭　　＿＿＿＿＿＿＿＿＿＿＿＿＿＿＿

2.　手机 / 玩游戏　　＿＿＿＿＿＿＿＿＿＿＿＿＿＿＿

3.　关系 / 找工作　　＿＿＿＿＿＿＿＿＿＿＿＿＿＿＿

4.　录音 / 练习听力　＿＿＿＿＿＿＿＿＿＿＿＿＿＿＿

5.　信用卡 / 付钱　　＿＿＿＿＿＿＿＿＿＿＿＿＿＿＿

STRUCTURE NOTES

语法

STRUCTURE NOTE 14.2
Use 着 to indicate an ongoing action

Structure Note 8.14 introduced 在 *as a way of describing ongoing action, as in* 我们在说中文, *"we are speaking Chinese." A similar effect is created by adding the particle* 着 *(zhe) after a verb. Rather than describing an ongoing action, however,* 着 *tends to indicate an ongoing or settled state. As a result, activities that involve a significant duration of time, such as "waiting" and "sitting," are often paired with* 着. *Like* 在, 着 *is negated by* 没.

> Subject + Verb + 着 (+ Object)

From the Lesson Text:

我穿着红袜子！
Wǒ chuānzhe hóng wàzi!
I'm wearing red socks!

Other examples:

他戴着一顶帽子。
Tā dàizhe yì dǐng màozi.
He's wearing a hat.

我们在餐厅里坐着。
Wǒmen zài cāntīng lǐ zuòzhe.
We're sitting in the cafeteria.

NOTE: （正）在 …… （呢）*and* 着 *are not mutually exclusive. They can both be used in the same sentence to emphasize an ongoing action.*

Practice: Change the following sentences into Chinese using the ongoing state particle 着.

Example: They are sitting on the sofa. → 他们在沙发上坐着。

1. He's waiting outside.

   _____

2. The children are carrying red envelopes.

   _____

3. She's sitting in the kitchen.

   _____

4. That musician is wearing black clothes.

   _____

5. Xiaomei is wearing yellow socks.

   _____

STRUCTURE NOTE 14.3
Use 快要……了 to say "be about to"

快要……了 (kuài yào……le) expresses that an event is about to take place. The 了 in this pattern denotes imminent action. It can be seen as an extension of the change of state 了 discussed in Structure Note 3.10, as it implies that the situation will soon be changing.

Subject + 快要 + Verb Phrase + 了

From the Lesson Text:
元宵节快要到了。
Yuánxiāojié kuài yào dào le.
The lantern festival is fast approaching.

Other examples:
我们快要走了。
Wǒmen kuài yào zǒu le.
We are about to leave.

他们快要放烟火了。
Tāmen kuài yào fàng yānhuǒ le.
They are about to set off fireworks.

Practice: Complete the sentences below using the 快要……了 pattern and the verb in parentheses.

Example: 你不用泡茶，我……（走）
→ 你不用泡茶，我快要走了。

1. 请大家安静点，表演……（开始）

   _____

2. 你们别吃糖果，我们……（吃饭）

   _____

3. 四点十七分的火车……（到）

   _____

4. 他给我打电话，说……（来）

   _____

5. 已经十点了，弟弟……（睡觉）

   _____

STRUCTURE NOTE 14.4

Use 到时候 *to express "when the time comes"*

到时候 (dào shíhou) *is a phrase equivalent to the English "when the time comes," "at that time," or simply "then." Unlike* 的时候 *sentences,* 到时候 *precedes the verb phrase or sentence.*

到时候 + Verb Phrase

到时候 + Main sentence

From the Lesson Text:

到时候欢迎你们再来玩儿！
Dào shíhou huānyíng nǐmen zài lái wánr!
You're all welcome to come back and visit then!

Other examples:

到时候再说吧。
Dào shíhou zài shuō ba.
We'll talk about it when the time comes.

到时候你就知道了。
Dào shíhou nǐ jiù zhīdào le.
You'll know when the time comes.

Practice: Add 到时候 to the expressions below to form complete sentences, following the example given.

Example: 考试要好好儿地准备
→ 到时候要好好儿地准备。

1. 上课要带课本。   _____
2. 下星期再联系吧。   _____
3. 付钱要刷卡。   _____
4. 表演不要紧张。   _____
5. 回家要坐飞机。   _____

PRACTICE 14.1

Working with a partner, ask whether each of the pictures shown below is a Chinese New Year custom, then describe the custom.

Example:

A: 这是过春节的传统习惯吗？

B: 是，中国人过春节喜欢用红色来装饰。

PRACTICE 14.2

Go on the Internet or ask your teacher to try to find out more about traditional foods eaten during Spring Festival. Ask your classmates which Spring Festival food they like the most. What does it taste like?

Name	Favorite Food	Taste

PRACTICE 14.3

Working in a group, act out a dialogue that might occur on a visit to a Chinese friend's house during Chinese New Year. In your dialogue, cover the following points:
1. Spring Festival greetings
2. Traditional decorations
3. Traditional foods

PRACTICE 14.4

Working with a partner, ask and describe the means of doing something.

接待客人

Example:
A: 他用什么接待客人？
B: 他用咖啡接待客人。

付钱

写信

吃饺子

打电话

PRACTICE 14.5

Make an audio recording and send it to your teacher. In the recording, describe what you have learned about the traditions of Chinese New Year.

PRACTICE 14.6

	Radical	Stroke Order
闹	门 mén door	、 丶 门 门 闩 闩 闹 闹
装	衣 yī clothing	、 丷 丬 壮 壯 壮 壮 壮 婺 娤 娤 裝 裝 装
春	日 rì sun	一 二 三 声 夫 未 春 春 春
节	⺾(草) cǎo grass	一 十 艹 艹 节 节
传	亻(人) rén person	丿 亻 仁 仁 传 传
统	纟(丝) sī silk	纟 纟 纟 纟 纟 纺 纺 统 统
恭	小(心) xīn heart	一 十 艹 艹 艹 共 恭 恭 恭
财	贝 bèi shell	丨 冂 贝 贝 贝 财 财
包	勹 bāo wrap	丿 勹 勹 匀 包
万	一 yī one	一 丆 万
如	女 nǚ female	𡿨 𡿨 女 如 如 如
果	木 mù wood	丨 冂 口 日 旦 甲 里 果
元	儿 rén person	一 二 テ 元
火	火 huǒ fire	、 丷 少 火
热	灬(火) huǒ fire	一 扌 扌 扒 执 执 热 热 热

PRACTICE 14.7

Type the following sentences on your computer and provide an answer to the question.

1. 为什么你家有这么多红色的装饰？
2. 这是中国人的传统习惯。
3. 春节时，要对别人说"恭喜发财"！
4. 祝你身体健康、万事如意。
5. 元宵节时我们会挂花灯、放烟火。

PRACTICE 14.8

Write three more Spring Festival greetings on the red banners below. Refer to the Language Notes for more on phrases related to the Spring Festival.

Example:

PRACTICE 14.9

Sender	王小美
Subject	春节

明天是中国的春节，你来我家玩吧！中国人过年都会穿红色的衣服，你可以穿上我给你买的中国传统衣服。春节前我们会先把家里打扫干净，再准备过年吃的晚饭。我们会准备饺子和年糕，可是你也要带点儿小礼物来。还有，你看到我爸妈的时候，记得说"恭喜发财"！

Read Wang Xiaomei's e-mail and answer the following questions.
1. What will Wang Xiaomei's family do to prepare for the Spring Festival?
2. What does Wang Xiaomei ask Chen Dadong to remember?

PRACTICE 14.10

张安娜：小美，我来了！

王小美：你真的穿了红色的衣服呀！

张安娜：我还穿了红袜子，戴了红手套。

王小美：来，我给你介绍一下，这是我爸爸和妈妈。

张安娜：伯父伯母，恭喜发财！

王爸爸：来来来，这个红包给你。

张安娜：谢谢伯父！

王妈妈：这是中国人的传统习惯，祝你学业进步。

Read the dialogue and answer the following questions.
1. What does Zhang Anna wear to the Chinese New Year celebration?
2. What do Wang Xiaomei's parents give to Zhang Anna?

PRACTICE 14.11

今天，我的中国朋友请我去她家过春节。我学了一些中国人的传统习惯。过年时去中国人家，要注意这些事：第一，要说些新年应该说的话，像"恭喜发财、"新年快乐"、"万事如意"。第二，要带点儿小礼物去，像糖果或者水果都可以。

Read Chen Dadong's diary and answer the following questions.
1. What Spring Festival greetings did Chen Dadong learn?
2. What kinds of gifts does Chen Dadong suggest are appropriate to give the hosts?

Tomb Sweeping Festival

清明节 (Qīngmíngjié: "Qingming Festival," also known as "Ancestors Day," and "Tomb Sweeping Day") is a traditional Chinese festival that is celebrated in early April. Qingming is a time to honor one's ancestors, so it is common for people to spend the day sweeping away the dust and dirt from their family tombs, hence the English translation of "Tomb Sweeping Day." During this festival, prayers are given and symbolic offerings are made in order to pay respect to one's departed ancestors. The most common offerings are paper replicas of luxurious items including money, gold, houses, and cars. Although it is a traditional festival, Qingming has certainly kept up with the times. In 2011, the most in-demand offering was an iPad2 replica boasting a capacity of 888 gigabytes!

The Dragon Boat Festival

端午节 (Duānwǔjié: "the Dragon Boat Festival") is held on the fifth day of the fifth month of the Chinese calendar. In addition to the consumption of 粽子 (zòngzi: "rice dumplings"), this midsummer celebration involves a lively boat race, from which it derives its name. These races feature long, slender vessels called 龙舟 (lóngzhōu: "dragon boats") and can have as many as eighty rowers in participation.

The Dragon Boat Festival has a long history. Among the various explanations of its origins, one ranks as the most popular. In 278 BC the famous poet 屈原 (Qū Yuán) drowned himself in the Miluo River, when the kingdom to which he belonged was conquered by the state of Qin. The locals took boats out onto the river to search for the poet, which is said to be the origin of the dragon boat race. In addition, in an attempt to keep fish from eating his body, they threw rice dumplings into the river, which is why this food is eaten during the Dragon Boat Festival today.

The Mid-Autumn Festival

中秋节 (Zhōngqiūjié: the Mid-Autumn Festival) is another festival with a long and rich history. It is celebrated on the fifteenth day of the eighth month of the Chinese lunar calendar, which falls in September or October. The Mid-Autumn Festival celebrates the successful completion of the harvest cycle and represents a time of rest after hard work and strain.

The traditional delicacy of the festival is the moon cake, which is usually placed in a gift box and exchanged between friends. In cities and some larger towns, performances and street fairs are held to celebrate the festival, which include popular customs such as burning incense and hanging lanterns.

孙玛丽：	小美，你家真漂亮，有这么多红色的装饰。	Xiaomei, your house is so pretty. There are so many red decorations.
王小美：	中国人过春节喜欢用红色来装饰，这是传统习惯。	During Spring Festival, Chinese people like to decorate with the color red. This has been a long-standing tradition.
张安娜：	难怪你要我们今天穿红色的衣服。你看，我戴着红帽子。祥安，你呢？	No wonder you had us wear red clothing today. Look, I'm wearing a red hat. What about you, Xiang'an?
黄祥安：	我穿着红袜子！	I'm wearing red socks!
王小美：	你们见到我爸妈的时候，要说"恭喜发财"！	When you see my parents, you must say "may you be happy and prosperous!"
大家：	伯父伯母，恭喜发财！	Mr. and Mrs. Wang, may you be happy and prosperous!

小美妈：	新年快乐！	Happy New Year!
小美爸：	来来来，每个人都有一个红包，祝你们学业进步，万事如意。	Here you go, everyone gets a red envelope. I wish you progress in your studies and success in all things.
孙玛丽：	谢谢！祝伯父伯母身体健康。	Thank you! May you both enjoy the best of health.
小美妈：	请坐，先吃些糖果，我去拿年糕和瓜子。	Please have a seat. First have some candies and I'll go get the New Year's rice cake and the melon seeds.
李中平：	伯父，您这儿有那么多的花灯啊！	Mr. Wang, you have a lot of lanterns here!

小美爸： 是啊，元宵节快要到了，我们会挂花灯，放烟火，那一天会非常热闹。到时候欢迎你们再来玩儿！

Indeed, the Lantern Festival is fast approaching. We will hang lanterns and set off firecrackers. It will be very festive on that day. You're all welcome to come back and visit then!

What Can You Do?

INTERPRETIVE
- I can understand the traditional greetings given at Chinese New Year.
- I can understand the meanings of some Chinese idioms.

INTERPERSONAL
- I can offer and receive Chinese New Year's greetings using culturally appropriate expressions.
- I can discuss some of the features of Chinese New Year and the Lantern Festival with someone.

PRESENTATIONAL
- I can give a presentation about Chinese New Year and its customs.

中国和西方节日
Chinese and Western Holidays

今天我们吃年夜饭(nián yè fàn)。
过年(guò nián)的时候，我们习惯吃鱼(yú)。
因为"鱼(yú)"听起来像"多余(duō yú)"的
"余(yú)"，所以吃鱼(yú)就是希望
"年年有余(nián nián yǒu yú)。"

吃年夜饭(nián yè fàn)，最重要的是全(quán)家人
在一起，跟圣诞节(shèng dàn jié)一样耶(ye)。

我们过节(guò jié)都
有传统的食物(shí wù)。
中秋节(zhōng qiū jié)要吃月饼(yuè bǐng)，
春节吃鱼(yú)、饺子
或者年糕。
你们呢？

我们家感恩节(gǎn ēn jié)一定要吃火鸡(huǒ jī)。

我们家
好像(hǎo xiàng)每天都
在过节(guò jié)，每天
都吃大餐(dà cān)！

我记得有一个
jì de
中国节日是吃
jié rì
粽子的……
zòng zi

那是端午节。端午节的时候
duān wǔ jié   duān wǔ jié
还会有划龙舟比赛。
huá lóng zhōu

哇，中国的节日那么多，
中国人还过西方节日吗？
xī fāng

现在有一些
西方节日在
xī fāng
中国越来越
yuè lái yuè
流行。
liú xíng

比方说，有的年轻人会
bǐ fāng shuō   *nián qīng rén*
参加万圣节派对。
cān jiā wàn shèng jié

没想到中国人
连万圣节都会
lián wàn shèng jié
过啊！

LESSON TEXT 14.2

Chinese and Western Holidays 中国和西方节日

The group sits down for a reunion dinner on Chinese New Year with Wang Xiaomei's family and discusses various Chinese festivals.

王小美：	今天我们吃年夜饭。过年的时候，我们习惯吃鱼。因为"鱼"听起来像"多余"的"余"，所以吃鱼就是希望"年年有余"。	Jīntiān wǒmen chī niányèfàn. Guònián de shíhou, wǒmen xíguàn chī yú. Yīnwèi "yú" tīngqilai xiàng "duōyú" de "yú," suǒyǐ chī yú jiùshì xīwàng "niánnián-yǒu-yú."
李中平：	吃年夜饭，最重要的是全家人在一起，跟圣诞节一样耶。	Chī niányèfàn, zuì zhòngyào de shì quán jiā rén zài yìqǐ, gēn Shèngdànjié yíyàng ye.
小美爸：	我们过节都有传统的食物。中秋节要吃月饼，春节吃鱼、饺子或者年糕。你们呢？	Wǒmen guòjié dōu yǒu chuántǒng de shíwù. Zhōngqiūjié yào chī yuèbǐng, Chūnjié chī yú, jiǎozi huòzhě niángāo. nǐmen ne?
孙玛丽：	我们家感恩节一定要吃火鸡。	Wǒmen jiā Gǎn'ēnjié yídìng yào chī huǒjī.

黄祥安：	我们家好像每天都在过节，每天都吃大餐！	Wǒmen jiā hǎoxiàng měi tiān dōu zài guòjié, měi tiān dōu chī dàcān!
孙玛丽：	我记得有一个中国节日是吃粽子的……	Wǒ jìde yǒu yí gè Zhōngguó jiérì shì chī zòngzi de……
王小美：	那是端午节。端午节的时候还会有划龙舟比赛。	Nà shì Duānwǔjié. Duānwǔjié de shíhou hái huì yǒu huá lóngzhōu bǐsài.
张安娜：	哇，中国的节日那么多，中国人还过西方节日吗？	Wā, Zhōngguó de jiérì nàme duō, Zhōngguó rén hái guò Xīfāng jiérì ma?

字 词 VOCABULARY

王小美：	现在有一些西方节日在中国越来越流行。	Xiànzài yǒu yìxiē Xīfāng jiérì zài Zhōngguó yuèláiyuè liúxíng.
小美爸：	比方说，有的年轻人会参加万圣节派对。	Bǐfāngshuō, yǒude niánqīng rén huì cānjiā Wànshèngjié pàiduì.
陈大东：	没想到中国人连万圣节都会过啊！	Méi xiǎng dào Zhōngguó rén lián Wàn-shèngjié dōu huì guò a!

LESSON VOCABULARY 14.2

	SIMPLIFIED	TRADITIONAL	PINYIN	WORD CATEGORY	DEFINITION
1.	年夜饭	年夜飯	niányèfàn	*n*	a reunion dinner for the whole family on Chinese New Year's Eve
2.	过年	過年	guònián	*vo*	to celebrate the New Year
3.	鱼	魚	yú	*n*	fish
4.	像		xiàng	*v*	to resemble
5.	多余	多餘	duōyú	*n, adj*	surplus; superfluous
6.	年年有余	年年有餘	niánnián-yǒuyú	*ie*	may you have abundance every year (greeting used at New Year)
7.	全		quán	*adj, adv*	complete, whole; completely
8.	圣诞节	聖誕節	Shèngdànjié	*n*	Christmas
9.	耶		ye	*p*	(particle used at end of a sentence)
10.	过节	過節	guò jié	*vo*	to celebrate a festival
11.	食物		shíwù	*n*	food
12.	中秋节	中秋節	Zhōngqiūjié	*n*	Mid-Autumn Festival
13.	月饼	月餅	yuèbǐng	*n*	mooncake
14.	感恩节	感恩節	Gǎn'ēnjié	*n*	Thanksgiving
15.	火鸡	火鷄	huǒjī	*n*	turkey
16.	好像		hǎoxiàng	*adv*	apparently; it appears; it seems like
17.	大餐		dàcān	*n*	a large feast
18.	记得	記得	jìde	*v*	to remember

LESSON VOCABULARY 14.2 (continued)

	SIMPLIFIED	TRADITIONAL	PINYIN	WORD CATEGORY	DEFINITION
19.	节日	節日	jiérì	*n*	holiday; festival
20.	粽子		zòngzi	*n*	pyramid-shaped dumpling made of glutinous rice wrapped in bamboo leaves
21.	端午节	端午節	Duānwǔjié	*n*	Dragon Boat Festival
22.	划		huá	*v*	to row
23.	龙舟	龍舟	lóngzhōu	*n*	dragon boat
24.	西方		Xīfāng	*n*	the West
25.	越来越	越來越	yuèláiyuè	*adv*	more and more
26.	流行		liúxíng	*adj*	popular
27.	比方说	比方説	bǐfāngshuō	*ie*	for example
28.	年轻人	年輕人	niánqīng rén	*n*	young people
	年轻	年輕	niánqīng	*adj*	young
29.	万圣节	萬聖節	Wànshèngjié	*n*	Halloween
30.	连	連	lián	*prep*	even

REQUIRED VOCABULARY 14.2

HOLIDAYS

	SIMPLIFIED	TRADITIONAL	PINYIN	WORD CATEGORY	DEFINITION
31.	母亲节	母親節	Mǔqīnjié	*n*	Mother's Day
32.	父亲节	父親節	Fùqīnjié	*n*	Father's Day
33.	情人节	情人節	Qíngrénjié	*n*	Valentine's Day

OPTIONAL VOCABULARY 14.2

HOLIDAYS

	SIMPLIFIED	TRADITIONAL	PINYIN	WORD CATEGORY	DEFINITION
34.	光明节	光明節	Guāngmíngjié	*n*	Hanukkah
35.	复活节	復活節	Fùhuójié	*n*	Easter
36.	元旦		Yuándàn	*n*	New Year's Day
37.	清明节	清明節	Qīngmíngjié	*n*	Tomb Sweeping Festival

Holiday Foods

Spring Festival Foods			
Foods	**Pinyin**	**Meaning**	**Symbolism/Significance**
年糕	niángāo	New Year's rice cake	年年高升 (niánnián-gāoshēng): "advance every year"
饺子	jiǎozi	dumplings	symbolize wealth as they resemble old Chinese currency
汤圆	tāngyuán	rice dumplings	团圆 (tuányuán): family reunion and togetherness
鱼	yú	fish	年年有余 (niánnián-yǒuyú): "abundance every year"
瓜子	guāzǐ	melon seeds	a wish for offspring (子: "son")

Other Holiday Foods			
月饼	yuèbǐng	moon cakes	eaten at Mid-Autumn Festival, they represent the moon
粽子	zòngzi	leaf-wrapped dumplings	a commemoration of the poet Qu Yuan (see Cultural Spotlight 14.1)

Online Resources

Visit *http://college.betterchinese.com* for a list of other words related to Chinese festivals.

Horizontal and Vertical Text

Historically, Chinese script was written and read from top to bottom, right to left. Formal inscriptions in temples and palaces could be written horizontally. However, it was mostly still read from right to left. In the early twentieth century, reformers began to print magazines in horizontal script, citing the fact that this format was better suited to incorporating Western words and scientific formulae into the text. In territories that use traditional characters, such as Taiwan and Hong Kong, many newspapers and books continue to use vertical text, whereas publications in Mainland China are by and large printed in the Western style. Nevertheless, it is not unusual to see vertical or right to left text on a restaurant or shop in any Chinese community, a touch that gives the establishment a more traditional feel.

STRUCTURE NOTE 14.5
Use 像 to express "resemble" or "is like"

像 (xiàng) *can act as a verb meaning "to resemble" or as an adjective meaning "similar." When* 像 *is used as a verb, it is simply placed between the two noun phrases, as in the pattern A* 是 *B. When used as an adjective, it comes after the noun phrases, which are joined by a conjunction.*

Noun Phrase A (+ 不) + 像 + Noun Phrase B

From the Lesson Text:

因为 "鱼" 听起来像 "多余" 的 "余"。
Yīnwèi "yú" tīngqilai xiàng "duōyú" de "yú."
As a result of the Chinese word for "fish" sounding like the word for "plentiful" . . .

Other examples:

我不像我妈妈。
Wǒ bú xiàng wǒ māma.
I don't look like my mom.

他有点像我们老师
Tā yǒu diǎn xiàng wǒmen lǎoshī.
He looks a bit like our teacher.

Practice: Use the 像 structure pattern in conjunction with the information below to create complete sentences. Remember that you may negate the pattern.

Example:
这里的天气 / 北京的天气
→ 这里的天气不像北京的天气。

1. 母亲节 / 父亲节 _____
2. 黄祥安 / 李中平 _____
3. 中医 / 西医 _____
4. 拉小提琴 / 拉大提琴 _____
5. 英语 / 法语 _____

STRUCTURE NOTE 14.6
Use 越来越 to mean "increasingly"

To express that something is "becoming more and more (adjective)," Chinese uses the phrase 越来越 (yuèláiyuè) *followed by the relevant adjective.*

Subject + 越来越 + Adjective

From the Lesson Text:

现在有一些西方节日在中国越来越流行。
Xiànzài yǒu yìxiē Xīfāng jiérì zài Zhōngguó yuèláiyuè liúxíng.
There are several Western holidays that are becoming more and more popular in China now.

Other examples:

会说中文的人越来越多。
Huì shuō Zhōngwén de rén yuèláiyuè duō.
More and more people can speak Chinese.

我们的公司越来越大。
Wǒmen de gōngsī yuèláiyuè dà.
Our company is getting bigger and bigger.

Practice: Complete the following sentences using 越来越 and an adjective of your choice.

Example: 最近天气…… → 最近天气越来越冷。

1. 爸爸最近看起来……

   _____

2. 中文语法好像……

   _____

3. 快要考试了……

   _____

4. 这家商店的东西……

   _____

5. 最近飞机票……

   _____

STRUCTURE NOTE 14.7
Use 比方说 to say "for example"

The phrase 比方说 (bǐfāngshuō) *can be used to introduce an example. It is equivalent to the English "for example" or "to give an example."*

比方说 + Example Sentence

From the Lesson Text:

比方说，有的年轻人会参加万圣节派对。
Bǐfāngshuō, yǒude niánqīng rén huì cānjiā Wànshèngjié pàiduì.
For example, some young people go to Halloween parties.

Other examples:

中国人过春节有很多传统。比方说，吃饺子、穿红色的衣服。
Zhōngguórén guò Chūnjié yǒu hěn duō chuántǒng. Bǐfāngshuō, chī jiǎozi, chuān hóngsè de yīfu.
Chinese people have many Spring Festival traditions. For example, the tradition of eating dumplings and wearing red clothing.

有的人不喜欢过节。比方说，我妹妹就不太喜欢。
Yǒude rén bù xǐhuan guò jié. Bǐfāngshuō, wǒ mèimei jiù bú tài xǐhuan.
Some people don't like to celebrate holidays. For example, my younger sister doesn't like to celebrate very much.

Practice: Provide examples to support the following statements, using 比方说.

Example: 周末有很多活动。 → 比方说，去看电影。

1. 手机现在可以用来做很多事，

   _____

2. 出国旅行可以去很多国家，

   _____

3. 北京好玩儿的地方很多，

   _____

4. 我的同学会玩很多乐器，

   _____

5. 大东有很多打工的经验，

   _____

STRUCTURE NOTE 14.8
Use 连······都 to say "even . . ."

连······都 (lián......dōu) *is a pattern used to express "even," as in "even he came to my party." Remember to pay attention to the position of the subject and object in relation to* 连. *For example,* 连他们都不会写那个字 *means "even they can't write that character," but* 他们连那个字都不会写 *means "they can't even write that character." Note that the* 都 *in this pattern can also be replaced with* 也.

连 + Subject + 都/也 + Verb Phrase

Subject + 连 + Object / Time Phrase + 都/也 + Verb Phrase

From the Lesson Text:

没想到中国人连万圣节都会过啊！
Méi xiǎng dào Zhōngguó rén lián Wànshèngjié dōu huì guò a!
Who would have thought that Chinese people even celebrate Halloween!

Other examples:

连我的奶奶都喜欢玩电子游戏。
Lián wǒ de nǎinai dōu xǐhuan wán diànzǐ yóuxì.
Even my grandmother likes to play video games.

她连星期天也练习中文。
Tā lián Xīngqī tiān yě liànxí Zhōngwén.
She even practices Chinese on Sundays.

Practice: Change the following sentences into Chinese using the 连……都 pattern.

Example: She doesn't even drink coffee. →她连咖啡都不喝。

1.   Even Chinese people forget how to write that character.

_____

2.   My roommate doesn't even eat dumplings.

_____

3.   He doesn't even know where Spain is.

_____

4.   My classmate can even speak Russian.

_____

5.   She can't even find a place to intern.

_____

PRACTICE 14.12

In the space provided below, record the details of a Western or Chinese festival that you like. Share the details of the festival with your classmates.

Festival: _____ Date: _____

Country of Origin: _____ Customs: _____

PRACTICE 14.13

Working with a partner, identify the foods below and the festivals that they are related to. Then, practice the dialogue shown. Refer to Cultural Spotlight 14.1 if you need help.

Example:

A: 过年的时候你们习惯吃什么？

B: 过年的时候我们习惯吃糖果。

糖果

鱼　　年糕　　月饼　　粽子

PRACTICE 14.14

Take a survey of the class to find out which Chinese festival they like the most. Record your findings below.

Festival	Number of Students

PRACTICE 14.15

Working with a partner, use the Cultural Spotlights in Unit 14 to identify the holidays associated with the pictures and the traditions that they depict. Record the traditions in the spaces provided.

Example:

A: 春节的时候会有很多传统活动。

B: 比方说，春节的时候会舞龙舞狮。

舞龙舞狮

	Radical	Stroke Order
午	十 shí ten	丿 丨 乍 午
餐	食 shí food	丶 丿 卜 炸 夕 乡 夕 夕 炙 炙 奴 奴 奴 餐 餐 餐
划	刂(刀) dāo knife	一 七 戈 戈 划 划
夜	亠 tóu lid	丶 一 广 宀 广 产 夜 夜
像	亻(人) rén person	丿 亻 亻 伫 伫 伆 伆 像 像 像 像 像
余	人 rén person	丿 人 人 令 令 余 余
秋	禾 hé grain	丿 二 千 禾 禾 禾 秒 秋
食	食 shí food	丿 人 人 今 今 今 食 食 食
端	立 lì stand	丶 亠 六 亠 立 立 妙 竔 妙 竔 竔 端 端 端
龙	龙 lóng dragon	一 大 尤 龙 龙
越	走 zǒu walk	一 十 土 丰 丰 走 走 赴 赴 越 越 越
流	氵(水) shuǐ water	丶 冫 氵 氵 汸 泸 泸 济 流 流
轻	车 chē cart	一 七 车 车 轺 轺 轻 轻 轻
亲	立 lì stand	丶 二 六 亠 立 立 辛 辛 亲
连	辶 chuò walk	一 七 乍 车 车 迮 连

PRACTICE 14.16

Make an audio recording and send it to your teacher. In the recording, use what you have learned to compare and contrast a Western holiday and a Chinese holiday of your choosing.

PRACTICE 14.17

Typing the following sentences on your computer.

1. 过春节的时候，中国人一定要回家吃年夜饭。
2. 每个节日都有传统的食物。
3. 现在有一些西方节日在中国越来越流行。
4. 你会参加学校的万圣节派对吗？
5. 没想到中国的年轻人也会过圣诞节！

PRACTICE 14.19

陈大东：昨天我跟小美的家人一起吃年夜饭了。

李中平：你吃了些什么？

陈大东：小美的妈妈做了很多中国菜，每个菜都有特别的意思。

李中平：你说说看！

陈大东：比方说，吃鱼就是希望"年年有余"。

李中平：你吃没吃年糕？

陈大东：当然吃了！

李中平：中国人吃年糕有什么特别的意思？

陈大东：哎呀！我吃完就忘了。

Read the dialogue and answer the following questions.
1. What did Chen Dadong eat with Xiaomei's family?
2. What symbolic value do the food represent?

中国的春节跟西方的圣诞节一样，是一年中最重要的节日，也是全家人一起过的节日。圣诞节的时候很多西方人吃火鸡，春节的时候中国人吃饺子、年糕。现在有一些西方节日，像圣诞节、万圣节，在中国越来越流行。中国的传统节日，像元宵节、端午节、中秋节，以后可能也会在西方越来越流行。

Read the passage and answer the following questions.
1. What are the similarities and differences between Chinese New Year and Christmas?
2. What Western festivals are becoming popular in China?

Chinese New Year

春节 (Chūnjié: "the Spring Festival," also referred to as "Chinese New Year") is celebrated by millions every year and is undoubtedly the most important annual celebration for the Chinese. The Spring Festival is a time to be with one's family and enjoy foods such as 饺子 (jiǎozi: "dumplings") and to celebrate by setting off firecrackers and fireworks.

The Spring Festival is typically a weeklong festival in Mainland China. It is China's busiest travel season. Only those prepared enough (and indeed lucky enough) to get tickets well in advance are able to go traveling. During this time, migrant workers around the country also make the trip to their ancestral homes to reunite with their families and celebrate the New Year.

The New Year period typically involves some vigorous spring cleaning, which, aside from its practical benefits, is believed to rid the house of negative energy from the previous year and to make room for good luck to move in. Children are given 红包 (hóngbāo: "red envelopes") containing money from their parents or older relatives, and new clothes and haircuts are frequently in order for a fresh start to the New Year.

Spring Festival is so important in Chinese culture that even other countries with large Chinese populations such as Indonesia and Malaysia have adopted it as a national holiday. In addition, major cities in the West also recognize the significance of the holiday by holding parades and celebrations for Chinese New Year.

Lantern Festival

元宵节 (Yuánxiāojié: "the Lantern Festival") marks the end of the Chinese New Year celebrations. It takes place on the fifteenth day of the New Year. It is also the first full moon of the year and an auspicious night to celebrate. Traditional activities associated with the Lantern Festival include solving puzzles and riddles, eating 汤圆 (tāngyuán: "glutinous rice balls"), and making colorful paper lanterns for children to carry around. Like most of the oldest Chinese festivals, the exact origin of the holiday is unclear. One legend states that the festival derives its name from 元宵 (Yuán Xiāo), a lonely palace maid who concocted a complex plan to reunite with her family. Whatever its origins, the Chinese people have been celebrating the Lantern Festival in one form or another for centuries.

Originally, the lanterns used at the festival were made of simple, unadorned paper. These days, they come in all shapes and sizes and are decorated with a variety of elaborate and eye-catching designs. In major cities like Shanghai and Hangzhou, competitions are held to find the most attractive lantern, an event that draws visitors from far and wide.

王小美：	今天我们吃年夜饭。过年的时候，我们习惯吃鱼。因为"鱼"听起来像"多余"的"余"，所以吃鱼就是希望"年年有余"。
李中平：	吃年夜饭，最重要的是全家人在一起，跟圣诞节一样耶。
小美爸：	我们过节都有传统的食物。中秋节要吃月饼，春节吃鱼、饺子或者年糕。你们呢？
孙玛丽：	我们家感恩节一定要吃火鸡。
黄祥安：	我们家好像每天都在过节，每天都吃大餐！
孙玛丽：	我记得有一个中国节日是吃粽子的……
王小美：	那是端午节。端午节的时候还会有划龙舟比赛。
张安娜：	哇，中国的节日那么多，中国人还过西方节日吗？
王小美：	现在有一些西方节日在中国越来越流行。
小美爸：	比方说，有的年轻人会参加万圣节派对。
陈大东：	没想到中国人连万圣节都会过啊！

Today, we are having a Chinese New Year's Eve dinner. During Chinese New Year, it is a tradition to have fish. As a result of the Chinese word for "fish" sounding like the word for "plentiful," eating fish represents a wish to "enjoy abundance year after year."

The most important thing about the Chinese New Year's Eve dinner is to have the whole family together, just like Christmas.

When we celebrate Chinese holidays, there are always traditional foods. For the Mid-Autumn Festival, we have moon cakes. For Chinese New Year, we have fish, dumplings, or New Year's rice cake. How about you?

At Thanksgiving, my family must have turkey.

My family seems like it's celebrating a holiday every day. Every day we have a feast!

I remember there is a Chinese festival where people eat leaf-wrapped dumplings . . .

That is the Dragon Boat Festival. During that festival, there are also dragon boat races.

Wow, there are so many Chinese holidays. Do Chinese people also celebrate Western holidays?

There are several Western holidays that are becoming more and more popular in China now.

For example, some young people go to Halloween parties.

Who would have thought that Chinese people even celebrate Halloween!

What Can You Do?

INTERPRETIVE

- I can understand why certain foods are eaten at certain festivals.
- I can interpret the significance of customs and activities associated with Chinese festivals.

INTERPERSONAL

- I can discuss holidays and festivals with others.
- I can inquire as to what kinds of food or activities are traditionally associated with a festival.

PRESENTATIONAL

- I can present information about a variety of Chinese holidays.
- I can compare and contrast Western festivals with Chinese festivals.

ACT IT OUT

Working in groups, compose an original three-minute skit that utilizes the vocabulary and structures introduced in Unit 14. Each of you should assume a role and have a roughly equal number of lines in the skit. Be prepared to perform your skit in class. You can either come up with your own story or choose from one of the following situations:

A) You visit your Chinese friend for Chinese New Year and he or she explains the customs of Chinese New Year to you.

B) You work in a store that sells party supplies and some customers want to buy supplies for a Chinese festival.

C) You and your spouse decide whose family to visit for the different holidays of the year.

CHECK WHAT YOU CAN DO

RECOGNIZE

Adjectives
- □ 传统
- □ 健康
- □ 热闹
- □ 全
- □ 流行
- □ 年轻

Adverbs
- □ 好像
- □ 越来越

Idiomatic Expressions
- □ 恭喜发财
- □ 万事如意
- □ 年年有余

- □ 比方说

Nouns
- □ 春节
- □ 习惯
- □ 伯父
- □ 伯母
- □ 新年
- □ 红包
- □ 学业
- □ 糖果
- □ 年糕
- □ 瓜子
- □ 花灯
- □ 元宵节

- □ 烟火
- □ 年夜饭
- □ 鱼
- □ 多余
- □ 圣诞节
- □ 食物
- □ 中秋节
- □ 月饼
- □ 感恩节
- □ 火鸡
- □ 大餐
- □ 节日
- □ 粽子
- □ 端午节
- □ 龙舟
- □ 西方
- □ 年轻人

- □ 万圣节
- □ 母亲节
- □ 父亲节
- □ 情人节

Particles
- □ 着
- □ 耶

Preposition
- □ 连

Verbs
- □ 装饰
- □ 过
- □ 恭喜
- □ 挂
- □ 放
- □ 过年

- □ 像
- □ 过节
- □ 记得
- □ 划

WRITE

- □ 闹
- □ 装
- □ 春
- □ 节
- □ 传
- □ 统
- □ 恭
- □ 财
- □ 包
- □ 万
- □ 如
- □ 果
- □ 元
- □ 火
- □ 热

- □ 午
- □ 餐
- □ 划
- □ 夜
- □ 像
- □ 余
- □ 秋
- □ 食
- □ 端
- □ 龙
- □ 越
- □ 流
- □ 轻
- □ 亲
- □ 连

USE

- □ 用···(来)··· to describe the means of doing something.
- □ 着 to indicate an ongoing action.
- □ 快要······了 to say "be about to."
- □ 到时候 to express "when the time comes."

- □ 像 to express "resemble" or "is like."
- □ 越来越 to mean "increasingly."
- □ 比方说 to say "for example."
- □ 连······都 to say "even ..."

礼

Chinese Ways

第十五单元
UNIT 15

Communication Goals

Lesson 1: 有礼貌 **Being Respectful**
- Politely ask someone to do something.
- Understand and follow Chinese social conventions.
- Use the correct etiquette towards one's elders.

Lesson 2: 了解中国文化 **Understanding Chinese Culture**
- Name some features of traditional Chinese culture.
- Express that one has "just" done something.
- Make basic comparisons between ancient and modern Chinese culture.

有礼貌
Being Respectful

服务员，麻烦您，请问
má fan
洗手间在哪儿？
xǐ shǒu jiān

我也去。

今天我请客，
让我来买单吧。
mǎi dān

今天晚饭是我父母
请我们。
fù mǔ

这样可以吗？

不用担心。
长辈请客也是
zhǎng bèi
对晚辈的
wǎn bèi
照顾。
zhàogù

我今天正好拿到薪水，就
zhèng hǎo *xīn shuǐ*
给我个面子。
miàn zi

下次吧。如果想要表示尊敬，
biǎo shì zūn jìng
你可以送一份礼物。

哎呀！我没有准备，怎么办？

小美，你太好了！

没关系，我知道你还不太了解中国传统。
（liǎo jiě）
这次我先帮你准备了一盒茶叶，你可以送给他们。
（hé chá yè）

那我下次请他们好了，要不然就是我不懂礼貌了。
（yào bu rán）

谢谢伯父伯母。

哪里哪里。

这是一份小礼物，希望下次有机会可以请伯父伯母吃饭。

别客气。你们还是大学生，我们是长辈，应该照顾你们。
（kè qi）
（zhǎng bèi）（zhào gù）

LESSON TEXT 15.1

Being Respectful 有礼貌

At a dinner with Wang Xiaomei and her parents, Chen Dadong wants to pay for the check, but Wang Xiaomei tells him to let her parents pay. Following social etiquette, Chen Dadong gives a gift instead.

小美爸:	服务员，麻烦您，请问洗手间在哪儿？	Fúwùyuán, máfan nín, qǐng wèn xǐshǒujiān zài nǎr?
小美妈:	我也去。	Wǒ yě qù.
陈大东:	今天我请客，让我来买单吧。	Jīntiān wǒ qǐngkè, ràng wǒ lái mǎidān ba.
王小美:	今天晚饭是我父母请我们。	Jīntiān wǎnfàn shì wǒ fùmǔ qǐng wǒmen.
陈大东:	这样可以吗？	Zhèiyàng kěyǐ ma?
王小美:	不用担心。长辈请客也是对晚辈的照顾。	Bú yòng dānxīn. Zhǎngbèi qǐngkè yě shì duì wǎnbèi de zhàogù.

陈大东:	我今天正好拿到薪水，就给我个面子。	Wǒ jīntiān zhènghǎo ná dào xīnshuǐ, jiù gěi wǒ gè miànzi.
王小美:	下次吧。如果想要表示尊敬，你可以送一份礼物。	Xià cì ba. Rúguǒ xiǎngyào biǎoshì zūnjìng, nǐ kěyǐ sòng yí fèn lǐwù.
陈大东:	哎呀！我没有准备，怎么办？	Āiyā! Wǒ méiyǒu zhǔnbèi, zěnmebàn?
王小美:	没关系，我知道你还不太了解中国传统。这次我先帮你准备了一盒茶叶，你可以送给他们。	Méi guānxi, wǒ zhīdào nǐ hái bú tài liǎojiě Zhōngguó chuántǒng. Zhèi cì wǒ xiān bāng nǐ zhǔnbèile yì hé cháyè, nǐ kěyǐ sòng gěi tāmen.
陈大东:	小美，你太好了！	Xiǎoměi, nǐ tài hǎo le!

陈大东：	那我下次请他们好了，要不然就是我不懂礼貌了。	Nà wǒ xià cì qǐng tāmen hǎo le, yàobùrán jiù shì wǒ bù dǒng lǐmào le.
陈大东：	谢谢伯父伯母。	Xièxie bófù bómǔ.
小美爸：	哪里哪里。	Nǎlǐ nǎlǐ.
陈大东：	这是一份小礼物，希望下次有机会可以请伯父伯母吃饭。	Zhè shì yí fèn xiǎo lǐwù, xīwàng xià cì yǒu jīhuì kěyǐ qǐng bófù bómǔ chīfàn.
小美妈：	别客气。你们还是大学生，我们是长辈，应该照顾你们。	Bié kèqi! Nǐmen hái shì dàxuéshēng, wǒmen shì zhǎngbèi, yīnggāi zhàogù nǐmen.

LESSON VOCABULARY 15.1

	SIMPLIFIED	TRADITIONAL	PINYIN	WORD CATEGORY	DEFINITION
1.	麻烦	麻煩	máfan	v, n, adj	to trouble someone to do something; trouble; troublesome
2.	洗手间	洗手間	xǐshǒujiān	n	restroom
3.	买单	買單	mǎidān	vo	to pay the bill
4.	父母		fùmǔ	n	parents (formal)
5.	长辈	長輩	zhǎngbèi	n	elder generation
6.	晚辈	晚輩	wǎnbèi	n	younger generation
7.	照顾	照顧	zhàogù	v	to take care of
8.	正好		zhènghǎo	adv	happen to, as it happens
9.	薪水		xīnshuǐ	n	salary
10.	面子		miànzi	n	reputation; face; feelings
11.	表示		biǎoshì	v	to express
12.	尊敬		zūnjìng	v	to pay respect to (used for people)
13.	了解		liǎojiě	v	to understand
14.	盒		hé	n, mw	box; a box of
15.	茶叶	茶葉	cháyè	n	tea leaves

LESSON VOCABULARY 15.1 (continued)

	SIMPLIFIED	TRADITIONAL	PINYIN	WORD CATEGORY	DEFINITION
16.	要不然		yàoburán	*cj*	otherwise
17.	礼貌	禮貌	lǐmào	*n*	manners; politeness
18.	客气	客氣	kèqi	*adj, v*	polite; to be polite

REQUIRED VOCABULARY 15.1

PEOPLE

19.	大人		dàrén	*n*	adults
20.	老人		lǎorén	*n*	elders

OTHER

21.	就是说	就是說	jiùshìshuō	*ie*	that is to say; in other words

OPTIONAL VOCABULARY 15.1

ETIQUETTE

22.	孝顺	孝順	xiàoshùn	*v, adj*	to show filial obedience; filial
	孝		xiào	*n, v*	filial piety; to be filial
23.	侮辱		wǔrǔ	*n, v*	insult; to insult; to humiliate
24.	得罪		dézuì	*v*	to offend; to displease
25.	谦虚	謙虛	qiānxū	*adj*	modest
26.	高傲		gāo'ào	*adj*	arrogant

Face

One of the most important features of Chinese etiquette is "face." Face refers to a person's public image. When someone is embarrassed or weakened in public, they "lose face" (丢脸: diū liǎn). When one allows someone to display or maintain their social status, one "gives them face" (给他面子: gěi tā miànzi). Chinese has a few different terms that refer to face. Here are some common expressions.

Phrase	Pinyin	Meaning	Use
请给我点儿面子	qǐng gěi wǒ diǎnr miànzi	Please give me some face	Request for someone not to embarrass the speaker
很丢脸啊！	hěn diūliǎn a!	It's disgraceful!	Something is embarrassing
你让我没面子！	nǐ ràng wǒ méi miànzi!	You made me lose face!	The addressee has embarrassed the speaker

Terms for Politeness

The term 客气 is primarily used as an adjective meaning "polite," and 礼貌 is primarily used as a noun meaning "politeness" or "manners." They can express the same meaning, but as they are different parts of speech, they are generally used in different ways.

Phrase	Pinyin	Meaning
他很客气	tā hěn kèqi	He is very polite
他很有礼貌	tā hěn yǒu lǐmào	
客气的话	kèqi de huà	polite words
有礼貌的话	yǒu lǐmào de huà	

Certain expressions can only use one term or the other:

Phrase	Pinyin	Meaning
不客气	bú kèqi	You're welcome (lit: Don't be polite)
不懂礼貌	bù dǒng lǐmào	doesn't have manners (lit: doesn't understand manners)
没礼貌	méi lǐmào	doesn't have manners

STRUCTURE NOTE 15.1
Use 麻烦 to make requests

As a noun, 麻烦 *(máfan) means "trouble," and as an adjective it is "troublesome" or "inconvenient." It can also be used as a verb when one wishes to make a request, in which case it is the same as the English "could I trouble you to . . ." As this is a polite form of request,* 麻烦 *is often used with the polite second person pronoun* 您.

> 麻烦 + 你/您 + Verb Phrase

From the Lesson Text:

服务员，麻烦您，请问洗手间在哪儿？
Fúwùyuán, máfan nín, qǐng wèn xǐshǒujiān zài nǎr?
Excuse me waiter, can you please tell me where the restroom is?

Other examples:

麻烦你把纸给我。
Máfan nǐ bǎ zhǐ gěi wǒ.
Please could you give the paper to me.

对不起，麻烦你了。
Duìbuqǐ, máfan nǐ le.
Sorry to have troubled you.

Practice: Change the sentences below into Chinese using the expression 麻烦.

Example: Could you please help me for a moment? → 麻烦你帮我一下，好吗？

1. Could please you read my résumé for me?

   _____

2. Could you please help me hang this lantern?

   _____

3. Could I trouble you to call him again?

   _____

4. Please help me clean up the living room.

   _____

5. Could you please carry those textbooks for me?

   _____

STRUCTURE NOTE 15.2
Use 来 before verbs to express commencing an activity

When it is placed before a verb phrase, 来 serves the purpose of emphasizing that someone will commence or engage in an activity presently.

Subject + 来 + Verb Phrase

From the Lesson Text:

让我来买单吧。
Ràng wǒ lái mǎidān ba.
Let me pay the bill.

Other examples:

请你来说一说你的建议。
Qǐng nǐ lái shuō yi shuō nǐ de jiànyì.
Please go ahead and share some of your thoughts on this.

现在我们来看一下这个问题。
Xiànzài wǒmen lái kàn yí xià zhèi gè wèntí.
Now we're going to take a look at this question.

Practice: Change the following into English.

Example: 让我来看一下。 → Let me take a look.

1.   你不喜欢吃饺子吗？ 那我来吃。

   _____

2.   让我们来看第十五课的练习。

   _____

3.   你去休息吧，厨房我来打扫。

   _____

4.   明天我们来放烟火吧。

   _____

5.   我们今天晚上去什么地方你来选吧。

   _____

STRUCTURE NOTE 15.3
Use 要不然 *to say "or else" or "otherwise"*

In Chinese, there are no special verb forms used to express counterfactual or hypothetical situations. Instead, context and certain key words indicate when a situation has not actually taken place. The conjunction 要不然 *(yàoburán) expresses the meaning "otherwise. . ." It is preceded by a condition and followed by what would result if this condition were not met.*

Condition + 要不然 + Sentence

From the Lesson Text:

那我下次请他们好了，要不然就是我不懂礼貌了。
Nà wǒ xià cì qǐng tāmen hǎo le, yàobùrán jiù shì wǒ bù dǒng lǐmào le.
Then, I'll treat them next time. Otherwise, I'll be perceived as being impolite.

Other examples:

你先把作业做好，要不然不可以去跳舞。
Nǐ xiān bǎ zuòyè zuò hǎo, yàoburán bù kěyǐ qù tiàowǔ.
Finish your homework first, otherwise you may not go dancing.

我应该学点中文，要不然去中国的时候会有很多问题。
Wǒ yīnggāi xué diǎn Zhōngwén, yàoburán qù Zhōngguó de shíhou huì yǒu hěn duō wèntí.
I should study some Chinese, otherwise I'll have a lot of problems when I go to China.

Practice: Complete the follow sentences using 要不然.

Example:　　我周末得复习，……
　　　　　　→ 我周末得复习，要不然考试一定考不好。

1.　明天是母亲节，你要给妈妈买花，……

　　_____

2.　春节快要到了，我们快去买火车票，……

　　_____

3.　你应该准备一份简历，……

　　_____

4.　你要对女朋友好，……

　　_____

5.　你要注意身体，……

　　_____

STRUCTURE NOTE 15.4

Use 正好 to express "as it happens"; "happen to . . ."

The adverb 正好 (zhènghǎo) expresses that the following event is a coincidence, similar to "as it happens." As in English, this pattern is generally used to describe a positive event.

Subject + 正好 + Verb Phrase

From the Lesson Text:

我今天正好拿到薪水，就给我个面子。
Wǒ jīntiān zhènghǎo ná dào xīnshuǐ, jiù gěi wǒ gè miànzi.
I received my paycheck today, so give face.

Other examples:

我想找玛丽借书，正好在街上看到她。
Wǒ xiǎng zhǎo Mǎlì jiè shū, zhènghǎo zài jiēshang kàn dào tā.
I wanted to go and find Mali to borrow a book, and I just happened to spot her on the street.

我今天没带我的笔记本，他正好带了很多纸，我去问他要几张。
Wǒ jīntiān méi dài wǒ de bǐjìběn, tā zhènghǎo dàile hěn duō zhǐ, wǒ qù wèn tā yào jǐ zhāng.
I didn't bring my notebook today. However, he happened to have brought a lot of paper, so I'll go ask for some.

Practice: Match the sentence beginnings below with the appropriate 正好 phrase to form complete expressions.

Example:　　你说你想学西班牙语，我正好认识一位西班牙语老师。

你说你想学西班牙语，	那边正好有个公园。
没想到今天有客人来，	我今天正好打扫客厅了。
她想去散散步，	我正好在那边实习。
我的手机没电了，	我正好带了一点糖果。
他去北京玩的时候，	他正好带了他的。
她的孩子开始哭了，	我正好认识一位西班牙语老师。

PRACTICE 15.1

Working with a partner, use the word box and the pictures below to enact dialogues containing the appropriate respectful language.

Example:

A: 让我请你吃饭吧。

B: 谢谢伯父。

A: 哪里哪里。我是长辈，应该照顾你。

伯父请她吃饭

谢谢　别客气　哪里哪里　长辈　晚辈　照顾　尊敬　礼貌

爷爷送他们去机场

孙小姐带他去看医生

小丽帮她们拿东西

奶奶帮她们做饭

PRACTICE 15.2

Use the following pattern to politely request something from your classmates. Record the requests you have made in the table below. Remember to respond politely by using the phrases you have learned.

Example:

A: 玛丽，麻烦你借一张纸给我。

B: 没问题。

A: 谢谢。

B: 不客气。

Name	Request
Example: 玛丽	麻烦你借一张纸给我

PRACTICE 15.3

Find two partners to script a roleplay based on the following scenario. You are invited by a Chinese friend to have dinner with his or her father. At the dinner, discuss the idea of 'face,' showing respect to older generations and who will pay the bill.

PRACTICE 15.4

Make an audio recording and send it to your teacher. In the recording, discuss what you have learned about being respectful to one's elders in Chinese culture.

PRACTICE 15.5

Type the following sentences on your computer.

1. 今天晚饭让我来买单吧！
2. 请你给我父母一点儿面子。
3. 服务员！麻烦您，我要买单。

	Radical	Stroke Order
单	`ˇ`(八) bā eight	丶 丷 丷 㐅 㘣 㘣 旦 单
客	宀 mián roof	丶 丷 宀 宀 夕 安 安 客 客
盒	人 rén person	丿 人 亼 亼 合 合 合 盒 盒 盒 盒
气	气 qì air	丿 气 气 气
父	父 fù father	丶 丷 父 父
母	毋 wú not	乚 母 母 母 母
麻	麻 má hemp	丶 亠 广 广 厈 庁 床 府 麻 麻
烦	火 huǒ fire	丶 丷 少 火 灯 灯 烦 烦 烦
辈	车 chē cart	丨 冂 刁 刁 非 非 非 非 韭 韭 韭 辈
尊	寸 cùn inch	丶 丷 丷 丷 酋 酋 酋 酋 酋 酋 尊 尊
敬	攵(攴) pū knock	一 十 艹 艹 芍 芍 苟 苟 苟 敬 敬 敬
照	灬(火) huǒ fire	丨 冂 日 日 昭 昭 昭 昭 昭 照 照 照 照
顾	页 yè page	一 厂 厂 厄 厄 顾 顾 顾 顾 顾
茶	艹(草) cǎo grass	一 十 艹 艹 艾 茶 茶 茶 茶
叶	口 kǒu mouth	丨 丨 口 口 叶 叶

王小美：大东，你记得下个周末要来我家过节吗？

陈大东：当然！

王小美：第一次来我家，要对我父母表示尊敬，
最好带一份礼物。

陈大东：我打算买一盒月饼送给你父母。

王小美：别开玩笑了，现在是春节，不是中秋节！

陈大东：我只是骗骗你！我昨天已经买了一盒茶叶了。

王小美：我爸爸最喜欢喝茶！他一定会喜欢你的礼物。

陈大东：太好了！我昨天还在担心你父母会不喜欢。

Read the dialogue and answer the following questions.
1. What does Wang Xiaomei advise Chen Dadong to do when he comes to her home?
2. What did Chen Dadong buy?

陈大东：伯父伯母，你们好！这是送你们的小礼物。

王妈妈：你太客气了！你还是学生，不要花钱给我
们买东西。

陈大东：第一次见面，一定要送礼物给你们。

王爸爸：大东，虽然你不是中国人，可是很懂中国的传
统。

陈大东：哪里哪里，都是小美教我的。

王妈妈：欢迎你以后常常来我们家玩。

陈大东：我有空会常常来看伯父伯母。

Read the dialogue and answer the following questions.
1. How do Wang Xiaomei's parents respond when Chen Dadong gives them a present?
2. How do Wang Xiaomei's parents praise Chen Dadong?

中国人喜欢请客吃饭。长辈常常请晚辈吃饭是因为他们觉得应该照顾晚辈，晚辈也想请客是因为他们觉得要尊敬长辈，所以在饭馆会常常看到中国人吵着谁应该请客。中国人觉得面子是很重要的，可是我想西方的请客习惯是比较简单的。

Read Huang Xiang'an's diary and answer the following questions.
1. What does Huang Xiang'an say that you might see Chinese people doing in a restaurant?
2. What does Huang Xiang'an think about the idea of 'face'?

Confucius and Confucianism

孔子 (Kǒngzǐ: "Confucius") is the most influential philosopher and teacher in the history of China. His ideas are based on ethical, respectful relationships between individuals and emphasize the importance of moral righteousness when interacting with family members and the outside community.

Confucius lived during the Spring and Autumn period (770 – 476 BC). During this time of instability, Confucianism arose as a philosophy which addressed issues of governance and correct social behavior. Confucius saw filial relationships within the family as a model for relationships between a ruler and his subjects, and preached that rulers who wished to unify the scattered Chinese states could only do so by practicing benevolence toward their people.

Confucian Ideals

Confucian ideals are a series of abstract ideas and noble characteristics that, according to Confucius, all people must work tirelessly to attain. One who exemplifies these traits is considered to be a 君子 (jūnzi: "ideal gentleman"). The ideal gentleman is said to follow the 道 (Dào: "the Way"), the ideal path of moral existence for man.

孝 (xiào: "filial piety") is one of the key concepts of Confucian philosophy. Confucius saw filial piety as the cornerstone of society. He expected people to treat their elders with respect, to care for them in their old age, and to acknowledge their teachings. This respect also extended to one's ancestors, who were still considered honored parts of the Chinese family even though they had passed on.

Even today, the Confucian emphasis on filial piety is extremely prevalent in Chinese culture. Grandparents and other elders are considered the most respected members of the family, and their children and grandchildren are expected to tend to their needs before their own.

Shaping Chinese Culture

Confucian philosophy has played a huge part in defining Chinese civilization, as well as the cultures of other East Asian nations. During the Han Dynasty (202 BC – 220 BC), Confucianism was adopted as the official national ideology. The Civil Service Examination, designed to appoint government officials based on merit, assessed proficiency in Confucian concepts from his writings and sayings. Testing candidates on these ideas did not necessarily evaluate their ability to contribute to governmental affairs; instead, the exam determined their moral character. Beyond the Civil Service Examination, Confucianism became the foundation of education and schooling in China, and the philosophy continues to exert a strong influence on Chinese culture today.

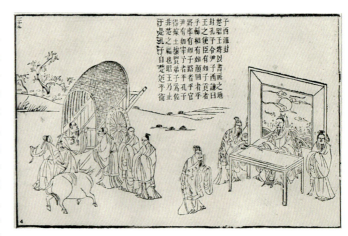

小美爸：	服务员，麻烦您，请问洗手间在哪儿？	Excuse me waiter, can you please tell me where the restroom is?
小美妈：	我也去。	I'll go too.
陈大东：	今天我请客，让我来买单吧。	Dinner is my treat today, let me pay the bill.
王小美：	今天晚饭是我父母请我们。	Tonight my parents are treating us to dinner.
陈大东：	这样可以吗？	Is that appropriate?
王小美：	不用担心。长辈请客也是对晚辈的照顾。	Don't worry. In Chinese culture, when the older generation treats their children to a meal, it is a way that the older generation takes care of the younger generation.

陈大东：	我今天正好拿到薪水，就给我个面子。	I received my paycheck today, so give face.
王小美：	下次吧。如果想要表示尊敬，你可以送一份礼物。	You can do it next time. If you want to show them proper respect, you can give them a gift.
陈大东：	哎呀！我没有准备，怎么办？	Oh! I didn't prepare anything, what should I do?
王小美：	没关系，我知道你还不太了解中国传统。这次我先帮你准备了一盒茶叶，你可以送给他们。	It's alright. I know you are still unfamiliar with Chinese traditions. So, I prepared a box of tea for you this time that you can give to them.
陈大东：	小美，你太好了！	Xiaomei, you're the best!
陈大东：	那我下次请他们好了，要不然就是我不懂礼貌了。	Then, I'll treat them next time. Otherwise, I'll be perceived as being impolite.
陈大东：	谢谢伯父伯母。	Thank you Mr. and Mrs. Wang.
小美爸：	哪里哪里。	Don't mention it.

陈大东： 这是一份小礼物，希望下次有机会可以请伯父伯母吃饭。

小美妈： 别客气！你们还是大学生，我们是长辈，应该照顾你们。

Here's a small token of my appreciation. I hope next time I get to treat you both to dinner.

You're welcome! You are still college students, and we are your elders. We should take care of you.

What Can You Do?

INTERPRETIVE
- I can respond using the proper social etiquette in various social situations.
- I can respond to a situation to allow someone to save face.

INTERPERSONAL
- I can interact with elders whilst showing them the proper respect.
- I can have a discussion to decide who will pay the bill at a restaurant.

PRESENTATIONAL
- I can give a presentation on aspects of manners and etiquette in Chinese culture.
- I can give a presentation on the meaning and significance of "face" in Chinese culture.

UNIT 15
礼
LESSON 2

了解中国文化
Understanding Chinese Culture

中平，快来看看这些书，我 **刚刚**（gāng gāng）在中文书店买的。
（kuài）

武术（wǔ shù）、**京剧**（jīng jù）、**书法**（shū fǎ）……怎么都是中国传统**文化**（wén huà）的东西？

我暑假要去中国实习，所以想先了解一下中国的**文化**（wén huà）。

什么？那些都太**古老**（gǔ lǎo）了，**现代**（xiàn dài）的中国很不一样吧。

虽然中国已经现代化了，可是传统文化还很重要。
比方说，孔子的思想还是很被重视的。

中国人的礼节很复杂，如果你做得不对，很容易发生误会。

没错，比如，一个人把东西交给你，你该怎么样？

我要用双手接受。用一只手接是不礼貌的。

这样我就放心了，你已经学了很多了。
你会在中国交到很多新朋友的！

有了新朋友，不要忘记老朋友喔！

LESSON TEXT 15.2

Understanding Chinese Culture 了解中国文化

Sun Mali has bought some books on Chinese culture and asks Li Zhongping to take a look with her. They discuss the influence of traditional culture on modern China and Sun Mali gives Li Zhongping some pointers.

孙玛丽：	中平，快来看看这些书，我刚刚在中文书店买的。	Zhōngpíng, kuài lái kànkan zhèi xiē shū, wǒ gānggāng zài Zhōngwén shūdiàn mǎi de.
李中平：	武术、京剧、书法……怎么都是中国传统文化的东西？	Wǔshù, Jīngjù, shūfǎ……zěnme dōu shì Zhōngguó chuántǒng wénhuà de dōngxi?
孙玛丽：	我暑假要去中国实习，所以想先了解一下中国的文化。	Wǒ shǔjià yào qù Zhōngguó shíxí, suǒyǐ xiǎng xiān liǎojiě yí xià Zhōngguó de wénhuà.
李中平：	什么？那些都太古老了，现代的中国很不一样吧。	Shénme? Nà xiē dōu tài gǔlǎo le, xiàndài de Zhōngguó hěn bù yíyàng ba.
孙玛丽：	虽然中国已经现代化了，可是传统文化还很重要。比方说，孔子的思想还是很被重视的。	Suīrán Zhōngguó yǐjīng xiàndài huà le, kěshì chuántǒng wénhuà hái hěn zhòngyào. Bǐfāngshuō, Kǒngzǐ de sīxiǎng hái shì hěn bèi zhòngshì de.

孙玛丽：	中国人的礼节很复杂，如果你做得不对，很容易发生误会。	Zhōngguó rén de lǐjié hěn fùzá, rúguǒ nǐ zuò de bu duì, hěn róngyì fāshēng wùhuì.
黄祥安：	没错，比如，一个人把东西交给你，你该怎么样？	Méi cuò, bǐrú, yí gè rén bǎ dōngxi jiāogěi nǐ, nǐ gāi zěnmeyàng?
孙玛丽：	我要用双手接受。用一只手接是不礼貌的。	Wǒ yào yòng shuāngshǒu jiēshòu. Yòng yì zhī shǒu jiē shì bù lǐmào de.
黄祥安：	这样我就放心了，你已经学了很多了。你会在中国交到很多新朋友的！	Zhèiyàng wǒ jiù fàngxīn le, nǐ yǐjīng xué le hěn duō le. Nǐ huì zài Zhōngguó jiāo dào hěn duō xīn péngyou de!
李中平：	有了新朋友，不要忘记老朋友喔！	Yǒu le xīn péngyou, bú yào wàngjì lǎo péngyou ō!

LESSON VOCABULARY 15.2

	SIMPLIFIED	TRADITIONAL	PINYIN	WORD CATEGORY	DEFINITION
1.	快		kuài	*adv*	soon; quickly
2.	刚刚	剛剛	gānggāng	*adv*	just
3.	武术	武術	wǔshù	*n*	martial arts
4.	京剧	京劇	Jīngjù	*n*	Peking opera
5.	书法	書法	shūfǎ	*n*	calligraphy
6.	文化		wénhuà	*n*	culture
7.	古老		gǔlǎo	*adj*	ancient; old-fashioned
8.	现代	現代	xiàndài	*adj, n*	modern; modern times
9.	现代化	現代化	xiàndàihuà	*adj, v, n*	modernized; modernize; modernization
10.	孔子		Kǒngzǐ	*name*	Confucius
11.	思想		sīxiǎng	*n*	thought, idea
12.	重视	重視	zhòngshì	*v*	think highly of; attach importance to
13.	礼节	禮節	lǐjié	*n*	etiquette; courtesy
14.	复杂	複雜	fùzá	*adj*	complex, complicated
15.	误会	誤會	wùhuì	*v*	to misunderstand
16.	没错	沒錯	méi cuò	*adj*	not wrong; (that's) right
17.	比如		bǐrú	*cj*	for instance
18.	交给	交給	jiāogěi	*v*	to hand or give to
19.	双手	雙手	shuāngshǒu	*n*	both hands
20.	接受		jiēshòu	*v*	to accept
21.	放心		fàngxīn	*v*	to put one's mind at ease
22.	交朋友		jiāo péngyou	*vo*	to make friends

REQUIRED VOCABULARY 15.2

	SIMPLIFIED	TRADITIONAL	PINYIN	WORD CATEGORY	DEFINITION
NOUNS					
23.	想法		xiǎngfǎ	*n*	idea; opinion; way of thinking
24.	太极拳	太極拳	Tàijíquán	*n*	Tai Chi

OPTIONAL VOCABULARY 15.2

RELATED TO CLASSICAL CULTURE

	SIMPLIFIED	TRADITIONAL	PINYIN	WORD CATEGORY	DEFINITION
25.	哲学家	哲學家	zhéxuéjiā	*n*	philosopher
26.	孟子		Mèngzǐ	*name*	Mencius
27.	庄子	莊子	Zhuāngzǐ	*name*	Zhuangzi
OTHER					
28.	办法	辦法	bànfǎ	*n*	method; means
29.	看法		kànfǎ	*n*	opinion; perspective
30.	古代		gǔdài	*adj, n*	ancient; ancient times

Classical and Modern Chinese

Until the early twentieth century, the majority of written Chinese was composed in 文言文 (wényánwén: "Classical Chinese"). In one form or another, 文言文 had existed since as early as the Spring and Autumn Period (771 – 403 BC). 文言文 was notably different from the spoken vernacular, but the latter was not considered appropriate for refined writing and so it remained largely a means of verbal communication. Momentous changes in China during the 1920s swept away the ancient language and replaced it with 白话 (báihuà: literally, "plain speech"). This was done so that written Chinese resembled the everyday spoken variety, unifying the language into the form we know today.

Although the structures and vocabulary of 文言文 are by and large completely different from present day Mandarin, the historical continuity of Chinese characters still allows the student of the modern language to understand some classical texts. Here, for example, is the poem 静夜思 (Jìng Yè Sī: "Thoughts On a Quiet Night") by the famous Tang Dynasty (618 – 907) poet 李白 (Lǐ Bái):

Poem	Pinyin	Meaning
床前明月光，	Chuáng qián míng yuè guāng	The moon shines bright before my bed,
疑是地上霜。	Yí shì dì shàng shuāng	I wonder if it is frost on the ground.
举头望明月，	Jǔ tóu wàng míng yuè	Lifting my head, I look at the bright moon,
低头思故乡。	Dī tóu sī gù xiāng	Lowering it, I think of my home.

It is important to note that Classical Chinese still exerts a significant influence on the modern language, particularly in formal written Chinese. There is a predilection for 'balanced' sentences or phrases consisting of four characters, as was often the classical style, as well as the many 成语 (chéngyǔ: "idioms") derived from classical stories. In addition, certain particles of Classical Chinese grammar still find their way into modern written Chinese. When writing formally, one may replace 的 with 之 (zhī), its classical equivalent. Similarly, formal notices may substitute 的人 with 者 (zhě), for example 年长者 (年长的人: "elderly people").

语法

STRUCTURE NOTE 15.5
Use 刚 *or* 刚刚 *to express "just now"*
刚 *(gāng) and* 刚刚 *(gānggāng) can both express the meaning "just now" or "only just." The single-character version* 刚 *is slightly more formal than* 刚刚.

Subject + 刚(刚) + Verb Phrase

From the Lesson Text:

我刚刚在中文书店买的。
Wǒ gānggāng zài Zhōngwén shūdiàn mǎi de.
I just bought them at a Chinese bookstore.

Other examples:

你是刚来的吗？
Nǐ shì gāng lái de ma?
Did you just get here?

我刚看到你的女儿。
Wǒ gāng kàn dào nǐ de nǚér.
I just saw your daughter.

Practice: Change the following sentences into Chinese using 刚 or 刚刚.

Example:　　I just finished my homework.　→　我刚把作业做完了。

1.　I'm sorry, the manager just left.

　　_____

2.　He only just broke up with his girlfriend, no wonder he's so sad.

　　_____

3.　Dad just finished putting up the lanterns.

　　_____

4.　They've just returned from China.

　　_____

5.　It's no problem; the match only just started.

　　_____

STRUCTURE NOTE 15.6

Use nouns with 化 to form "-ize" verbs or "-ized" adjectives

化 (huà), *when added onto certain adjectives and nouns, is equivalent to the English suffixes "-ize" and "-ized," as in "modernize." Depending on the context, a noun or an adjective with the* 化 *suffix in Chinese will become a verb or an adjective when translated into English.*

> Adjective/Noun + 化

From the Lesson Text:

虽然中国已经现代化了，可是传统文化还很重要。
Suīrán Zhōngguó yǐjīng xiàndàihuà le, kěshì chuántǒng wénhuà hái hěn zhòngyào.
Even though China has become modernized, old traditions and customs are still important.

Other examples:

北京人说话常常带儿化音。
Běijīng rén shuō huà chángcháng dài érhuà yīn.
People from Beijing often rhotacize their words.
("rhotacize": to add an "-r" sound to the end of a word)

住在西方这么多年了，他们当然西化了。
Zhù zài Xīfāng zhème duō nián le, tāmen dāngrán Xīhuà le.
They've lived in the West all these years. Of course they've become westernized.

Practice: Select the appropriates phrases from the word bank below to complete each sentence.

> 儿化音，中国化，现代化，加州化，西化，美国化

Example: 这本书跟中国<u>现代化</u>的问题有关。

1. 每天打太极拳、用筷子吃饭，看起来你已经 _____ 了！

2. 他说的 _____ 是什么意思呢？

3. 长辈重视传统文化，可是被 _____ 的年轻人没有这个想法。

4. 北京人说话带 _____ 我有的时候听不懂。

5. 他看了那么多美国电影以后，朋友都说他 _____ 了。

STRUCTURE NOTE 15.7
Use 比如(说) to say "for instance" and give examples

In Structure Note 14.7, the phrase 比方说 *was introduced as a way to present examples.* 比如(说) *(bǐrú [shuō]) is a another way to do this, but it carries a slightly more formal tone.*

比如(说), + Example Sentence

From the Lesson Text:

比如，一个人把东西交给你，你该怎么样？

Bǐrú, yí ge rén bǎ dōngxi jiāogěi nǐ, nǐ gāi zěnmeyàng?

For example, if someone hands you something, what should you do?

Other examples:

我很喜欢中国电影，比如说，《一个都不能少》。

Wǒ hěn xǐhuan Zhōngguó diànyǐng, bǐrú shuō, *Yí Ge Dōu Bù Néng Shǎo.*

I really like Chinese movies, for example, *Not One Less.*

他交了很多朋友。比如，小美、玛丽和中平。

Tā jiāo le hěn duō péngyou. Bǐrú, Xiǎoměi, Mǎlì, and Zhōngpíng.

He made a lot of friends. For example, Xiaomei, Mali, and Zhongping.

Practice: Complete the following statements using 比如(说) and one or more examples.

Example: 她会说很多语言，……
→ 她会说很多语言，比如英语、法语，跟中文。

1. 中国有很多节日，……

_____

2. 他在家里常常帮妈妈的忙，……

_____

3. 我爸爸对中国传统文化有兴趣，……

_____

4. 中国的春节跟西方的新年不太一样，……

_____

5. 我妈妈做过很多工作，……

_____

STRUCTURE NOTE 15.8
Use double-了 to describe an action continuing up to the present

It has been shown that the particle 了 is sometimes placed after the verb and sometimes at the end of a sentence. When the verb-suffix 了 and the sentence-final 了 are both used in the same sentence, it indicates that an action is continuing up to the present. For example, 我学了三年的中文 *means that the speaker studied Chinese for three years at some point in the past but is not studying it anymore. However,* 我学了三年的中文了 *means the speaker has studied for three years now and is still studying. The first* 了 *in this pattern is followed by a quantity (see Structure Note 6.11) or a duration (see Structure Note 10.11).*

Subject + Verb + 了 + Quantity (+ Object) + 了

Subject + Verb + Object + Verb + 了 + Duration + 了

Subject + Verb + 了 + Duration + 的 + Object + 了

From the Lesson Text:
你已经学了很多了。
Nǐ yǐjīng xuéle hěn duō le.
You've already learned a lot.

Other examples:
我们学中文学了一年半了。
Wǒmen xué Zhōngwén xuéle yì nián bàn le.
We have been studying Chinese for a year and a half.

这儿已经下了三天的雨了。
Zhèr yǐjīng xiàle sān tiān de yǔ le.
It has been raining for three days here.

Practice: Use double-了 to change the meaning of these sentences so that they indicate an action continuing up to the present.

Example: 我学了六个月的西班牙语。
→ 我学了六个月的西班牙语了。

1. 弟弟吃了十五个饺子！他真能吃。
   _____

2. 元宵节的花灯你已经挂了很多，休息一下吧！
   _____

3. 她学了四年的钢琴，现在弹得很不错。
   _____

4. 今天下了一个早上的雪，你快来看！
   _____

5. 老板讲了两个小时，大家好像快要睡着了。
   _____

PRACTICE 15.10

Working with a partner, enact a dialogue based on the information below. Following the structure in the example, person A should list a number of items associated with the picture and form a question about them, and person B should offer a corresponding explanation.

Example:

A: 武术、京剧、书法……怎么都是中国传统文化的书？

B: 因为我想了解中国传统文化。书店里卖关于中国传统文化的书还有很多，比如说太极拳、中国节日，还有孔子思想。

我在图书馆借了很多出国旅游的书。

我在饭馆点了很多中国菜。

我在商店买了很多红色的东西。

我在中国参加了很多庆祝节日的传统活动。

PRACTICE 15.11

Take a survey of the class to find out which aspect of traditional Chinese culture your classmates would most like to learn. Write the most popular response below.

Aspect of Traditional Culture	Number of Students

PRACTICE 15.12

Make an audio recording and send it to your teacher. In the recording, talk about some of the ways in which the influence of traditional Chinese culture can still be seen in China today.

PRACTICE 15.13

Type the following sentences on your computer.

1. 我在图书馆借了一本介绍中国京剧的书。
2. 虽然中国已经现代化了，可是传统文化还很重要。
3. 中国人很重视孔子的想法。
4. 中国人的礼节很复杂，你要多学习！
5. 如果做得不对，很容易发生误会。

PRACTICE 15.14

Help Chen Dadong to reply to his dad's postcard from Beijing. Respond to his dad's inquiry about Chinese customs.

大东：

　　我到北京了，这里天气很热。我打算工作完以后，去长城看看再回加拿大。

　　我很喜欢这里，大家都对我很好，可是我不太了解这里的文化。昨天我去了一位中国朋友的家，他送了我一份礼物。我很高兴，想马上看看里面是什么，可是他叫我回家再看。我不明白，为什么我不可以马上看看他送我什么礼物呢？

爸爸

✏ **PRACTICE 15.15**

	Radical	Stroke Order
放	攵(攴) pū knock	丶 亠 方 方 扩 扩 放
刚	刂(刀) dāo knife	丨 刀 冈 冈 刚 刚
武	止 zhǐ stop	一 二 于 于 武 正 武 武
术	木 mù wood	一 十 才 木 术
剧	刂(刀) dāo knife	乛 コ 尸 尸 尸 尸 居 居 剧 剧
化	亻(人) rén person	丿 亻 化 化
拳	手 shǒu hand	丶 丷 丷 半 关 关 差 差 拳
古	口 kǒu mouth	一 十 古 古 古
代	亻(人) rén person	丿 亻 仁 代 代
复	夊 suī go slowly	丿 亻 亻 亇 旬 旬 复 复 复
杂	朩(木) mù wood	丿 九 杂 杂 杂 杂
误	讠(言) yán speech	丶 讠 讠 讠 讠 误 误 误
双	又 yòu again	乛 又 双 双
接	扌(手) shǒu hand	一 十 扌 扩 扩 扩 护 拉 接 接 接
受	又 yòu again	一 爫 爫 爫 严 严 受 受

PRACTICE 15.16

王小美：玛丽，这是我送你的生日礼物。

孙玛丽：哦！是跟中国书法有关的书，谢谢你！

王小美：我刚刚在中文书店买的，希望你喜欢。

孙玛丽：我非常喜欢，最近我正好想学习写书法。

王小美：真的吗？我也对书法很有兴趣。

孙玛丽：你可以教我吗？

王小美：那我先带你去书店买写书法的文具。

孙玛丽：怎么才能把书法学好呢？

王小美：你得多多练习，每天练习一个小时，你很快就会有进步了。

孙玛丽：那我明天就开始练习！

Read the dialogue and answer the following questions.
1. What did Wang Xiaomei buy for Sun Mali at the bookshop?
2. What else do they plan to buy?

PRACTICE 15.17

Sender	玛丽
Subject	中国文化

爸爸：

我暑假要去中国实习，想先了解一下中国的文化。我特别喜欢中国的传统文化，可是不知道应该从哪里开始学习。还有，我朋友说中国的礼节很复杂，如果做得不对，很容易发生误会。所以请你教教我应该特别注意中国人的哪些礼节。

Sender	爸爸
Subject	re:中国文化

玛丽：

你可以到图书馆去借一些中国文化的书来看。你也可以在中文书店买一些跟中国传统文化有关的书，比如说京剧、武术、中国画，还有中国菜。中国的礼节需要注意的地方很多，比方说，别人送礼物给你，你不能用一只手接受，要用双手接受才有礼貌。

Read the e-mails and answer the following questions.
1. Why does Sun Mali want to know about traditional Chinese culture?
2. What kind of books does her dad suggest that she should buy?

孔子是中国历史上一位很有名的老师。孔子很受大家尊重，有些地方在孔子的生日那天会有敬师的活动。学校也会有很多文化活动，让学生学习孔子思想。虽然中国已经现代化，但孔子的思想还是很受重视。

Read the passage and answer the following questions.
1. What do some places do to mark Confucius' birthday?
2. What do some schools do to mark the occasion?

Daoism

道教 (Dàojiào: "Daoism") is a philosophy with ancient origins that is commonly associated with the philosopher 老子 (Lǎozǐ) and his text 道德经 (Dàodéjīng: "The Daodejing"). As Daoism became more popular over time, more organized rituals and practices emerged, and the philosophy eventually evolved into a religious faith.

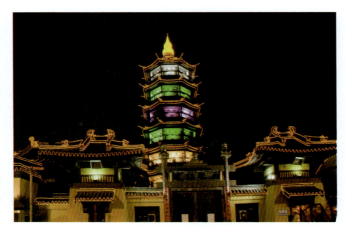

Daoism espouses belief in the 道 (Dào: "the Way"), which represents the basis of all living things and dictates the flow of the universe. Daoist ideas encourage one to embrace the simplicity of life and acknowledge the nature of reality.

Among the central themes associated with Daoism are balance and interdependence. This idea is represented by the well-known Daoist symbol, the 阴阳 (yīnyáng: "yin and yang"). Yin, the black portion of the symbol, represents passivity, softness and femininity, while yang, the white portion of the symbol, represents solidity, aggression, and masculinity. However, each side still contains a portion of the other, representing the interaction of opposites and the balance of complementary forces that brings order to nature.

One of Laozi's most famous disciples, 庄子 (Zhuāngzǐ), is also credited with developing many Daoist ideas. Zhuangzi emphasized the importance of recognizing relativity in all situations. Famously, he once dreamt that he was a carefree butterfly, roaming the skies. Once he awoke, he proclaimed, "I do not know whether I was then a man dreaming I was a butterfly, or whether I am now a butterfly dreaming I am a man."

Enduring Influence

Despite the great prominence of Confucian philosophy and Daoist beliefs in Chinese culture, the schools of thought have undergone a number of challenges throughout Chinese history. During the Qin dynasty (221 – 207 BC), the emperor 秦始皇 (Qín Shǐhuáng) governed by one philosophy, Legalism, and sought to eliminate all other schools of thought. He ordered that all non-Legalist texts be burned and is rumored to have ordered hundreds of Confucian scholars to be buried alive.

In more recent years, too, traditional philosophies have had to endure tough times. During the Cultural Revolution (1966 – 1976), mass movements were undertaken to rid China of old influences, with Confucianism and Daosim being identified as targets for criticism. Despite these setbacks, however, Confucian and Daoist influences are still found in Chinese society, a fact that stands as a testament to how deeply ingrained they are in the fabric of Chinese civilization.

孙玛丽： 中平，快来看看这些书，我刚刚在中文书店买的。

Zhongping, come take a look at these books. I just bought them at the Chinese bookstore.

李中平： 武术、京剧、书法……怎么都是中国传统文化的东西？

Martial arts, Peking opera, calligraphy…… how come they're all about traditional Chinese culture?

孙玛丽： 我暑假要去中国实习，所以想先了解一下中国的文化。

I am going to China for a summer internship, so I thought I should first learn more about Chinese culture.

李中平： 什么？那些都太古老了，现代的中国很不一样吧。

What? Those things are all so old-fashioned, China nowadays is probably very different.

孙玛丽： 虽然中国已经现代化了，可是传统文化还很重要。比方说，孔子的思想还是很被重视的。

Even though China has become modernized, old traditions and customs are still important. For example, Confucius' ideas are still very much respected.

孙玛丽： 中国人的礼节很复杂，如果你做得不对，很容易发生误会。

Chinese customs are very complicated. If you commit a cultural faux pas, it's very easy for misunderstandings to occur.

黄祥安： 没错，比如，一个人把东西交给你，你该怎么样？

That's right. For example, if someone hands you something, what should you do?

孙玛丽： 我要用双手接受。用一只手接是不礼貌的。

I should receive it with both hands. If you use only one hand, it is impolite.

黄祥安： 这样我就放心了，你已经学了很多了。你会在中国交到很多新朋友的！

You have set my mind at ease; you've already learned a lot. You'll make lots of new friends in China!

李中平： 有了新朋友，不要忘记老朋友喔！

Once you've made new friends, don't forget about your old ones!

What Can You Do?

Interpretive
- I can understand some of the significant features of traditional Chinese culture.

Interpersonal
- I can hold a discussion with someone on aspects of traditional and modern Chinese culture, and support my statements by giving examples.

Presentational
- I can give a presentation about the main aspects of traditional Chinese culture.
- I can compare some features of traditional and modern culture in China.

ACT IT OUT

Working in groups, compose an original three-minute skit that utilizes the vocabulary and structures introduced in Unit 15. Each of you should assume a role and have a roughly equal number of lines in the skit. Be prepared to perform your skit in class. You can either come up with your own story or choose from one of the following situations:

A) You and a group of friends discuss where you were all born and your families' history.

B) Your friend will be studying abroad next semester. You discuss how your local customs differ from those of his or her destination.

C) You will be staying with a host family in Beijing for a week. You ask your friend from China for tips regarding Chinese etiquette.

CHECK WHAT YOU CAN DO

RECOGNIZE

Adjectives
- □ 客气
- □ 古老
- □ 现代
- □ 现代化
- □ 复杂
- □ 没错

Adverbs
- □ 快
- □ 正好
- □ 刚刚

Conjunctions
- □ 要不然
- □ 比如

Idiomatic Expression
- □ 就是说

Measure Word
- □ 盒

Name
- □ 孔子

Nouns
- □ 洗手间
- □ 父母
- □ 长辈
- □ 晚辈
- □ 薪水
- □ 面子
- □ 茶叶

- □ 礼貌
- □ 大人
- □ 老人
- □ 武术
- □ 京剧
- □ 书法
- □ 文化
- □ 思想
- □ 礼节
- □ 双手
- □ 想法
- □ 太极拳

Verbs
- □ 麻烦
- □ 买单
- □ 照顾
- □ 尊敬
- □ 表示
- □ 了解
- □ 重视
- □ 误会
- □ 交给
- □ 接受
- □ 放心
- □ 交朋友

WRITE

- □ 单
- □ 客
- □ 盒
- □ 气
- □ 父
- □ 母
- □ 麻烦
- □ 辈
- □ 尊
- □ 敬
- □ 照
- □ 顾
- □ 茶
- □ 叶

- □ 放
- □ 刚
- □ 武
- □ 术
- □ 剧
- □ 化
- □ 券
- □ 古
- □ 代
- □ 复
- □ 杂
- □ 误
- □ 双
- □ 接
- □ 受

USE

- □ 麻烦 to make requests.
- □ 来 before verbs to express commencing an activity.
- □ 要不然 to say "or else" or "otherwise."
- □ 正好 to express "as it happens"; "happen to . . ."

- □ 刚 or 刚刚 to express "just now."
- □ Nouns with 化 to form "-ize" verbs or "-ized" adjectives.
- □ 比如(说) to say "for instance" and give examples.
- □ Double-了 to describe an action continuing up to the present.

Technology & Modern China

Communication Goals

Lesson 1: 线上聊天 **Chatting Online**
- Use expressions related to computers and the Internet.
- Discuss city lifestyles.
- Understand and use the "besides" construction.

Lesson 2: 一路平安！ **Have a Safe Trip!**
- Express that you will miss someone.
- Use terms for posting letters and packages as well as sending e-mails.
- Wish someone a safe trip.

线上聊天
Chatting Online

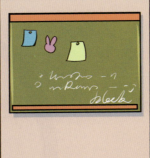

小美，我在北京找到一份暑假实习的工作了！

恭喜你啊！
chú le
除了了解中国的
qíng kuàng yǐ wài
工作情况以外，你
cān guān
还可以参观北京
yǒu míng jǐng diǎn
有名的景点。

北京那么大，人那么多，我
pà
怕我会不习惯
shēng huó
那儿的生活。

biǎo gē
别担心，我的表哥
住在北京。

来，我们看看他
zài xiàn
在不在线上。

嗨，
biǎo gē
表哥，这是
我的好朋友
孙玛丽，

她今年暑假要去北京，你一定要照顾她喔！

没问题！

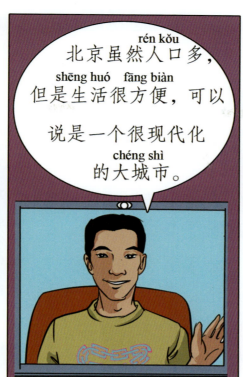

北京虽然人口多（rén kǒu），但是生活（shēng huó）很方便（fāng biàn），可以说是一个很现代化的大城市（chéng shì）。

有什么好玩儿的活动？

什么都有！可以逛胡同（guàng hú tong）、吃很多不同（bù tóng）的食物、去博物馆（bó wù guǎn），还可以去逛街（guàng jiē）、看电影。

听起来真不错。在北京怎么上网（shàng wǎng）呢？

你可以带自己（zì jǐ）的笔记本电脑（bǐ jì běn diàn nǎo）来，买无线上网卡（wú xiàn shàng wǎng kǎ），或者去网吧（wǎng bā）。

好，等（děng）我到北京以后，再麻烦你！

LESSON TEXT 16.1

Chatting Online 线上聊天

Sun Mali tells Wang Xiaomei that she will be going to Beijing for an internship but that she is worried about her inability to adjust to life in a new place. Wang Xiaomei suggests they talk to her cousin, who lives there.

孙玛丽：	小美，我在北京找到一份暑假实习的工作了！	Xiǎoměi, wǒ zài Běijīng zhǎo dào yí fèn shǔjià shíxí de gōngzuò!
王小美：	恭喜你啊！除了了解中国的工作情况以外，你还可以参观北京有名的景点。	Gōngxǐ nǐ a! Chúle liǎojiě Zhōngguó de gōngzuò qíngkuàng yǐwài, nǐ hái kěyǐ cānguān Běijīng yǒumíng de jǐngdiǎn.
孙玛丽：	北京那么大，人那么多，我怕我会不习惯那儿的生活。	Běijīng nàme dà, rén nàme duō, wǒ pà wǒ huì bù xíguàn nàr de shēnghuó.
王小美：	别担心，我的表哥住在北京。来，我们看看他在不在线上。	Bié dānxīn, wǒ de biǎogē zhù zài Běijīng. Lái, wǒmen kànkan tā zài bu zài xiàn shàng.

王小美：	嗨，表哥，这是我的好朋友孙玛丽，她今年暑假要去北京，你一定要照顾她喔！	Hēi, biǎogē, zhèi shì wǒ de hǎo péngyou Sūn Mǎlì, tā jīnnián shǔjià yào qù Běijīng, nǐ yídìng yào zhàogù tā ō!
小美的表哥：	没问题！北京虽然人口多，但是生活很方便，可以说是一个很现代化的大城市。	Méi wèntí! Běijīng suīrán rénkǒu duō, dànshì shēnghuó hěn fāngbiàn, kěyǐ shuō shì yí gè hěn xiàndài huà de dà chéngshì.
孙玛丽：	有什么好玩儿的活动？	Yǒu shénme hǎo wánr de huódòng?
小美的表哥：	什么都有！可以逛胡同、吃很多不同的食物、去博物馆，还可以去逛街、看电影。	Shénme dōu yǒu! Kěyǐ guàng hútong, chī hěn duō bù tóng de shíwù, qù bówùguǎn, hái kěyǐ qù guàng jiē, kàn diànyǐng.

孙玛丽：	听起来真不错。在北京怎么上网呢？	Tīngqilai zhēn bú cuò. Zài Běijīng zěnme shàngwǎng ne?
小美的表哥：	你可以带自己的笔记本电脑来，买无线上网卡，或者去网吧。	Nǐ kěyǐ dài zìjǐ de bǐjìběn diànnǎo lái, mǎi wúxiàn shàngwǎng kǎ, huòzhě qù wǎngbā.
孙玛丽：	好，等我到北京以后，再麻烦你！	Hǎo, děng wǒ dào Běijīng yǐhòu, zài máfan nǐ!

LESSON VOCABULARY 16.1

	SIMPLIFIED	TRADITIONAL	PINYIN	WORD CATEGORY	DEFINITION
1.	除了		chúle	cj	in addition to; apart from; besides
2.	情况	情況	qíngkuàng	n	situation
3.	以外		yǐwài	cj	other than; except
4.	参观	參觀	cānguān	v	to tour; to visit
5.	有名		yǒumíng	adj	famous
6.	景点	景點	jǐngdiǎn	n	scenic spot
7.	怕		pà	v	to fear, to be afraid of
8.	生活		shēnghuó	n	life; lifestyle
9.	表哥		biǎogē	n	older male cousin
10.	在线	在綫	zài xiàn	vo, adj	to be online; online
11.	人口		rénkǒu	n	population
12.	方便		fāngbiàn	adj	convenient
13.	城市		chéngshì	n	city
14.	逛		guàng	v	to stroll
15.	胡同		hútong	n	*hutong* (old-fashioned alleys in Beijing); lane, alley
16.	不同		bù tóng	adj	different
17.	博物馆	博物館	bówùguǎn	n	museum

	SIMPLIFIED	TRADITIONAL	PINYIN	WORD CATEGORY	DEFINITION
18.	逛街		guàng jiē	vo	to go shopping
19.	上网	上網	shàngwǎng	vo	to go online
20.	自己		zìjǐ	pr	oneself
21.	笔记本电脑	筆記本電腦	bǐjìběn diànnǎo	n	laptop computer
	笔记本	筆記本	bǐjìběn	n	laptop computer
22.	无线上网卡	無綫上網卡	wúxiàn shàngwǎng kǎ	n	wireless Internet card
23.	网吧	網吧	wǎngbā	n	Internet café
24.	等		děng	cj	wait until; when

REQUIRED VOCABULARY 16.1

ACTIVITIES

25.	舞会	舞會	wǔhuì	n	dance party

OPTIONAL VOCABULARY 16.1

RELATED TO THE INTERNET

26.	网站	網站	wǎngzhàn	n	website
27.	网页	網頁	wǎngyè	n	webpage
28.	博客		bókè	n	blog

RELATED TO CELLPHONES

29.	发短信	發短信	fā duǎnxìn	vo	to send a text message

ACTIVITIES AND SIGHTS IN BEIJING

30.	卡拉OK		kǎlā OK	n	karaoke
31.	天安门	天安門	Tiān'ānmén	n	Tian'anmen (Gate of Heavenly Peace)

Terms for "Online"

This lesson covers the term 在线 (zài xiàn: "to be online; online"). There are, in fact, a number of words that convey this meaning. Both 线上 (xiàn shàng) and 网上 (wǎng shàng) can also be used to mean "online." Some common phrases involving these different terms are listed opposite. Remember also that, just as in English, there are separate terms for "to be online" (在线) and "to go online" (上网).

Terms	Pinyin	Meaning
在线音乐	zàixiàn yīnyuè	online music (streaming)
在线辞典	zàixiàn cídiǎn	online dictionary
线上游戏	xiànshàng yóuxì	online games
网上购物	wǎngshàng gòu wù	online shopping
网上银行	wǎngshàng yínháng	online banking

Review of Measure Words

This book has introduced a number of measure words that apply to different nouns. Presented below is a review of these measure words and some examples of what they can be paired with. It is worth remembering that other nouns in this book are partnered with measure words that may not be listed here.

Measure Word	Pinyin	Usage	Noun Examples
个	gè	most nouns	礼物，手机，人，地方
只	zhī	birds and some mammals	鸡，猫，狗，鸟
口	kǒu	people	人
条	tiáo	long, thin objects	项链，鱼，裤子
杯	bēi	cups of liquid	茶，咖啡，汽水，果汁
盘	pán	plates of food	青菜，饺子
份	fèn	portions of food; share	麻婆豆腐，米饭；工作
碗	wǎn	bowls of food or liquid	米饭，酸辣汤，茶
家	jiā	businesses	饭馆，公司，商店
瓶	píng	bottles of liquid	水，汽水，饮料
本	běn	books	书
张	zhāng	flat objects	书桌，床，卡，票，照片
间	jiān	rooms	卧室，厨房，客厅
块	kuài	money; a piece of something	钱，肉，鱼，蛋糕
门	mén	courses	课
件	jiàn	items; articles of clothing	事，毛衣，衬衫，外套
双	shuāng	pairs	鞋子，袜子，眼睛，手
顶	dǐng	hats	帽子
部	bù	films	电影
盒	hé	boxes of something	茶叶，糖果

Some measure words may also act as nouns in themselves. The words for "cup," "bottle," and "box" are the same as the measure words, with the addition of 子 (杯子，瓶子，盒子). Sometimes, a measure word and a noun may be reversed to form a new noun which carries a plural or generic connotation. For example, 一口人 (a person) becomes 人口 (population), and 一本书 (a book) becomes 书本 (books).

STRUCTURE NOTE 16.1

Use 除了……以外 *to say "besides"*

除了……以外 (chúle……yǐwài) *is a pattern that can be used to form a number of meanings with slightly different variations. When used on its own, the construction indicates "with the exception of" or "in addition to," depending on the context. The meaning can be clarified by adding an adverb to the following clause. This can either be* 还 *or* 也*, in which case the pattern means "in addition to" or "besides," or* 都*, in which case it means "with the exception of." In all cases,* 以外 *is optional.*

> Subject + 除了 + Noun/Verb/Adjective (+ 以外) , + Verb Phrase

> Subject + 除了 + Noun/Verb/Adjective (+ 以外) ,+ 还 / 也 + Verb Phrase

> Subject + 除了 + Noun/Verb/Adjective (+ 以外) + 都 + Verb Phrase

From the Lesson Text: 除了了解中国的工作情况以外，你还可以参观北京有名的景点。

Chúle liǎojiě Zhōngguó de gōngzuò qíngkuàng yǐwài, nǐ hái kěyǐ cānguān Běijīng yǒumíng de jǐngdiǎn.

Not only will you get to learn about the work environment in China, you will also get to visit a lot of Beijing's famous attractions.

Other examples: 除了肉以外, 我什么都可以吃。

Chúle ròu yǐwài, wǒ shénme dōu kěyǐ chī.

I can eat anything except for meat.

我很忙，除了明天以外，我没有时间去银行。

Wǒ hěn máng, chúle míngtiān yǐwài, wǒ méiyǒu shíjiān qù yínháng.

I'm really busy; apart from tomorrow, I don't have time to go to the bank.

Practice: Create complete sentences using 除了……以外 and the information provided below.

Example: 我 / 安娜 / 也 / 喜欢打网球
→ 除了我以外，安娜也喜欢打网球。

1. 她 / 中文 / 也 / 会说法语

   _____

2. 王老师 / 我们的老师 / 都 / 是男的

   _____

3. 中国的节日 / 中国人 / 还 / 过西方的节日

   _____

4. 大东 / 周末 / 每天 / 都 / 要上班

   _____

5. 带笔记本电脑 / 你 / 也 / 可以去网吧上网

   _____

STRUCTURE NOTE 16.2
Use question words with 都 to express "any" or "every"

Chinese does not have special words for "everything/anything," "everywhere/anywhere," or "everyone/every-thing." These meanings are instead created by placing 都 *after the question words* 什么, 谁, *and* 哪儿 *or* 哪里. *Because the* 都 *phrase must precede the verb, the object is placed before the verb when it is modified by* 都.

Subject + Question Word + 都 + Verb Phrase

Subject + Question Word + Object + 都 + Verb Phrase

From the Lesson Text: 有什么好玩儿的活动？
什么都有。
Yǒu shénme hǎowánr de huódòng?
Shénme dōu yǒu.
What fun things are there to do?
Beijing has everything!

Other examples: 哪儿都有网吧。　　我们什么地方都可以去。
Nǎr dōu yǒu wǎngbā.　　Wǒmen shénme dìfang dōu kěyǐ qù.
There are Internet cafés every-　　We can go anywhere.
where.

Practice: Answer the following questions using the question word in brackets and 都, following the example given.

Example: 　她在北京没有朋友吗？（谁）
　　　　→ 她刚来几天，谁都不认识。

1. 第十六课的练习容易吗？（谁）

　　_____

2. 这家商店卖什么东西？（什么）

　　_____

3. 你的课本找到了吗？（哪儿）

　　_____

4. 你今天晚上想去哪儿？（哪儿）

　　_____

5. 你去北京的时候想看哪些景点？（什么）

　　_____

STRUCTURE NOTE 16.3

Use 自己 *to refer to oneself or another*

自己 (zìjǐ) *usually corresponds to "my own," "your own," "his/her own," or "their own" in English. Watch out for the context to figure out who is being referred to.*

> Pronoun + 自己

From the Lesson Text:　你可以带自己的笔记本电脑来，买无线上网卡，或者去网吧。
Nǐ kěyǐ dài zìjǐ de bǐjìběn diànnǎo lái, mǎi wúxiàn shàng wǎng kǎ, huòzhě qù wǎngbā.
You can bring your own laptop and buy a wireless Internet card or go to an Internet café.

Other examples:　每个人都有自己的想法。　　这个蛋糕是他自己做的。
Měi gè rén dōu yǒu zìjǐ de xiǎngfǎ.　　Zhèige dàngāo shì tā zìjǐ zuò de.
Everyone has his or her own opinions.　　He made this cake himself.

Practice: Change the following sentences into Chinese using 自己.

Example: I cleaned the living room myself. → 客厅是我自己打扫的。

1. If you still don't believe me, go and look for yourself.

   _____

2. I don't have time to help you, you'll have to do your homework by yourself.

   _____

3. This isn't the school's textbook, it's the teacher's own copy.

   _____

4. He has a job now; he can pay for the sweater himself.

   _____

5. The kids made the dinner themselves.

   _____

STRUCTURE NOTE 16.4

Use 等 to express "at the point when / by the time"

等 (děng) *generally means "to wait," but in some contexts it can preface a time expression in order to convey the meaning "by the time" or "when."*

等 + Time Expression + Sentence

From the Lesson Text:　等我到北京以后，再麻烦你！
Děng wǒ dào Běijīng yǐhòu, zài máfan nǐ!
When I get to Beijing, I will have to trouble you again!

Other examples:　等你买好了衣服天都黑了。
Děng nǐ mǎi hǎole yīfu, tiān dōu hēi le.
By the time you finished buying clothes, it was dark.

等你长大了，我就带你去旅行。
Děng nǐ zhǎngdà le, wǒ jiù dài nǐ qù lǚxíng.
When you grow up, I'll take you traveling.

Practice: Complete the following sentences by matching the appropriate beginnings with the appropriate endings.

Example:　　　　等我们去中国旅行的时候，我就给你介绍我的中国朋友。

等我们去中国旅行的时候，	我们就可以吃年糕和饺子。
等你吃完饭，	我们可以去逛街。
等你长大了，	你就可以自己付钱买东西。
等元宵节的时候，	别的客人都走了。
等考完试以后，	我们会挂花灯。
等春节到来的时候，	我就给你介绍我的中国朋友。

PRACTICE 16.1

Working with a partner, answer the questions below by placing 都 after the question words 什么, 谁, or 哪儿／哪里, and provide an explanation for your answer. You may then practice the dialogues that you have created.

Example:

A: 这儿的服务员你都认识吗？

B: 我在这儿工作了两年了，所以谁都认识。

这儿的服务员你都认识吗？

北京有名的景点你都去过吗？

你有没有关系好的同事？

医生开了什么药给你？

找工作需要的东西你准备好了吗？

PRACTICE 16.2

Conduct a survey to find out what students would most want to do in Beijing. Record the most popular answer below.

Activity in Beijing	Number of Students

PRACTICE 16.3

Sun Mali is chatting online with Wang Xiaomei's cousin. Working with a partner, fill in appropriate responses and questions in the spaces provided, then practice the dialogue that you have made.

嗨，我下个月要去北京。我有点紧张，因为我怕我会不习惯那儿的生活。

玛丽，你别担心，你来了以后我会好好地照顾你。

你可以问问你的公司有没有宿舍。要不然到时候我可以再帮你找找。

从车站到你的公司，走路只要十分钟。你最好不要坐出租车，因为那会比较贵。

这儿有中医也有西医。

长城和故宫是一定要去的。你也可以逛胡同、去博物馆。

这儿的食物有辣的也有不辣的。你来到北京一定要吃北京烤鸭！如果这次来不吃的话，就像去北京不去故宫一样。

那我一定要吃！对了，在北京怎么上网呢？

好，等我到了北京以后，再麻烦你了！

PRACTICE 16.5

	Radical	Stroke Order
便	亻(人) rén person	丿 亻 仁 仨 佰 佰 便 便
城	土 tǔ earth	一 十 土 圠 圳 圻 城 城 城
市	巾 jīn cloth	丶 亠 宀 市 市
街	彳 chì walk	丿 彳 彳 彳 彳 往 往 往 往 街 街
除	阝(阜) fù hill	阝 阝 阝 队 险 险 除 除 除
况	冫(冰) bīng ice	丶 冫 冫 沪 沪 沪 况
观	见 jiàn see	𠃌 又 𮤕 观 观 观
怕	忄(心) xīn heart	丶 丷 忄 忄 忄 怕 怕 怕
无	无 wú negative	一 二 无 无
线	纟(丝) sī silk	乚 纟 纟 纟 纟 线 线 线
卡	卜 bǔ divination	丨 卜 上 卡 卡
胡	月(肉) ròu meat	一 十 古 古 古 胡 胡 胡 胡
博	十 shí ten	一 十 博 博 博 博 博 博 博 博 博 博
自	自 zì self	丿 亻 冂 自 自 自
己	己 jǐ self	𠃌 𠃍 己

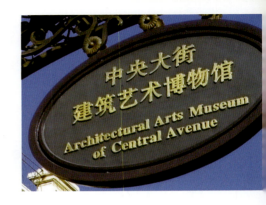

PRACTICE 16.6

Type the following sentences on your computer.

1. 除了工作以外，你还可以参观有名的景点。
2. 我在北京找到了一份暑假实习的工作。
3. 我怕我会不习惯这儿的生活。
4. 北京是一个很现代化的大城市。
5. 我要带自己的笔记本电脑去。

PRACTICE 16.7

中平：

我快要去北京了。我问了小美的表哥关于在北京上网的问题，他说我可以带自己的笔记本电脑去，或者去网吧。我觉得带自己的笔记本去上网会比较方便，可是我不知道在哪里能买无线上网卡。你可以帮我找找看能在哪里买到吗？谢谢。

——玛丽

Read Sun Mali's note and answer the following questions.
1. What does Sun Mali think will be the most convenient way to go online in Beijing?
2. What does Sun Mali ask Li Zhongping to help her look for?

PRACTICE 16.8

陈大东：这次去北京你打算去哪儿玩儿？

孙玛丽：第一个地方当然是故宫！你听说过吗？"没去故宫就像是没去北京一样。"

陈大东：我听说过。故宫是北京最有名的景点，而且是了解中国历史的好地方。

孙玛丽：小美的表哥还建议我多逛北京的胡同和博物馆，了解一下中国的生活和文化。

陈大东：你打算去这么多地方，你知道在北京坐车方便吗？

孙玛丽：现在的北京可以说是一个很现代化的大城市，生活非常方便，所以不用担心坐车的问题。

Read the dialogue and answer the following questions.
1. What does Chen Dadong think about the Forbidden City?
2. Is Sun Mali worried about transportation in Beijing? Why?

Modern Architecture

With the construction frenzy surrounding the 2008 Beijing Olympics, the Chinese capital city emerged on the global stage as a modern metropolis and a budding architectural mecca. A number of contemporary masterpieces designed by famous architects from around the globe were erected in time for the opening ceremony of the games, and they now stand as memorable landmarks of the new-look Beijing. These are four of Beijing's most eye-catching works of modern architecture:

The Beijing National Stadium
(鸟巢 niǎocháo: "the bird's nest")

Originally designed with the practical use of concealing support beams in mind, the "nest" shape of the stadium brings to mind the Chinese culinary delicacy of a bird's nest.

The Beijing National Aquatics Center
(水立方 shuǐ lìfāng: "the water cube")

The National Aquatics center is a cube-like structure clad in plastic "bubbles," which express the purpose of the structure while cutting energy costs by allowing light and heat into the building.

The National Center for the Performing Arts
(巨蛋 jùdàn: "the giant egg")

Located near Tian'anmen Square, this giant glass-and-steel opera house sits in the center of a man-made lake, accessible only by an underwater tunnel. The curved dome makes it look like an enormous egg, hence its colloquial name.

China Central Television Headquarters
(大裤衩 dà kùchǎ: "big boxer shorts")

The CCTV headquarters is one of central Beijing's most iconic skyscrapers. Comprised of 44 stories enclosed in a complex loop, the building was designed with radical angles to appear almost as a visual puzzle. It is said that the unofficial name for this unusual structure was coined by a Beijing taxi driver.

The Internet in China

While the Internet is of course a sensation all around the world, there is no denying that it has achieved particular popularity in the People's Republic of China. As early as 2008, China had already surpassed the United States as the country with the most Internet users worldwide.

Homegrown websites have developed rapidly in China and have on the whole proved more popular than their Western counterparts. Among other things, China has its own social networking websites, online encyclopedias, search engines, auction sites, photo sharing forums, and blog hosts. Online gaming is another popular Internet activity in China, and many games are created specifically for the Chinese market.

In order to get online, people will often go to a 网吧 (wǎngbā: "Internet café"). Another conspicuous feature of the Internet in China, these "cafés" are usually large spaces with rows and rows of terminals, like a college computer room. While personal computer ownership is on the rise, paying a small fee to go to an Internet café and chat with your friends or play online games remains a favorite pastime of many young Chinese.

孙玛丽： 小美，我在北京找到一份暑假实习的工作了！

Xiaomei, I found a summer internship in Beijing!

王小美： 恭喜你啊！除了了解中国的工作情况以外，你还可以参观北京有名的景点。

Congratulations! Not only will you get to learn about the work environment in China, you will also get to visit a lot of Beijing's famous attractions.

孙玛丽： 北京那么大，人那么多，我怕我会不习惯那儿的生活。

Beijing is so big, and there are so many people, I'm worried that I won't be able to get used to life there.

王小美： 别担心，我的表哥住在北京。来，我们看看他在不在线上。

Don't worry. My cousin lives in Beijing. Let's see if he's online.

王小美： 嗨，表哥，这是我的好朋友孙玛丽，她今年暑假要去北京，你一定要照顾她喔！

Hi, cousin, this is my good friend Sun Mali. She's going to Beijing this summer. You better take care of her!

小美的表哥： 没问题！北京虽然人口多，但是生活很方便，可以说是一个很现代化的大城市。

Not a problem! Even though there are a lot of people in Beijing, life here is very convenient. It's a very modern city.

孙玛丽： 有什么好玩儿的活动？

What fun things are there to do in Beijing?

小美的表哥： 什么都有！可以逛胡同、吃很多不同的食物、去博物馆，还可以去逛街、看电影。

Beijing has everything! You can walk around the old alleys, eat different types of foods, visit museums, and also go shopping and watch movies.

孙玛丽： 听起来真不错。在北京怎么上网呢？

Sounds good. How can I access the Internet in Beijing?

小美的表哥：	你可以带自己的笔记本电脑来，买无线上网卡，或者去网吧。	You can bring your own laptop and buy a wireless Internet card or go to an Internet café.
孙玛丽：	好，等我到北京以后，再麻烦你！	OK. When I get to Beijing, I will have to trouble you again!

What Can You Do?

INTERPRETIVE
- I can understand an article or a discussion that uses terms related to computing and the Internet.

INTERPERSONAL
- I can engage in an online chat or phone call with someone.
- I can discuss tourism and city life.

PRESENTATIONAL
- I can give a presentation about a city or place which includes its size, population, and what one can do there.

一路平安！
Have a Safe Trip!

玛丽，你一个人在那么远的地方，要保重身体。我会很想念你的。
xiǎng niàn

wǎng luò
现在网络这么方便，
diàn zǐ yóu jiàn
我们可以用电子邮件和
liáo tiān ruǎn jiàn
聊天软件，还是可以
天天联系的。

可是，我们不能一起吃饭，一起看电影……

你这样说，玛丽
ān xīn   la
就不能安心实习啦。

玛丽，记得多拍些照片，
pāi zhào piàn
放在网上给我们看看。

今年暑假，我和小美会去欧洲旅行，我们会给大家买纪念品的！

真羡慕你们，我们要去南非乡下陪我外婆。

现在那里是冬天，会冷死我的！

没关系，我们多带几件大衣就没事了！

玛丽，别忘了告诉我你的地址。我会给你寄包裹的。

时间到了，你应该登机了。

到了那边，有人接你吗？

有。小美的表哥会来接我。

祝你一路平安！

LESSON TEXT 16.2

Have a Safe Trip! 一路平安！

The group gathers at the airport to bid farewell to Sun Mali and talk about their respective plans for the summer break.

李中平： 玛丽，你一个人在那么远的地方，要保重身体。我会很想念你的。

Mǎlì, nǐ yí gè rén zài nàme yuǎn de dìfang, yào bǎozhòng shēntǐ. Wǒ huì hěn xiǎngniàn nǐ de.

孙玛丽： 现在网络这么方便，我们可以用电子邮件和聊天软件，还是可以天天联系的。

Xiànzài wǎngluò zhème fāngbiàn, wǒmen kěyǐ yòng diànzǐ yóujiàn hé liáotiān ruǎnjiàn, háishì kěyǐ tiāntiān liánxì de.

李中平： 可是，我们不能一起吃饭，一起看电影……

Kěshì, wǒmen bù néng yìqǐ chī fàn, yìqǐ kàn diànyǐng . . .

张安娜： 你这样说，玛丽就不能安心实习啦。玛丽，记得多拍些照片，放在网上给我们看看。

Nǐ zhèiyàng shuō, Mǎlì jiù bù néng ānxīn shíxí la. Mǎlì, jìde duō pāi xiē zhàopiàn, fàng zài wǎngshàng gěi wǒmen kànkan.

陈大东： 今年暑假，我和小美会去欧洲旅行，我们会给大家买纪念品的！

Jīnnián shǔjià, wǒ hé Xiǎoměi huì qù Ōuzhōu lǚxíng, wǒmen huì gěi dàjiā mǎi jìniàn pǐn de!

黄祥安： 真羡慕你们，我们要去南非乡下陪我外婆。现在那里是冬天，会冷死我的！

Zhēn xiànmù nǐmen, wǒmen yào qù Nánfēi xiāngxia péi wǒ wàipó. Xiànzài nàli shì dōngtiān, huì lěng sǐ wǒ de!

张安娜： 没关系，我们多带几件大衣就没事了！

Méi guānxi, wǒmen duō dài jǐ jiàn dàyī jiù méi shì le!

李中平： 玛丽，别忘了告诉我你的地址。我会给你寄包裹的。

Mǎlì, bié wàng le gàosu wǒ nǐ de dìzhǐ. Wǒ huì gěi nǐ jì bāoguǒ de.

王小美： 时间到了，你应该登机了。

Shíjiān dào le, nǐ yīnggāi dēng jī le.

李中平：	到了那边，有人接你吗？	Dào le nèi biān, yǒu rén jiē nǐ ma?
孙玛丽：	有。小美的表哥会来接我。	Yǒu. Xiǎoměi de biǎogē huì lái jiē wǒ.
大家：	祝你一路平安！	Zhù nǐ yílù píng'ān!

LESSON VOCABULARY 16.2

	SIMPLIFIED	TRADITIONAL	PINYIN	WORD CATEGORY	DEFINITION
1.	想念		xiǎngniàn	v	to miss (someone)
2.	网络	網絡	wǎngluò	n	the Internet
3.	电子邮件	電子郵件	diànzǐ yóujiàn	n	e-mail
4.	聊天软件	聊天軟件	liáotiān ruǎnjiàn	n	chat software
	聊天		liáotiān	vo	to chat
	软件	軟件	ruǎnjiàn	n	software
5.	安心		ānxīn	adj, vo	relieved; at ease; to rest assured
6.	啦		la	p	(exclamation particle, a combination of 了 and 啊)
7.	拍		pāi	v	to shoot; to take (photos)
8.	照片		zhàopiàn	n	photograph
9.	欧洲	歐洲	Ōuzhōu	n	Europe
10.	纪念品	紀念品	jìniànpǐn	n	souvenir
11.	羡慕		xiànmù	v	to envy
12.	南非		Nánfēi	n	South Africa
13.	乡下	鄉下	xiāngxia	n	countryside
14.	陪		péi	v	to accompany; to keep somebody company
15.	外婆		wàipó	n	maternal grandmother
16.	死		sǐ	v, adv	to die; extremely
17.	地址		dìzhǐ	n	address
18.	寄		jì	v	to send
19.	包裹		bāoguǒ	n	package

LESSON VOCABULARY 16.2 (continued)

SIMPLIFIED	TRADITIONAL	PINYIN	WORD CATEGORY	DEFINITION
20. 登机	登機	dēng jī	*vo*	to board a plane
21. 接		jiē	*v*	to receive, to pick up, to meet (someone)
22. 一路平安		yílù píng'ān	*ie*	have a safe trip!

REQUIRED VOCABULARY 16.2

OTHER

SIMPLIFIED	TRADITIONAL	PINYIN	WORD CATEGORY	DEFINITION
23. 安全		ānquán	*adj*	safe
24. 发	發	fā	*v*	to send (e-mail, text message)
25. 邮局	郵局	yóujú	*n*	post office

OPTIONAL VOCABULARY 16.2

TRAVEL AND THE AIRPORT

SIMPLIFIED	TRADITIONAL	PINYIN	WORD CATEGORY	DEFINITION
26. 护照	護照	hùzhào	*n*	passport
27. 签证	簽證	qiānzhèng	*n*	visa
28. 大使馆	大使館	dàshǐguǎn	*n*	embassy
29. 海关	海關	hǎiguān	*n*	customs
30. 旅游	旅遊	lǚyóu	*v, n*	to travel; tour; tourism
31. 报纸	報紙	bàozhǐ	*n*	newspaper
32. 杂志	雜誌	zázhì	*n*	magazine

Sentence-Final Particle Review

"Sentence-final particle" is the commonly-used term for a particle that can go at the end of certain phrases in Chinese. While a few sentence-final particles have a definite grammatical function, such as 吗, which turns a sentence into a question, most sentence-final particles have a more vague function of adding a certain type of emphasis to a sentence. Often the rules about when to use particular particles are very subtle — some particles imply surprise, some imply agreement, etc.

Chinese speakers use sentence-final particles more frequently in casual speech, and particles differ considerably from region to region. Because of this, many particles do not have one standard representation in Chinese characters — for example, the sentence-final particle 喔 is also sometimes written as 哦. The particles introduced in this textbook are some of the more common particles used across different regions.

吗	ma	question	玛丽，你好吗？
吧	ba	suggestion, softening	我们点菜吧！
呢	ne	question (what about x?), marks progressive aspect	（我）没什么活动。你呢？玛丽他们呢？
啊	a	emphasis, surprise	我很高兴啊！
呀	ya	variant of 啊, most often following vowels	哇，她还是个音乐家呀！
啦	la	variant of 啊, combination of 了 plus 啊	你这样说，玛丽就不能安心实习啦。
喔/哦	ō	surprise, emphatic reminder	玛丽，别忘了告诉我你的地址喔。
耶	ye	emphasis, surprise	吃年夜饭，最重要的是全家人在一起，跟圣诞节一样耶。

STRUCTURE NOTE 16.5

Use Verb Phrase 给 Someone 看/听 to express doing something to show someone else

In Structure Note 12.6, the pattern Subject + 帮 + Someone + Verb Phrase was introduced to express doing something for someone (帮他买东西). In the present pattern, 给 is used in a similar way. It comes after the main verb and is used to express the meaning "to do something for the purpose of showing someone," either through seeing or listening.

> Subject + Verb Phrase + 给 + Someone + 看/听

From the Lesson Text:
记得多拍些照片，放在网上给我们看看。
Jìde duō pāi xiē zhàopiàn, fàng zài wǎngshàng gěi wǒmen kànkan.
Remember to take some photos and put them on the Internet for us to see.

Other examples:

请说给我听。
Qǐng shuō gěi wǒ tīng.
Please explain it to me.

他喜欢画画儿给妈妈看。
Tā xǐhuan huà huàr gěi māma kàn.
He likes to paint paintings to show his mother.

Practice: Match the phrases below to create complete sentences, following the example given.

Example: 饺子有点难做，来，我做给你看。

我最近开始学吉他，	那我就唱给你听。
你刚才说的那个字是什么字？	我做给你看。
如果你有建议的话，	可以写给我看吗？
中国的国歌你没听过吗？	你要我穿给你看吗？
我今天买了一件毛衣，	我弹给你听好不好？
饺子有点难做，来，	你就说给我听。

STRUCTURE NOTE 16.6

Use 陪 to express keeping someone company

Unlike 送, which means to transport or escort, 陪 (péi) specifically means to accompany someone somewhere, or to stay with someone and keep them company.

> Subject + 陪 + Someone (+ Verb Phrase)

From the Lesson Text:
我们要去南非乡下陪我外婆。
Wǒmen yào qù Nánfēi xiāngxia péi wǒ wàipó.
We're going to the countryside in South Africa to visit my grandmother.

Other examples:

他陪我去参加比赛。
Tā péi wǒ qù cānjiā bǐsài.
He accompanied me to the match.

我希望你今天晚上可以陪我。
Wǒ xīwàng nǐ jīntiān wǎnshang kěyǐ péi wǒ.
I hope you can stay with me tonight.

Practice: Fill in the blanks in the following sentences by adding 送 or 陪, as appropriate.

Example:　我们下班以后，你想 ___ 我吃晚饭吗？
→ 我们下班以后，你想陪我吃晚饭吗？

1. 我也要往那边去，我 ___ 你回家吧。
2. 妈妈说我上班以前得 ___ 弟弟去学校。
3. 你可以帮我把这本书 ___ 到图书馆吗？
4. 爸爸生病了，我应该去医院 ___ 他。
5. 你今天晚上想 ___ 我去看电影吗？

STRUCTURE NOTE 16.7
Use 会……的 to stress that something will be the case

In Structure Note 3.1, it was noted that 会 *can be used to indicate the possibility of an action taking place in the future. Adding sentence-final* 的 *to this kind of expression gives the assertion a greater deal of certainty, equivalent to including the phrase* 一定 *in the sentence.*

Subject + 会 + Verb Phrase + 的

From the Lesson Text:　我会很想念你的。
Wǒ huì hěn xiǎngniàn nǐ de.
I will miss you very much.

Other Examples:

我们会找到它的。　　她会记住的。
Wǒmen huì zhǎo dào tā de.　Tā huì jì zhù de.
We're going to find it.　　She will keep it in mind.

Practice: Change the following 会……的 sentences into English.

Example:　她的派对听起来很好玩，我一定会参加的。
→ Her party sounds like a lot of fun; I will definitely attend.

1. 回到家我会打电话给你的。
_____

2. 到了中国以后我会寄照片给你看的。
_____

3. 看这么让人难过的电影，我一定会哭的！
_____

4. 你自己出门妈妈一定会不放心的。
_____

5. 你要小心，你说这样的话别人会误会你的。
_____

STRUCTURE NOTE 16.8
Use 死 to mean "extremely" or "to death"

Like the intensifier 极了 *(see Structure Note 13.8),* 死 *(sǐ) can be placed after certain adjectives as an adverb used to express a high degree. Its literal meaning is "so (adjective) that I'm going to die." Some common expressions using* 死 *are:* 冷死 *(lěng sǐ: "really cold"),* 气死 *(qì sǐ: "really angry"), and* 饿死 *(è sǐ: "really hungry").* 死 *is often followed by* 了.

Adjective + 死 (+ 了)

From the Lesson Text:　　会冷死我的！
Huì lěng sǐ wǒ de!
I'm going to freeze to death!

Other Examples:　　我饿死啦！　　　　　　我真的气死了！
Wǒ è sǐ la!　　　　　　Wǒ zhēnde qì sǐ le!
I'm starving!　　　　　　I'm so angry!

Practice: Fill in the blanks in the following sentences with an appropriate adjective and the intensifier 死.

Example:　　你做了这么多辣的菜，___ 我了！
→ 你做了这么多辣的菜，辣死我了！

1.　我今天没有时间吃早饭，___ 我了！
2.　北京的夏天 ___ 我了！
3.　我下了课就得去上班，___ 我了！
4.　老师说儿子昨天又没有去上课，___ 我了！
5.　你妈妈做的酸辣汤 ___ 我了！

PRACTICE 16.9

Working with a partner, look at the information below and take turns describing the problems indicated and potential solutions to those problems.

这里的手机很贵！

Example:
A: 这里的手机很贵！可是我得跟爸爸妈妈联系，怎么办？
B: 你可以用电子邮件，上网比较便宜。

这里的网吧很贵。

我没有他的地址。

写信很麻烦。

这里不能上网。

PRACTICE 16.10

Take a survey of the class to find out what mode of communication your classmates use most frequently to keep in touch with people. Record the most popular answer below.

Mode of Communication	Number of Students

PRACTICE 16.11

Working in groups of three or four, act out a scenario in which your friend is leaving for summer vacation and you are seeing him or her off at the airport. Talk about how you are going to keep in touch with each other and what everyone's plans are for the summer.

PRACTICE 16.12

Imagine that you are Sun Mali. Write an e-mail to Li Zhongping explaining to him that you have taken pictures and you have put them on the Internet. In addition, discuss life in Beijing. Describe the souvenirs you have bought and tell him that you have sent them to him. Read your e-mail to the class after you have finished.

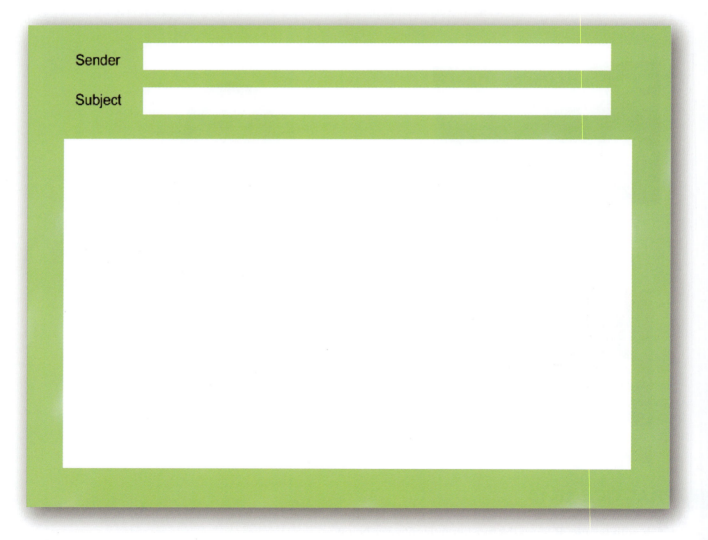

PRACTICE 16.13

Make an audio recording and send it to your teacher. In the recording, discuss what you plan to do during the summer vacation. Will you find a job or an internship? Will you go traveling? Explain the reasons for your decisions.

	Radical	Stroke Order
品	口 kǒu mouth	丶 口 口 吕 品 品 品 品 品
软	车 chē cart	一 ㄊ 车 车 轧 轫 软 软
片	片 piàn slice	丿 丿 片 片
纪	纟(丝) sī silk	乙 纟 纟 纪 纪 纪
邮	阝(邑) yì city	丶 口 曰 由 由 由阝 邮
陪	阝(阜) fù hill	阝 阝 阝 阽 阽 陪 陪 陪 陪
址	土 tǔ earth	一 十 土 圤 圤 址 址
乡	乙 yǐ secon heavenly stem	乙 纟 乡
婆	女 nǚ female	丶 冫 氵 汙 汙 泸 波 波 婆 婆
寄	宀 mián roof	丶 丷 宀 宀 宇 安 宝 宝 寄 寄 寄
登	癶 bò legs	丿 丬 夕 夕 癶 癶 癶 咎 咎 登 登 登
路	𧾷(足) zú foot	丶 口 口 𧾷 𧾷 𧾷 跋 趴 跋 路 路 路
欧	欠 qiàn lack	一 丆 㐅 区 区 欧 欧 欧
洲	氵(水) shuǐ water	丶 冫 氵 氵 汌 沙 洲 洲 洲
安	宀 mián roof	丶 丷 宀 宀 安 安

Type the following sentences on your computer.
1. 我会很想念你的。
2. 我们可以用电子邮件和聊天软件联系。
3. 祝你一路平安！
4. 你会寄包裹给我吗？
5. 南非的冬天冷死我了！

PRACTICE 16.16

Sender	中平
Subject	实习

玛丽：

　　我寄给你的包裹你收到了吗？那是我去西班牙玩的时候买的纪念品，是一条很特别的项链，希望你会喜欢。

　　最近你好像都不在线上，你不是说每天都会写电子邮件给我吗？上个月你把两三张照片放在网上以后，就没有再放了。你实习的工作很忙吗？听朋友说这个星期北京的天气冷了，你要记得多穿衣服。我下个月也要去加拿大实习，以后可能会更忙，但是我们一定要继续联系喔！

Read the e-mail and answer the following questions.
1. What did Li Zhongping buy for Sun Mali?
2. What does Li Zhongping hope that he and Sun Mali can continue to do in the future?

PRACTICE 16.17

Sender	祥安
Subject	南非

大东：

你好吗？我跟安娜都很想念你。我们快要从南非回来了！来了南非以后，我一直陪着安娜去逛街买东西，累死我了！因为这样，我外婆有点不高兴。

Read the e-mail and answer the following questions.
1. Where was Huang Xiang'an when he wrote the e-mail?
2. Why has he been so tired?

PRACTICE 16.18

陈大东：小美，你来看看祥安发给我的电子邮件，还有他们在南非拍的照片。

王小美：真羡慕他们，安娜看起来玩得很开心。

陈大东：安娜怎么买了这么多东西啊？

王小美：我们也把在欧洲旅行的照片放在网上给他们看吧！告诉他们我们在欧洲买了纪念品，还有问问他们什么时候回来，要不要我们去机场接……

陈大东：好，好，好，说慢一点。

王小美：快一点吧！时间到了，你忘了我们八点要跟中平去看电影了吗？

Read the dialogue and answer the following questions.
1. What does Chen Dadong show to Wang Xiaomei?
2. What does Wang Xiaomei ask Chen Dadong to write in the e-mail?

Cell Phones in China

China has become the world's largest mobile phone market in recent years, with the total number of cellphone user accounts surpassing 900 million in 2011. That number seems even larger when one considers the number of accounts was just over 400 million in 2006. The market expansion has grown rapidly as the wealth of the average Chinese citizen steadily increases and luxuries like a smartphone, which are simultaneously dropping in price, become more readily available. Cellphone use is not restricted to the major metropolitan areas, either. All over the country, people are buying mobile phones and getting hooked on their ease and efficiency.

High-Speed Rail and the Maglev Train

The Maglev

The Maglev is a railway system that works by using magnets to suspend the train above the tracks, a method that makes the ride smoother and quicker. Shanghai's Maglev Train, or 上海磁浮示范运营线 (Shànghǎi Cífú Shìfàn Yùnyíng Xiàn: "Shanghai Magnetic Levitation Demonstration Operation Line") was the first commercial high-speed Maglev line in the world, with record speeds of over 248.55 mi/h (400 km/h). The journey from Shanghai Pudong International Airport to the Longyang Road station in central Shanghai spans roughly 18.64 miles (30 kilometers) and takes only 7.5 minutes. The train's top speed is around 267.81 mi/h (431 km/h), making it the world's fastest train in regular commercial service to date.

China's HSR Network

Following the launch of a number of joint projects between Chinese and foreign companies, China's 中国高速铁路 (Zhōngguó Gāosù Tiělù: "China High-Speed Rail") has expanded at astronomical rates. To date, this system already spans over 4,971 miles (8,000 kilometers) and is the longest high-speed rail network in the world. Certain lines have reached speeds of up to 217.48 mi/h (350 km/h), and it is projected that the network will span roughly 15,534 miles (25,000 kilometers) upon scheduled completion in 2020. These higher-speed trains are expected to allow more trains to share the tracks and improve overall rail transport capacity. As a result, the Chinese government not only expects an increase in job opportunities for rail laborers, but also anticipates elevated levels of transport efficiency and economic growth.

李中平： 玛丽，你一个人在那么远的地方，要保重身体。我会很想念你的。

Mali, you're going to be on your own in such a far-off place; you must take care of yourself. I will miss you very much.

孙玛丽： 现在网络这么方便，我们可以用电子邮件和聊天软件，还是可以天天联系的。

The Internet is so convenient these days; we can use e-mail and chat services to talk to each other every day.

李中平： 可是，我们不能一起吃饭，一起看电影……

But, we won't be able to have meals together or watch movies together.

张安娜： 你这样说，玛丽就不能安心实习啦。玛丽，记得多拍些照片，放在网上给我们看看。

If you keep on like that, Mali won't be able to keep her mind on her internship. Mali, remember to take some photos and put them on the Internet for us to see.

陈大东： 今年暑假，我和小美会去欧洲旅行，我们会给大家买纪念品的！

This summer, Xiaomei and I are going traveling in Europe. We'll buy souvenirs for all of you!

黄祥安： 真羡慕你们，我们要去南非乡下陪我外婆。现在那里是冬天，会冷死我的！

I'm so envious of you. We're going to the countryside in South Africa to be with my grandmother. It's winter there right now; I'm going to freeze to death!

张安娜： 没关系，我们多带几件大衣就没事了！

Don't worry, we'll bring a few extra jackets and we'll be fine!

李中平： 玛丽，别忘了告诉我你的地址。我会给你寄包裹的。

Mali, don't forget to tell me your address. I will send you packages.

王小美： 时间到了，你应该登机了。

It's time. You should get on the plane.

李中平： 到了那边，有人接你吗？

Is someone picking you up when you get there?

| 孙玛丽： | 有。小美的表哥会来接我。 | Yeah. Xiaomei's cousin will come pick me up. |
| 大家： | 祝你一路平安！ | Have a safe trip! |

What Can You Do?

INTERPRETIVE
- I can understand the terms used for posting letters, packages, and e-mails.

INTERPERSONAL
- I can discuss and use different modes of communication such as e-mail and chat software.
- I can exchange the appropriate leave-taking expressions when seeing someone off.

PRESENTATIONAL
- I can give a detailed presentation about a trip I have taken or plan to take.

ACT IT OUT

Working in groups, compose an original three-minute skit that utilizes the vocabulary and structures introduced in Unit 16. Each of you should assume a role and have a roughly equal number of lines in the skit. Be prepared to perform your skit in class. You can either come up with your own story or choose from one of the following situations:

A) Your cousins from out of town just flew in to visit you for the first time.
B) You and your friends look online to decide what to do when you visit China.
C) You and your friends are planning a vacation and need to compare various modes of transportation.

CHECK WHAT YOU CAN DO

RECOGNIZE

Adjectives
- 有名
- 方便
- 不同
- 安心
- 安全

Conjunctions
- 除了
- 以外
- 等

Idiomatic Expression
- 一路平安

Nouns
- 情况
- 景点
- 生活
- 表哥
- 人口
- 城市
- 胡同
- 博物馆
- 笔记本电脑
- 无线上网卡
- 网吧
- 舞会
- 网络
- 电子邮件
- 聊天软件

- 照片
- 欧洲
- 纪念品
- 南非
- 乡下
- 外婆
- 地址
- 包裹
- 邮局

Particle
- 啦

Pronoun
- 自己

Verbs
- 参观
- 怕
- 在线
- 逛
- 逛街
- 上网
- 保重
- 想念
- 拍
- 羡慕
- 陪
- 死
- 寄
- 登机
- 接
- 发

WRITE
- 便
- 城
- 市
- 街
- 除
- 况
- 观
- 怕
- 无
- 线
- 卡
- 胡
- 博
- 自
- 己

- 品
- 软
- 片
- 邮
- 陪
- 址
- 乡
- 婆
- 寄
- 登
- 路
- 欧
- 洲
- 安

USE

- 除了……以外 to say "besides."
- Question words with 都 to express "any" or "every."
- 自己 to refer to oneself or another.
- 等 to express "at the point when / by the time."
- Verb Phrase 给 Someone 看/听 to express doing something to show someone else.
- 陪 to express keeping someone company.
- 会……的 to stress that something will be the case.
- 死 to mean "extremely" or "to death."

附录
APPENDIX

第九單元

第一課　買衣服

售貨員：	歡迎光臨！
張安娜：	你想買什麼衣服？
孫瑪麗：	我想買毛衣和襯衫，還想買裙子。走，我們先去看毛衣。
張安娜：	這件毛衣太大了，你應該穿中號的或者小號的。

孫瑪麗：	這件很漂亮，你覺得呢？
張安娜：	我覺得這件看起來比那件更大！
孫瑪麗：	可是這件比那件便宜一點兒。
張安娜：	你看，這件紅色的毛衣有中號的，又漂亮又便宜。
孫瑪麗：	不錯啊！裙子呢？
張安娜：	這條裙子跟那件毛衣一樣便宜，也很配。你買這條吧！

孫瑪麗：　嗨，祥安，進來吧！我看，你應該買新褲子了。

黃祥安：　不用，這條還好好的。我很喜歡這條長褲 ——

孫瑪麗：　安娜，我先走了，祥安需要幫忙，幫他找一找吧！

張安娜：　没問題！祥安，你喜歡什麼顏色？

————————————

黃祥安：　我最喜歡藍色。黑色、灰色或者黃色也可以。

張安娜：　明白了。這條黑色的牛仔褲怎麼樣？大小合適嗎？試試看！

黃祥安：　這條有一點兒短……

張安娜：　不短！我觉得很合适，你看起来真的好酷。

黃祥安：　是嗎？好！就買這條。

第一課　　星期六的活動

張安娜：　怎麼大家都這麼忙！看看祥安有沒有空。

黃祥安：　喂，安娜！你好！

張安娜：　嗨，祥安，你在做什麼？

黃祥安：　我一邊吃飯一邊跟你說話啊！

張安娜：　哈哈，我是說，今天是星期六，你有什麼活動嗎？

黃祥安：　沒什麼活動。你呢？瑪麗他們呢？

張安娜：　他們……有的去打球，有的去游泳，還有的去跑步了，可是我對這些活動都沒有興趣。

―――――――

黃祥安：　那你喜歡做什麼？

張安娜：　跳舞、唱歌我都喜歡，我也常常去看電影。

黃祥安：　是嗎？我今天晚上八點要去看一部新電影，是功夫片。你想跟我一起去嗎？

張安娜：　哦！聽起來很有意思。

黃祥安：　好吧，你能不能七點五十分在電影院門口等我？

第二課　　在音樂會

孫瑪麗：　大東，中平，你們下個周末有空嗎？

李中平：　有什麼特別的事嗎？

孫瑪麗：　星期六小美會在音樂會表演，我們一起去看，好不好？

陳大東：　哇，小美真是個天才！念書念得好，網球打得好，畫畫兒也畫得好，還是個音樂家呀！

李中平：　她今天表演什麼呢？

孫瑪麗：　彈吉他。她最近每天都練習五六個小時，很認真！

李中平：　瑪麗，你不是會拉小提琴嗎？你也是個天才！

孫瑪麗：　哪裏，哪裏！大東拉得比我好！

孫瑪麗：　小美出來了！你們看，她笑得多開心。

第十一單元

第一課　約會

陳大東：　小美，你的表演真棒！我可以請你吃晚飯嗎？

王小美：　好啊！瑪麗、中平他們也一起去嗎？

陳大東：　我祇想約你……

王小美：　哦……好的！

陳大東：　我晚點兒跟你説在哪兒見面。

王小美：　好，你再打電話告訴我吧！

———————————————

陳大東：　我真的緊張得不得了。這是我第一次跟小美約會。

黃祥安：　你喜歡小美什麼呢？

陳大東：　她又聰明又善良，也很可愛。

黃祥安：　女孩子都希望聽別人説她美。這點你別忘記對她説喔。

陳大東：　什麼！我記不住這麼多！

黃祥安：　你要讓她知道你對她是很有感情的！

陳大東：　祥安！別開玩笑了，你還有什麼建議嗎？

黃祥安：　吃完飯，你可以跟她去公園散散步，再約她下次出去玩。

———————————————

王小美：　嗨！

陳大東：　你今天真漂亮……

第二課　分手

孫瑪麗：　安娜，你怎麼了？發生什麼事了？可以跟我說說嗎？

張安娜：　我……跟我男朋友分手了。

孫瑪麗：　哦，別難過了！

張安娜：　我不是難過，我是非常生氣。

孫瑪麗：　他做什麼了？

張安娜：　我被他騙了。他跟我交往的時候，還一直跟他在俄羅斯的女朋友有聯系。

孫瑪麗：　真的嗎？怎麼會這樣？

張安娜：　我們還談過結婚的事，可是現在……

孫瑪麗：　唉，別哭了。忘了他吧。

張安娜：　可是我做不到，我從來沒有這麼愛過一個人。

孫瑪麗：　你會找到一個更好的男朋友。

第十二單元

黃祥安：　安娜，你看起來不太舒服，是不是生病了？

張安娜：　可能是吧。我跟男朋友分手以後，天天睡不着。現在身體很不舒服，肚子疼，頭也很疼。

黃祥安：　最近天氣冷得很，你要保重身體啊！你的眼睛和鼻子都紅了，你最好去看病。

張安娜：　可是現在下雨了，我不想出去……

黃祥安：　我可以送你去啊！你在這兒等我，我馬上回來。

張安娜：　好吧，謝謝！

黃祥安：　我認識一個很好的中醫。我帶你去他那兒看看，好不好？

張安娜：　中醫？爲什麽不去看西醫？

黃祥安：　這位中醫很不錯。

張安娜：　好，試試吧。

第二課　看病

醫生：　　來，請坐。你哪兒不舒服？

張安娜：　我有點發燒，頭疼……而且肚子也不舒服.

醫生：　　我幫你看看。請你張開嘴巴，讓我看看你的舌頭。

醫生：　　你的感冒不是很嚴重。

張安娜：　需要打針嗎？

醫生：　　中醫不用打針。 我給你開一周的藥，吃完就没事了。

張安娜：　中藥怎麽吃？ 會不會很苦？

醫生：　　有一點兒苦，別擔心。護士一會兒會告訴你怎麽吃。記
　　　　　住，你要多喝水，好好兒地休息。

張安娜：　謝謝醫生，我一定會記住。

———————

黃祥安：　醫生説什麽了？

張安娜：　還好，他説我感冒了。

護士：　　這是你的藥， 一天兩次，吃七天。

黃祥安：　穿好大衣，外面又下雨了。

護士：　　你男朋友對你真好。

張安娜：　我們……只是好朋友。

第十三單元

第一課　打工

陳大東：　小美！沒想到你會來這兒！

王小美：　我想看看你打工的地方。這兒環境真不錯，你每天在這兒工作幾小時？

陳大東：　四個小時，我每天晚上從八點到十二點在這兒上班。

王小美：　你十二點才下班，難怪晚上很少見到你。

———————

王小美：　你在這兒都做些什麼樣的事？

陳大東：　我要泡咖啡、收銀、還要打掃廚房。

王小美：　你要做的事真不少！

陳大東：　我以前祇管打掃，後來老闆看我很努力，慢慢地就讓我管更多的事了。

王小美：　你不但要上學，而且還要工作。這樣一天到晚都很忙，不會太累嗎？

陳大東：　雖然累一點，但是我想賺點兒錢，這樣的話，今年暑假就可以出國旅行了。

王小美：　聽起來不錯。加油！

第二課　去中國實習

孫瑪麗：　劉老師，我打算今年夏天去中國，在中國公司實習。您有什麼建議嗎？

我已經準備了一份簡歷，介紹了我的背景、學歷和工作經歷。

劉老師：　好極了！你想要找什麼樣的工作？在中國有很多工作機會。

孫瑪麗：　我畢業後想做跟商務有關的事。

刘老师：　在中国做商务，关系很重要。你可以先问问你的中国朋友。

他们可以帮你问一下他们认识的人，有很多外国公司和中国公司都需要你这样的人才。

孫瑪麗：　謝謝老師！

劉老師：　祝你今年夏天實習成功！

第一課　新年快樂！

孫瑪麗：　小美，你家真漂亮，有這麼多紅色的裝飾。

王小美：　中國人過春節喜歡用紅色來裝飾，這是傳統習慣。

張安娜：　難怪你要我們今天穿紅色的衣服。你看，我戴着紅帽子。祥安，你呢？

黃祥安：　我穿着紅襪子！

王小美：　你們見到我爸媽的時候，要説"恭喜發財"！

―――――――

大家：　　伯父伯母，恭喜發財！

小美媽：　新年快樂！

小美爸：　來來來，每個人都有一個紅包，祝你們學業進步，萬事如意。

孫瑪麗：　謝謝！祝伯父伯母身體健康。

小美媽：　請坐，先吃些糖果，我去拿年糕和瓜子。

李中平：　伯父，您這兒有那麼多的花燈啊！

小美爸：　是啊，元宵節快要到了，我們會挂花燈，放烟火，那一天會非常熱鬧。到時候歡迎你們再來玩兒！

第二課　　中國和西方節日

王小美：　今天我們吃年夜飯。過年的時候，我們習慣吃魚。因爲
　　　　　"魚"聽起來像"多餘"的　"餘"，所以吃魚就是希望
　　　　　"年年有餘"。

李中平：　吃年夜飯，最重要的是全家人在一起，跟聖誕節一樣
　　　　　耶。

小美爸：　我們過節都有傳統的食物。中秋節要吃月餅，春節吃
　　　　　魚、餃子或者年糕。你們呢？

孫瑪麗：　我們家感恩節一定要吃火雞。

─────────────────

黃祥安：　我們家好像每天都在過節，每天都吃大餐！

孫瑪麗：　我記得有一個中國節日是吃粽子的……

　　　　　那是端午節。端午節的時候還會有划龍舟比賽。

黃祥安：　哇，中國的節日那麼多，中國人還過西方節日嗎？

孫瑪麗：　現在有一些西方節日在中國越來越流行。

王小美：　比方說，有的年輕人會參加萬聖節派對。

張安娜：　沒想到中國人連萬聖節都會過啊！

王小美：　現在有一些西方節日在中國越來越流行。

小美爸：　比方說，有的年輕人會參加萬聖節派對。

陳大東：　沒想到中國人連萬聖節都會過啊！

第十五單元

第一課　有禮貌

小美爸：　服務員，麻煩您，請問洗手間在哪兒？

小美媽：　我也去。

陳大東：　今天我請客，讓我來買單吧。

王小美：　今天晚飯是我父母請我們。

陳大東：　這樣可以嗎？

王小美：　不用擔心。長輩請客也是對晚輩的照顧。

———————————

陳大東：　我今天正好拿到薪水，就給我個面子。

王小美：　下次吧。如果想要表示尊敬，你可以送一份禮物。

陳大東：　哎呀！我沒有準備，怎麼辦？

王小美：　沒關系，我知道你還不太了解中國傳統。這次我先幫你準備了一盒茶葉，你可以送給他們。

陳大東：　小美，你太好了！

陳大東：　那我下次請他們好了，要不然就是我不懂禮貌了。

陳大東：　謝謝伯父伯母。

小美爸：　哪裏哪裏。

陳大東：　這是一份小禮物，希望下次有機會可以請伯父伯母吃飯。

小美媽：　別客氣。你們還是大學生，我們是長輩，應該照顧你們。

第二課　了解中國文化

孫瑪麗：　中平，快來看看這些書，我剛剛在中文書店買的。

李中平：　武術、京劇、書法……怎麼都是中國傳統文化的東西？

孫瑪麗：　我暑假要去中國實習，所以想先了解一下中國的文化。

李中平：　什麼？那些都太古老了，現代的中國很不一樣吧。

孫瑪麗：　雖然中國已經現代化了，可是傳統文化還很重要。比方說，孔子的思想還是很被重視的。

孫瑪麗：　中國人的禮節很復雜，如果你做得不對，很容易發生誤會。

黃祥安：　没錯，比如，一個人把東西交給你，你該怎麼樣？

孫瑪麗：　我要用雙手接受。用一衹手接是不禮貌的。

黃祥安：　這樣我就放心了，你已經學了很多了。你會在中國交到很多新朋友的！

李中平：　有了新朋友，不要忘記老朋友喔！

第十六單元

孫瑪麗：　小美，我在北京找到一份暑假實習的工作了！

王小美：　恭喜你啊！除了了解中國的工作情況以外，你還可以參觀北京有名的景點。

孫瑪麗：　北京那麼大，人那麼多，我怕我會不習慣那兒的生活。

王小美：　別擔心，我的表哥住在北京。來，我們看看他在不在綫上。

———————————

王小美：　嗨，表哥，這是我的好朋友孫瑪麗，她今年暑假要去北京，你一定要照顧她喔！

小美的　　沒問題！北京雖然人口多，但是生活很方便，可以說是一個很現代化的大城市。

表哥：　　有什麼好玩兒的活動？

孫瑪麗：　什麼都有！可以逛胡同、吃很多不同的食物、去博物館，還可以去逛街、看電影。

小美的　　聽起來真不錯。在北京怎麼上網呢？

表哥：　　你可以帶自己的筆記本電腦來，買無綫上網卡，或者去網吧。

孫瑪麗：　好，等我到北京以後，再麻煩你！

第二課　　一路順風!

李中平：　瑪麗，你一個人在那麼遠的地方，要保重身體。我會很想念你的。

孫瑪麗：　現在網絡這麼方便，我們可以用電子郵件和聊天軟件，還是可以天天聯系的。

李中平：　可是，我們不能一起吃飯，一起看電影……

張安娜：　你這樣說，瑪麗就不能安心實習啦。瑪麗，記得多拍些照片，放在網上給我們看看。

陳大東：　今年暑假，我和小美會去歐洲旅行，我們會給大家買紀念品的!

黃祥安：　真羨慕你們，我們要去南非鄉下陪我外婆。現在那裏是冬天，會冷死我的!

張安娜：　没關系，我們多帶幾件大衣就没事了!

李中平：　瑪麗，別忘了告訴我你的地址。我會給你寄包裹的。

王小美：　時間到了，你應該登機了。

李中平：　到了那邊，有人接你嗎?

孫瑪麗：　有。小美的表哥會來接我。

大家：　　祝你一路平安!

Vocabulary Index (Chinese-English)

The Chinese-English index is alphabetized according to pinyin. Required Vocabulary is shown in purple. Optional Vocabulary is shown in green.

Characters	Pinyin	Word Category	Definition	Lesson
A				
唉	ài	interj	(expresses sadness, sympathy, disappointment etc.)	11.2
爱	ài	v	to love	11.2
安全	ānquán	adj	safe	16.2
安心	ānxīn	adj, vo	relieved; at ease; to rest assured	16.2
B				
白色	báisè	n	white	9.2
办法	bànfǎ	n	method; means	15.2
棒	bàng	adj	great; wonderful	11.1
帮忙	bāng máng	vo	to help	9.2
包裹	bāoguǒ	n	package	16.2
报纸	bàozhǐ	n	newspaper	16.2
保重	bǎozhòng	v	to take care (of oneself)	12.1
被	bèi	prep	by (passive)	11.2
背景	bèijǐng	n	background	13.2
悲剧	bēijù	n	tragedy	10.1
比	bǐ	prep	compared to	9.1
表哥	biǎogē	n	older male cousin	16.1
表示	biǎoshì	v	to express	15.1
表演	biǎoyǎn	v, n	to perform; performance	10.2
别人	biérén	n	other people	11.1
比方说	bǐfāngshuō	ie	for example	14.2
笔记本	bǐjìběn	n	laptop computer	16.1
笔记本电脑	bǐjìběn diànnǎo	n	laptop computer	16.1
比如	bǐrú	cj	for instance	15.2
毕业	bìyè	vo	to graduate	13.2
鼻子	bízi	n	nose	12.1

Characters	Pinyin	Word Category	Definition	Lesson
伯父	bófù	n	uncle (polite term of address for a man of one's parents' generation)	14.1
博客	bókè	n	blog	16.1
伯母	bómǔ	n	aunt (polite term of address for a woman of one's parents' generation)	14.1
博物馆	bówùguǎn	n	museum	16.1
部	bù	mw	(used for movies)	10.1
不要闹了	bú yào nào le	ie	Stop it! (used when others are not being serious, poking fun at someone)	11.1
不常	bùcháng	adv	not often; seldom	10.1
不但	búdàn	cj	not only	13.1
不得了	bùdéliǎo	adv	(to a degree)	11.1
不同	bùtóng	adj	different	16.1

C

Characters	Pinyin	Word Category	Definition	Lesson
猜谜	cāi mí	vo	to guess a riddle	14.1
参观	cānguān	v	to tour; to visit	16.1
唱歌	chàng gē	vo	to sing	10.1
常常	chángcháng	adv	often	10.1
长裤	chángkù	n	pants, trousers (lit. "long pants")	9.2
吵架	chǎojià	vo	to quarrel; to fight	11.2
茶叶	cháyè	n	tea leaves	15.1
成功	chénggōng	v, n	to succeed; success	13.2
橙色	chéngsè	n	orange	9.2
城市	chéngshì	n	city	16.1
衬衫	chènshān	n	shirt	9.1
吃药	chī yào	vo	to take medicine	12.2
穿	chuān	v	to wear	9.1
传统	chuántǒng	adj, n	traditional; tradition	14.1
厨房	chúfáng	n	kitchen	13.1
出国	chūguó	vo	to leave the country	13.1
出来	chūlai	dc	to emerge; come out	10.2
除了	chúle	cj	in addition to; apart from; besides	16.1
春节	Chūnjié	n	Spring Festival	14.1
春天	chūntiān	n	spring	12.1
出去	chūqu	dc	to go outside	11.1

Characters	Pinyin	Word Category	Definition	Lesson
出去玩(儿)	chūqu wán(r)	ie	to go out and play, have a good time	11.1
厨师	chúshī	n	cook, chef	13.1
除夕	Chúxī	n	(Chinese) New Year's Eve	14.1
次	cì	mw	(used to describe the frequency of an action)	11.1
从来	cónglái	adv	always, all along; never (when used in the negative)	11.2
聪明	cōngmíng	adj	smart, intelligent	11.1

D

Characters	Pinyin	Word Category	Definition	Lesson
打工	dǎ gōng	vo	to work part-time, to temp	13.1
打鼓	dǎ gǔ	vo	to play the drums	10.2
打球	dǎ qiú	vo	to play ball	10.1
大餐	dàcān	n	a large feast	14.2
戴	dài	v	to wear (for glasses and hats)	9.1
当	dāng	v	to serve as, to be (a profession)	13.2
担心	dānxīn	adj, vo	anxious; to worry	12.2
大人	dàrén	n	adults	15.1
打扫	dǎsǎo	v	to clean up; to sweep	13.1
大使馆	dàshǐguǎn	n	embassy	16.2
大提琴	dàtíqín	n	cello	10.2
大小	dàxiǎo	n	size	9.2
大衣	dàyī	n	overcoat	9.1
大衣	dàyī	n	overcoat	12.2
打针	dǎzhēn	vo	to give or have an injection	12.2
地	de	p	(used to express the manner in which an action is performed)	12.2
等	děng	v	to wait	10.1
等	děng	cj	wait until; when	16.1
登机	dēng jī	vo	to board a plane	16.2
得罪	dézuì	v	to offend; to displease	15.1
点	diǎn	n	point, characteristic	11.1
电影	diànyǐng	n	movie	10.1
电影院	diànyǐngyuàn	n	cinema, movie theater	10.1
电子邮件	diànzǐ yóujiàn	n	email	16.2
顶	dǐng	mw	(used for hats)	9.1

Characters	Pinyin	Word Category	Definition	Lesson
地址	dìzhǐ	n	address	16.2
冬天	dōngtiān	n	winter	12.1
短	duǎn	adj	short	9.2
端午节	Duānwǔjié	n	Dragon-Boat Festival	14.2
对	duì	prep	at; toward	10.1
多	duō	adv	how, however	10.2
多余	duōyú	n, adj	surplus; superfluous	14.2
肚子	dùzi	n	stomach	12.1

E

Characters	Pinyin	Word Category	Definition	Lesson
俄罗斯	éluósī	n	Russia	11.2
而且	érqiě	cj	furthermore; and also	12.2

F

Characters	Pinyin	Word Category	Definition	Lesson
发	fā	v	to send (email, text message)	16.2
发短信	fā duǎnxìn	vo	to send a text message	16.1
发烧	fā shāo	vo	to have a fever	12.2
放	fàng	v	to put; to set off	14.1
方便	fāngbiàn	adj	convenient	16.1
放心	fàngxīn	v	to put one's mind at ease	15.2
翻译	fānyì	v, n	to translate; translation; translator	13.2
发生	fāshēng	v	to happen	11.2
非常	fēicháng	adv	very, extremely	11.2
分手	fēnshǒu	vo	to break up	11.2
复活节	Fùhuójié	n	Easter	14.2
父母	fùmǔ	n	parents (formal)	15.1
父亲节	Fùqīnjié	n	Father's Day	14.2
复杂	fùzá	adj	complex, complicated	15.2

G

Characters	Pinyin	Word Category	Definition	Lesson
感恩节	Gǎn'ēnjié	n	Thanksgiving	14.2
刚刚	gānggāng	adv	just	15.2
钢琴	gāngqín	n	piano	10.2
干净	gānjìng	adj	clean	13.1
感冒	gǎnmào	v, n	to catch/have a cold; a cold	12.2
感情	gǎnqíng	n	feeling, emotion	11.1

Characters	Pinyin	Word Category	Definition	Lesson
高傲	gāo'ào	adj	arrogant	15.1
高尔夫球	gāo'ěrfūqiú	n	golf	10.1
告诉	gàosu	v	to tell	11.1
更	gèng	adv	even more	9.1
工程师	gōngchéngshī	n	engineer	13.2
功夫	gōngfu	n	kung fu	10.1
功夫片	gōngfu piàn	n	kung fu movie	10.1
公司	gōngsī	n	company	13.2
恭喜	gōngxǐ	v	to congratulate	14.1
恭喜发财	gōngxǐfācái	ie n	wishing you happiness and property (greeting used during the New Year)	14.1
公园	gōngyuán		park	11.1
挂	guà	v	to hang	14.1
管	guǎn	v	to be in charge of	13.1
逛	guàng	v	to stroll	16.1
逛街	guàng jiē	vo	to go shopping	16.1
光明节	Guāngmíngjié	n	Hanukkah	14.2
关系	guānxi	n	relation; relationship; connections	13.2
官员	guānyuán	n	official	13.2
瓜子	guāzǐ	n	melon seeds, dried seeds	14.1
古代	gǔdài	adj, n	ancient; ancient times	15.2
古典音乐	gǔdiǎn yīnyuè	n	classical music	10.2
古老	gǔlǎo	adj	ancient; old-fashioned	15.2
过	guo	p	(used after a verb to indicate a past experience)	11.2
过	guò	v	to spend (the holiday, an occasion)	14.1
过节	guò jié	vo	to celebrate a festival	14.2
过年	guònián	vo	to celebrate the New Year	14.2

H

Characters	Pinyin	Word Category	Definition	Lesson
哈哈	hā hā	on	(sound of laughter)	10.1
嗨	hāi	ie	hi	9.2
还好	hái hǎo	adj	not bad; OK; so-so	12.1
海关	hǎiguān	n	customs	16.2
号	hào	n	size	9.1
好听	hǎo tīng	adj	lovely; pleasant (to the ear)	10.2

Characters	Pinyin	Word Category	Definition	Lesson
好看	hǎokàn	adj	pretty; good-looking	11.1
好像	hǎoxiàng	adv	apparently; it appears; it seems like	14.2
盒	hé	n, mw	box; a box of	15.1
黑色	hēisè	n	black	9.2
很少	hěnshǎo	adv	very infrequently; rarely	10.1
合适	héshì	adj	suitable	9.2
红包	hóngbāo	n	red envelope	14.1
红色	hóngsè	n	red	9.1
后来	hòulái	adv	afterwards	13.1
划	huá	v	to row	14.2
画画(儿)	huà huà(r)	vo	to paint; to draw	10.2
花灯	huādēng	n	festive or decorative lantern	14.1
坏	huài	adj	bad	11.2
画家	huàjiā	n	artist	13.2
黄色	huángsè	n	yellow	9.2
环境	huánjìng	n	environment	13.1
画儿	huàr	n	painting; drawing	10.2
灰色	huīsè	n	gray	9.2
活动	huódòng	n	activity	10.1
火鸡	huǒjī	n	turkey	14.2
或者	huòzhě	cj	or	9.1
护士	hùshi	n	nurse	12.2
胡同	hútong	n	hutong (old-fashioned alleys in Beijing); lane, alley	16.1
护照	hùzhào	n	passport	16.2

J

Characters	Pinyin	Word Category	Definition	Lesson
寄	jì	v	to send	16.2
记不住	jì bu zhù	rv	to be unable to remember	11.1
家教	jiājiào	n	tutor	13.1
件	jiàn	mw	(used for articles of clothing such as shirts, dresses, jackets and coats)	9.1
见面	jiàn miàn	vo	to meet	11.1
健康	jiànkāng	adj, n	healthy; health	14.1
简历	jiǎnlì	n	résumé; curriculum vitae	13.2
建议	jiànyì	v, n	to suggest; suggestion, advice	11.1

Characters	Pinyin	Word Category	Definition	Lesson
脚	jiǎo	n	foot	12.1
交朋友	jiāo péngyou	vo	to make friends	15.2
交给	jiāogěi	v	to hand/give to	15.2
交往	jiāowǎng	v	to be in a relationship; to associate (with); to contact	11.2
家庭主妇	jiātíng zhǔfù	n	homemaker	13.2
加油	jiāyóu	ie	you can do it! (literally "add oil"; used when offering words of encouragement)	13.1
记得	jìde	v	to remember	14.2
接	jiē	v	to receive, to pick up, to meet (someone)	16.2
接待	jiēdài	v	to receive (guests)	13.1
结婚	jiéhūn	vo	to get married	11.2
节日	jiérì	n	holiday; festival	14.2
接受	jiēshòu	v	to accept	15.2
机会	jīhuì	n	opportunity	13.2
极了	jíle	adv	extremely	13.2
技能	jìnéng	n	skill	13.2
景点	jǐngdiǎn	n	scenic spot	16.1
京剧	Jīngjù	n	Peking opera	15.2
经历	jīnglì	n	experience	13.2
经验	jīngyàn	n	experience	13.2
纪念品	jìniànpǐn	n	souvenir	16.2
进来	jìnlai	dc	to come in	9.2
紧张	jǐnzhāng	adj	nervous	11.1
吉他	jítā	n	guitar	10.2
就是说	jiùshìshuō	ie	that is to say; in other words	15.1
记住	jìzhù	v	to remember, to bear in mind	12.2

K

Characters	Pinyin	Word Category	Definition	Lesson
咖啡色	kāfēisè	n	coffee color; brown	9.2
开药	kāi yào	vo	to prescribe medicine	12.2
开刀	kāidāo	vo	to perform/have an operation	12.2
开玩笑	kāiwánxiào	v	to joke	11.1
开心	kāixīn	adj	happy	10.2
卡拉OK	kǎlā OK	n	karaoke	16.1

Characters	Pinyin	Word Category	Definition	Lesson
看	kàn	v	(after a reduplicated verb) try and see, do something and see	9.2
看病	kànbìng	vo	to see a doctor	12.1
看法	kànfǎ	n	opinion; perspective	15.2
看起来	kànqilai	ie	it appears, it seems	9.1
可爱	kě'ài	adj	cute	11.1
客气	kèqi	adj, v	polite; to be polite	15.1
客人	kèrén	n	guests; customers	13.1
恐怖片	kǒngbù piàn	n	horror movie	10.1
孔子	Kǒngzǐ	name	Confucius	15.2
酷	kù	adj	cool	9.2
哭	kū	v	to cry	11.2
快	kuài	adj	fast	10.2
快	kuài	adv	soon; quickly	15.2
裤子	kùzi	n	pants, trousers	9.2

L

Characters	Pinyin	Word Category	Definition	Lesson
啦	la	p	(exclamation particle, a combination of 了 and 啊)	16.2
拉	lā	v	to play (an instrument with a bow); to pull	10.2
蓝色	lánsè	n	blue	9.2
老板	lǎobǎn	n	boss	13.1
老人	lǎorén	n	elders	15.1
冷	lěng	adj	cold	12.1
连	lián	prep	even	14.2
联络	liánluò	v	to contact; to have contact	11.2
联系	liánxì	v	to contact, to get in touch with	11.2
了解	liǎojiě	v	to understand	15.1
聊天	liáotiān	vo	to chat	16.2
聊天软件	liáotiān ruǎnjiàn	n	chat software	16.2
离婚	líhūn	vo	to divorce	11.2
礼节	lǐjié	n	etiquette; courtesy	15.2
礼貌	lǐmào	n	manners; politeness	15.1
流行	liúxíng	adj	popular	14.2
流行音乐	liúxíng yīnyuè	n	pop music	10.2
龙舟	lóngzhōu	n	dragon boat	14.2

Characters	Pinyin	Word Category	Definition	Lesson
锣鼓	luó gǔ	n	gong and drum	14.1
绿色	lǜsè	n	green	9.2
旅游	lǚyóu	v, n	to travel; tour; tourism	16.2

M

Characters	Pinyin	Word Category	Definition	Lesson
麻烦	máfan	v, n, adj	to trouble someone to do something; trouble; troublesome	15.1
买单	mǎidān	vo	to pay the bill	15.1
慢	màn	adj	slow	10.2
忙	máng	adj	busy	10.1
慢慢	mànmàn	adv	slowly; gradually	13.1
毛衣	máoyī	n	sweater	9.1
帽子	màozi	n	hat	9.1
每	měi	pr	every, each	10.2
美	měi	adj	beautiful	11.1
没错	méi cuò	adj	not wrong; (that's) right	15.2
没事	méi shì	vo	it doesn't matter; it's not a problem	12.2
没想到	méi xiǎng dào	ie	to not have expected or thought of	13.1
玫瑰花	méiguīhuā	n	rose	11.1
孟子	Mèngzǐ	name	Mencius	15.2
门口	ménkǒu	n	entrance	10.1
面子	miànzi	n	reputation; face; feelings	15.1
明白	míngbai	v	to understand	9.2
墨镜	mòjìng	n	sunglasses	9.1
母亲节	Mǔqīnjié	n	Mother's Day	14.2

N

Characters	Pinyin	Word Category	Definition	Lesson
哪里哪里	nǎlǐ nǎlǐ	ie	not at all (a polite reply to a compliment)	10.2
男朋友	nán péngyou	n	boyfriend	11.2
南非	Nánfēi	n	South Africa	16.2
难怪	nánguài	adv	no wonder	13.1
难过	nánguò	adj	sad	11.2
能	néng	av	can; be able to	10.1
念书	niàn shū	vo	to study; to read	10.2
年糕	niángāo	n	candy	14.1

Characters	Pinyin	Word Category	Definition	Lesson
年年有余	niánnián-yǒuyú	ie	may you have abundance every year (greeting used at New Year)	14.2
年轻	niánqīng	adj	young	14.2
年轻人	niánqīng rén	n	young people	14.2
年夜饭	niányèfàn	n	a reunion dinner for the whole family on Chinese New Year's Eve	14.2
牛仔裤	niúzǎikù	n	jeans (lit. "cowboy pants")	9.2
女朋友	nǚ péngyou	n	girlfriend	11.2
努力	nǔlì	adj, v	diligent; to work hard	13.1

O

Characters	Pinyin	Word Category	Definition	Lesson
喔	ō	interj	(used to indicate a reminder, admonition, or warning)	11.1
欧洲	Ōuzhōu	n	Europe	16.2

P

Characters	Pinyin	Word Category	Definition	Lesson
怕	pà	v	to fear, to be afraid of	16.1
拍	pāi	v	to shoot; to take (photos)	16.2
排球	páiqiú	n	volleyball	10.1
泡	pào	v	to make (coffee or tea); to steep	13.1
跑步	pǎobù	vo	to jog	10.1
陪	péi	v	to accompany; to keep sb. company	16.2
配	pèi	v, adj	to match, suit	9.1
骗	piàn	v	to trick, to fool, to cheat	11.2
漂亮	piàoliang	adj	pretty, beautiful	9.1
乒乓球	pīngpāngqiú	n	ping pong	10.1

Q

Characters	Pinyin	Word Category	Definition	Lesson
骑马	qí mǎ	vo	to ride a horse	10.1
谦虚	qiānxū	adj	modest	15.1
签证	qiānzhèng	n	visa	16.2
情况	qíngkuàng	n	situation	16.1
清明节	Qīngmíngjié	n	Tomb Sweeping Festival	14.2
情人	qíngrén	n	lover; sweetheart	11.2
情人节	Qíngrénjié	n	Valentine's Day	14.2
晴天	qíngtiān	n	clear day, sunny day	12.1

Characters	Pinyin	Word Category	Definition	Lesson
秋天	qiūtiān	n	autumn	12.1
求职意向	qiúzhí yìxiàng	n	work objective	13.2
全	quán	adj, adv	complete, whole; completely	14.2
裙子	qúnzi	n	skirt; dress	9.1

R

Characters	Pinyin	Word Category	Definition	Lesson
让	ràng	v	to allow or cause (somebody to do something)	11.1
热	rè	adj	hot (as in temperature)	12.1
热闹	rènao	adj	lively	14.1
人才	réncái	n	a person of ability/talent	13.2
人口	rénkǒu	n	population	16.1
认真	rènzhēn	adj	serious; conscientious; diligent	10.2
软件	ruǎnjiàn	n	software	16.2

S

Characters	Pinyin	Word Category	Definition	Lesson
散步	sàn bù	vo	to go for a stroll	11.1
上班	shàng bān	vo	to go to work	13.1
上次	shàng cì	n	last time	11.1
上网	shàng wǎng	vo	to go online	16.1
商务	shāngwù	n	business	13.2
上学	shàngxué	vo	to attend school	13.1
善良	shànliáng	adj	nice, kind, kind-hearted	11.1
生病	shēngbìng	vo	to get sick	12.1
圣诞节	Shèngdànjié	n	Christmas	14.2
生活	shēnghuó	n	life; lifestyle	16.1
生气	shēngqì	adj	mad, angry	11.2
什么样	shénme yàng	pr	what kind/sort	13.1
身体	shēntǐ	n	body	12.1
舌头	shétou	n	tongue	12.2
食物	shíwù	n	food	14.2
实习	shíxí	v	to intern; to have an internship	13.2
手	shǒu	n	hand	12.1
收银	shōuyín	vo	to collect money	13.1
帅	shuài	adj	handsome	11.1
双	shuāng	adj, mw	double, two; a pair	9.1

Characters	Pinyin	Word Category	Definition	Lesson
双手	shuāngshǒu	n	both hands	15.2
书法	shūfǎ	n	calligraphy	15.2
舒服	shūfu	adj	comfortable; feeling well	12.1
睡不着	shuìbuzháo	rv	to be unable to sleep	12.1
暑假	shǔjià	n	summer vacation	13.1
说话	shuō huà	vo	to talk	10.1
死	sǐ	v, adv	to die; extremely	16.2
思想	sīxiǎng	n	thought, idea	15.2
送花	sòng huā	vo	to give flowers	11.1
虽然	suīrán	cj	even though	13.1

T

Characters	Pinyin	Word Category	Definition	Lesson
T一恤衫	T-xùshān	n	T-shirt	9.1
太极拳	Tàijíquán	n	Tai Chi	15.2
弹	tán	v	to play (a musical instrument); to pluck	10.2
谈	tán	v	to talk, discuss	11.2
糖果	tángguǒ	adj, n	candy	14.1
特别	tèbié	adj	special	10.2
疼	téng	adj	painful; sore	12.1
踢	tī	v	to kick	10.1
天安门	Tiān'ānmén	n	Tian'anmen (Gate of Heavenly Peace)	16.1
天才	tiāncái	n	genius; talent	10.2
天气	tiānqì	n	weather	12.1
天天	tiāntiān	adv	every day	12.1
跳舞	tiào wǔ	vo	to dance	10.1
听起来	tīngqǐlái	ie	to sound like	10.1
痛	tòng	adj	painful	12.1
头	tóu	n	head	12.1
头疼	tóuténg	adj, n	to have a headache; headache	12.2

W

Characters	Pinyin	Word Category	Definition	Lesson
外国	wàiguó	adj, n	foreign; foreign country	13.2
外面	wàimian	n	outside	12.2
外婆	wàipó	n	maternal grandmother	16.2
外套	wàitào	n	coat, jacket	9.1
玩	wán	v	to play	10.1

Characters	Pinyin	Word Category	Definition	Lesson
晚辈	wǎnbèi	n	younger generation	15.1
晚点	wǎndiǎn	adv	(a bit) later	11.1
网吧	wǎngbā	n	Internet café	16.1
忘记	wàngjì	rv	to forget	11.1
网络	wǎngluò	n	the Internet	16.2
网球	wǎngqiú	n	tennis	10.2
网页	wǎngyè	n	webpage	16.1
网站	wǎngzhàn	n	website	16.1
万圣节	Wànshèngjié	n	Halloween	14.2
万事如意	wànshìrúyì	ie	healthy; health	14.1
袜子	wàzi	n	socks	9.1
吻	wěn	v, n	to kiss; kiss	11.1
文化	wénhuà	n	culture	15.2
误会	wùhuì	v	to misunderstand	15.2
舞会	wǔhuì	n	dance party	16.1
舞龙舞狮	wǔlóngwǔshī	n	dragon and lion dance	14.1
侮辱	wǔrǔ	n, v	insult; to insult; to humiliate	15.1
武术	wǔshù	n	martial arts	15.2
无线上网卡	wúxiàn shàngwǎng kǎ	n	wireless internet card	16.1

X

Characters	Pinyin	Word Category	Definition	Lesson
下班	xià bān	vo	to get off work	13.1
下雪	xià xuě	vo	to snow	12.1
下雨	xià yǔ	vo	to rain	12.1
下次	xiàcì	n	next time	11.1
现代	xiàndài	adj, n	modern; modern times	15.2
现代化	xiàndàihuà	adj, v, n	modernized; modernize; modernization	15.2
像	xiàng	v	to resemble	14.2
想	xiǎng	v	to think	11.1
想法	xiǎngfǎ	n	idea; opinion; way of thinking	15.2
想念	xiǎngniàn	v	to miss (someone)	16.2
乡下	xiāngxia	n	countryside	16.2
相信	xiāngxìn	v	to believe	11.2
想要	xiǎngyào	av	want; wish; would like	13.2
羡慕	xiànmù	v	to envy	16.2
笑	xiào	v	to smile; to laugh	10.2

Characters	Pinyin	Word Category	Definition	Lesson
孝	xiào	n, v	filial piety; to be filial	15.1
小	xiǎo	adj	small; little	9.1
孝顺	xiàoshùn	v, adj	to show filial obedience; filial	15.1
小提琴	xiǎotíqín	n	violin	10.2
夏天	xiàtiān	n	summer	12.1
些	xiē	mw	some	10.1
鞋(子)	xié (zi)	n	shoes	9.1
血	xiě, xuè	n	blood	12.2
西方	Xīfāng	n	the West	14.2
习惯	xíguàn	n, v	habit; to be used to	14.1
喜剧	xǐjù	n	comedy	10.1
心	xīn	n	heart	11.2
行	xíng	adj	OK, all right	10.1
兴趣	xìngqù	n	interest	10.1
新年	xīnnián	n	new year	14.1
薪水	xīnshuǐ	n	salary	15.1
洗手间	xǐshǒujiān	n	restroom	15.1
休息	xiūxi	v	to rest	12.2
希望	xīwàng	v, n	to hope; hope	11.1
西医	xīyī	n	(doctor of) Western medicine	12.1
西装	xīzhuāng	n	suit	9.1
学历	xuélì	n	educational background	13.2
学业	xuéyè	n	studies; academics	14.1
需要	xūyào	v	to need; to want	9.2

Y

Characters	Pinyin	Word Category	Definition	Lesson
呀	ya	p	(used to express surprise like 啊 but follows vowels)	10.2
演	yǎn	v	to perform, to act	10.2
烟火	yānhuǒ	n	fireworks	14.1
眼睛	yǎnjing	n	eyes	12.1
眼镜	yǎnjìng	n	glasses	9.1
眼泪	yǎnlèi	n	tears	11.2
颜色	yánsè	n	color	9.2
严重	yánzhòng	adj	serious	12.2
要不然	yàoburán	cj	otherwise	15.1

Characters	Pinyin	Word Category	Definition	Lesson
摇滚乐	yáogǔnyuè	n	rock music	10.2
耶	ye	p	(particle used at end of a sentence)	14.2
一会儿	yí huìr	adv	in a while, in a moment	12.2
一边	yìbiān	conj	on the one hand; at the same time	10.1
一定	yídìng	adj, adv	certain(ly), definite(ly)	12.2
一路平安	yílùpíng'ān	ie	have a safe flight!	16.2
阴天	yīntiān	n	cloudy day	12.1
音乐家	yīnyuèjiā	n	musician	10.2
以前	yǐqián	prep	before	13.1
医生	yīshēng	n	doctor	12.2
一天到晚	yìtiān-dàowǎn	adv	from morning until night; all day long	13.1
以外	yǐwài	cj	other than; except	16.1
一样	yíyàng	adj	same	9.1
医院	yīyuàn	n	hospital	12.2
又	yòu	adv	again; moreover	12.2
又⋯又⋯	yòu . . . yòu . . .	adv	both . . . and . . .	9.1
有空	yǒu kòng	vo	to have free time	10.1
有关	yǒuguān	vo	to be relevant; to be about; to do with	13.2
邮局	yóujú	n	post office	16.2
有名	yǒumíng	adj	famous	16.1
游戏	yóuxì	n	game	10.1
游泳	yóuyǒng	vo	to swim	10.1
鱼	yú	n	fish	14.2
元旦	Yuándàn	n	New Year's Day	14.2
元宵节	Yuánxiāojié	n	Lantern Festival	14.1
约	yuē	v	to arrange; to make an appointment	11.1
约会	yuē huì	vo, n	to go on a date; date	11.1
月饼	yuèbǐng	n	mooncake	14.2
越来越	yuèláiyuè	adv	more and more	14.2
乐器	yuèqì	n	musical instrument	10.2
羽毛球	yǔmáoqiú	n	badminton	10.1

Z

Characters	Pinyin	Word Category	Definition	Lesson
在线	zài xiàn	vo, adj	to be online; online	16.1
杂志	zázhì	n	magazine	16.2
怎么了	zěnme le	qph	what's wrong; what's the matter	11.2

Characters	Pinyin	Word Category	Definition	Lesson
长辈	zhǎngbèi	n	elder generation	15.1
张开	zhāngkāi	rv	to open	12.2
照顾	zhàogù	v	to take care of	15.1
照片	zhàopiàn	n	photograph	16.2
着	zhe	p	(added to verb or adjective to indicate a continued action or state)	14.1
真的	zhēnde	adv, ie	really	9.2
正好	zhènghǎo	adv	happen to, as it happens	15.1
整理	zhěnglǐ	v	to sort out; to put in order; to arrange	13.1
正月	zhēngyuè	n	first month of the lunar year	14.1
这些	zhèxiē	n	these	10.1
哲学家	zhéxuéjiā	n	philosopher	15.2
中	zhōng	adj	middle	9.1
中号	zhōnghào	adj	medium size	9.1
中秋节	Zhōngqiūjié	n	Mid-Autumn Festival	14.2
重视	zhòngshì	v	think highly of; attach importance to	15.2
中药	zhōngyào	n	Chinese herbal medicine	12.2
中医	zhōngyī	n	(doctor of) Traditional Chinese Medicine	12.1
周	zhōu	n	week	12.2
赚钱	zhuàn qián	vo	to earn money	13.1
装饰	zhuāngshì	v, n	to decorate; decoration	14.1
庄子	Zhuāngzǐ	name	Zhuangzi	15.2
专业技能	zhuānyè jìnéng	n	teaching assistant	13.2
助教	zhùjiào	n	professional skills	13.1
自己	zìjǐ	pr	oneself	16.1
紫色	zǐsè	n	purple	9.2
粽子	zòngzi	n	pyramid-shaped dumpling made of glutinous rice wrapped in bamboo leaves	14.2
最	zuì	adv	most (used to describe superlative degree)	9.2
嘴巴	zuǐba	n	mouth	12.2
最好	zuìhǎo	adv	had better	12.1
最近	zuìjìn	adv	recently	10.2
尊敬	zūnjìng	v	to pay respect to (used for people)	15.1
做生意	zuò shēngyì	vo	to do business	13.2
做事	zuò shì	vo	to work; to handle matters	13.1
作家	zuòjiā	n	writer, author	13.2

Vocabulary Index (English-Chinese)

The measure words and particles index is arranged according to the lesson. The Chinese-English index is alphabetized according to English. Required Vocabulary is shown in purple. Optional Vocabulary is shown in green.

Definition	Characters	Pinyin	Word Category	Lesson
Measure Words				
(used for articles of clothing such as shirts, dresses, jackets and coats)	件	jiàn	mw	9.1
(used for hats)	顶	dǐng	mw	9.1
(used for movies)	部	bù	mw	10.1
(used to describe the frequency of an action)	次	cì	mw	11.1
a box of	盒	hé	mw	15.1
a pair	双	shuāng	mw	9.1
some	些	xiē	mw	10.1
Particles				
(exclamation particle, a combination of 了 and 啊)	啦	la	p	16.2
(expresses sadness, sympathy, disappointment etc.)	唉	ài	interj	11.2
(particle used at end of a sentence)	耶	ye	p	14.2
(sound of laughter)	哈哈	hā hā	on	10.1
(used to express surprise like 啊 but follows vowels)	呀	ya	p	10.2
(used to indicate a reminder, admonition, or warning)	喔	ō	interj	11.1
hi	嗨	hāi	ie	9.2

Definition	Characters	Pinyin	Word Category	Lesson
A				
a large feast	大餐	dàcān	n	14.2
a person of ability/talent	人才	réncái	n	13.2
a reunion dinner for the whole family on Chinese New Year's Eve	年夜饭	niányèfàn	n	14.2
to accept	接受	jiēshòu	v	15.2
to accompany; to keep sb. company	陪	péi	v	16.2
activity	活动	huódòng	n	10.1
(added to verb or adjective to indicate a continued action or state)	着	zhe	p	14.1
address	地址	dìzhǐ	n	16.2
adults	大人	dàrén	n	15.1
afterwards	后来	hòulái	adv	13.1
again; moreover	又	yòu	adv	12.2
to allow or cause (somebody to do something)	让	ràng	v	11.1
always, all along; never (when used in the negative)	从来	cónglái	adv	11.2
ancient; ancient times	古代	gǔdài	adj, n	15.2
ancient; old-fashioned	古老	gǔlǎo	adj	15.2
anxious; to worry	担心	dānxīn	adj, vo	12.2
apparently; it appears; it seems like	好像	hǎoxiàng	adv	14.2
to arrange; to make an appointment	约	yuē	v	11.1
arrogant	高傲	gāo'ào	adj	15.1
artist	画家	huàjiā	n	13.2
at; toward	对	duì	prep	10.1
to attend school	上学	shàngxué	vo	13.1
aunt (polite term of address for a woman of one's parents' generation)	伯母	bómǔ	n	14.1
autumn	秋天	qiūtiān	n	12.1
B				
background	背景	bèijǐng	n	13.2
bad	坏	huài	adj	11.2
badminton	羽毛球	yǔmáoqiú	n	10.1
to be online; online	在线	zài xiàn	vo, adj	16.1

Definition	Characters	Pinyin	Word Category	Lesson
to be relevant; to be about; to do with	有关	yǒuguān	vo	13.2
beautiful	美	měi	adj	11.1
before	以前	yǐqián	prep	13.1
to believe	相信	xiāngxìn	v	11.2
black	黑色	hēisè	n	9.2
blog	博客	bókè	n	16.1
blood	血	xiě, xuè	n	12.2
blue	蓝色	lánsè	n	9.2
to board a plane	登机	dēng jī	vo	16.2
body	身体	shēntǐ	n	12.1
boss	老板	lǎobǎn	n	13.1
both . . . and . . .	又…又…	yòu . . . yòu . . .	adv	9.1
both hands	双手	shuāngshǒu	n	15.2
box	盒	hé	n	15.1
boyfriend	男朋友	nán péngyou	n	11.2
to break up	分手	fēnshǒu	vo	11.2
business	商务	shāngwù	n	13.2
busy	忙	máng	adj	10.1
by (passive)	被	bèi	prep	11.2

C

Definition	Characters	Pinyin	Word Category	Lesson
calligraphy	书法	shūfǎ	n	15.2
can; be able to	能	néng	av	10.1
candy	糖果	tángguǒ	n	14.1
to catch/have a cold; a cold	感冒	gǎnmào	v, n	12.2
to celebrate a festival	过节	guò jié	vo	14.2
to celebrate the New Year	过年	guònián	vo	14.2
cello	大提琴	dàtíqín	n	10.2
certain(ly), definite(ly)	一定	yídìng	adj, adv	12.2
chat software	聊天软件	liáotiān ruǎnjiàn	n	16.2
Chinese herbal medicine	中药	zhōngyào	n	12.2
(Chinese) New Year's Eve	除夕	Chúxī	n	14.1
Christmas	圣诞节	Shèngdànjié	n	14.2
cinema, movie theater	电影院	diànyǐngyuàn	n	10.1
city	城市	chéngshì	n	16.1
classical music	古典音乐	gǔdiǎn yīnyuè	n	10.2

Definition	Characters	Pinyin	Word Category	Lesson
clean	干净	gānjìng	adj	13.1
to clean up; to sweep	打扫	dǎsǎo	v	13.1
clear day, sunny day	晴天	qíngtiān	n	12.1
cloudy day	阴天	yīntiān	n	12.1
coat, jacket	外套	wàitào	n	9.1
coffee color; brown	咖啡色	kāfēisè	n	9.2
cold	冷	lěng	adj	12.1
to collect money	收银	shōuyín	vo	13.1
color	颜色	yánsè	n	9.2
to come in	进来	jìnlai	dc	9.2
comedy	喜剧	xǐjù	n	10.1
comfortable; feeling well	舒服	shūfu	adj	12.1
company	公司	gōngsī	n	13.2
compared to	比	bǐ	prep	9.1
complete, whole; completely	全	quán	adj, adv	14.2
complex, complicated	复杂	fùzá	adj	15.2
Confucius	孔子	Kǒngzǐ	name	15.2
to congratulate	恭喜	gōngxǐ	v	14.1
to contact, to get in touch with	联系	liánxì	v	11.2
to contact; to have contact	联络	liánluò	v	11.2
convenient	方便	fāngbiàn	adj	16.1
cook, chef	厨师	chúshī	n	13.1
cool	酷	kù	adj	9.2
countryside	乡下	xiāngxia	n	16.2
to cry	哭	kū	v	11.2
culture	文化	wénhuà	n	15.2
customs	海关	hǎiguān	n	16.2
cute	可爱	kě'ài	adj	11.1

D

Definition	Characters	Pinyin	Word Category	Lesson
to dance	跳舞	tiào wǔ	vo	10.1
dance party	舞会	wǔhuì	n	16.1
to decorate; decoration	装饰	zhuāngshì	v, n	14.1
to die; extremely	死	sǐ	v, adv	16.2
different	不同	bùtóng	adj	16.1
diligent; to work hard	努力	nǔlì	adj, v	13.1

Definition	Characters	Pinyin	Word Category	Lesson
to divorce	离婚	líhūn	vo	11.2
to do business	做生意	zuò shēngyì	vo	13.2
doctor	医生	yīshēng	n	12.2
(doctor of) Traditional Chinese Medicine	中医	zhōngyī	n	12.1
(doctor of) Western medicine	西医	xīyī	n	12.1
double, two	双	shuāng	adj	9.1
dragon and lion dance	舞龙舞狮	wǔlóngwǔshī	n	14.1
dragon boat	龙舟	lóngzhōu	n	14.2
Dragon-Boat Festival	端午节	Duānwǔjié	n	14.2

E

Definition	Characters	Pinyin	Word Category	Lesson
to earn money	赚钱	zhuàn qián	vo	13.1
Easter	复活节	Fùhuójié	n	14.2
educational background	学历	xuélì	n	13.2
elder generation	长辈	zhǎngbèi	n	15.1
elders	老人	lǎorén	n	15.1
email	电子邮件	diànzǐ yóujiàn	n	16.2
embassy	大使馆	dàshǐguǎn	n	16.2
to emerge; come out	出来	chūlai	dc	10.2
engineer	工程师	gōngchéngshī	n	13.2
entrance	门口	ménkǒu	n	10.1
environment	环境	huánjìng	n	13.1
to envy	羡慕	xiànmù	v	16.2
etiquette; courtesy	礼节	lǐjié	n	15.2
Europe	欧洲	Ōuzhōu	n	16.2
even	连	lián	prep	14.2
even more	更	gèng	adv	9.1
even though	虽然	suīrán	cj	13.1
every day	天天	tiāntiān	adv	12.1
every, each	每	měi	pr	10.2
experience	经历	jīnglì	n	13.2
experience	经验	jīngyàn	n	13.2
to express	表示	biǎoshì	v	15.1
extremely	极了	jíle	adv	13.2
eyes	眼睛	yǎnjing	n	12.1

Definition	Characters	Pinyin	Word Category	Lesson
F				
famous	有名	yǒumíng	adj	16.1
fast	快	kuài	adj	10.2
Father's Day	父亲节	Fùqīnjié	n	14.2
to fear, to be afraid of	怕	pà	v	16.1
feeling, emotion	感情	gǎnqíng	n	11.1
festive or decorative lantern	花灯	huādēng	n	14.1
filial piety; to be filial	孝	xiào	n, v	15.1
fireworks	烟火	yānhuǒ	n	14.1
first month of the lunar year	正月	zhēngyuè	n	14.1
fish	鱼	yú	n	14.2
food	食物	shíwù	n	14.2
foot	脚	jiǎo	n	12.1
for example	比方说	bǐfāngshuō	ie	14.2
for instance	比如	bǐrú	cj	15.2
foreign; foreign country	外国	wàiguó	adj, n	13.2
to forget	忘记	wàngjì	rv	11.1
from morning until night; all day long	一天到晚	yìtiān-dàowǎn	adv	13.1
furthermore; and also	而且	érqiě	cj	12.2
G				
game	游戏	yóuxì	n	10.1
genius; talent	天才	tiāncái	n	10.2
to get married	结婚	jiéhūn	vo	11.2
to get off work	下班	xià bān	vo	13.1
to get sick	生病	shēngbìng	vo	12.1
girlfriend	女朋友	nǚ péngyou	n	11.2
to give flowers	送花	sòng huā	vo	11.1
to give or have an injection	打针	dǎzhēn	vo	12.2
glasses	眼镜	yǎnjìng	n	9.1
to go for a stroll	散步	sàn bù	vo	11.1
to go on a date; date	约会	yuē huì	vo, n	11.1
to go online	上网	shàng wǎng	vo	16.1
to go out and play, have a good time	出去玩(儿)	chūqu wán(r)	ie	11.1
to go outside	出去	chūqu	dc	11.1
to go shopping	逛街	guàng jiē	vo	16.1

Definition	Characters	Pinyin	Word Category	Lesson
to go to work	上班	shàng bān	vo	13.1
golf	高尔夫球	gāo'ěrfūqiú	n	10.1
gong and drum	锣鼓	luó gǔ	n	14.1
to graduate	毕业	bìyè	vo	13.2
gray	灰色	huīsè	n	9.2
great; wonderful	棒	bàng	adj	11.1
green	绿色	lǜsè	n	9.2
to guess a riddle	猜谜	cāi mí	vo	14.1
guests; customers	客人	kèrén	n	13.1
guitar	吉他	jítā	n	10.2

H

Definition	Characters	Pinyin	Word Category	Lesson
habit; to be used to	习惯	xíguàn	n, v	14.1
had better	最好	zuìhǎo	adv	12.1
Halloween	万圣节	Wànshèngjié	n	14.2
hand	手	shǒu	n	12.1
to hand/give to	交给	jiāogěi	v	15.2
handsome	帅	shuài	adj	11.1
to hang	挂	guà	v	14.1
Hanukkah	光明节	Guāngmíngjié	n	14.2
to happen	发生	fāshēng	v	11.2
happen to, as it happens	正好	zhènghǎo	adv	15.1
happy	开心	kāixīn	adj	10.2
hat	帽子	màozi	n	9.1
to have a fever	发烧	fā shāo	vo	12.2
to have a headache; headache	头疼	tóuténg	adj, n	12.2
to have free time	有空	yǒu kòng	vo	10.1
have a safe flight!	一路平安	yílùpíng'ān	ie	16.2
healthy; health	健康	jiànkāng	adj, n	14.1
heart	心	xīn	n	11.2
to help	帮忙	bāng máng	vo	9.2
holiday; festival	节日	jiérì	n	14.2
homemaker	家庭主妇	jiātíng zhǔfù	n	13.2
to hope; hope	希望	xīwàng	v, n	11.1
horror movie	恐怖片	kǒngbù piàn	n	10.1
hospital	医院	yīyuàn	n	12.2

Definition	Characters	Pinyin	Word Category	Lesson
hot (as in temperature)	热	rè	adj	12.1
how, however	多	duō	adv	10.2
hutong (old-fashioned alleys in Beijing); lane, alley	胡同	hútong	n	16.1

I

Definition	Characters	Pinyin	Word Category	Lesson
idea; opinion; way of thinking	想法	xiǎngfǎ	n	15.2
to be in a relationship; to associate (with); to contact	交往	jiāowǎng	v	11.2
in a while, in a moment	一会儿	yí huìr	adv	12.2
in addition to; apart from; besides	除了	chúle	cj	16.1
to be in charge of	管	guǎn	v	13.1
insult; to insult; to humiliate	侮辱	wǔrǔ	n, v	15.1
interest	兴趣	xìngqù	n	10.1
to intern; to have an internship	实习	shíxí	v	13.2
Internet café	网吧	wǎngbā	n	16.1
it appears, it seems	看起来	kànqilai	ie	9.1
it doesn't matter; it's not a problem	没事	méi shì	vo	12.2

J

Definition	Characters	Pinyin	Word Category	Lesson
jeans (lit. "cowboy pants")	牛仔裤	niúzǎikù	n	9.2
to jog	跑步	pǎobù	vo	10.1
to joke	开玩笑	kāiwánxiào	v	11.1
just	刚刚	gānggāng	adv	15.2

K

Definition	Characters	Pinyin	Word Category	Lesson
karaoke	卡拉OK	kǎlā OK	n	16.1
to kick	踢	tī	v	10.1
to kiss; kiss	吻	wěn	v, n	11.1
kitchen	厨房	chúfáng	n	13.1
kung fu	功夫	gōngfu	n	10.1
kung fu movie	功夫片	gōngfu piàn	n	10.1

L

Definition	Characters	Pinyin	Word Category	Lesson
Lantern Festival	元宵节	Yuánxiāojié	n	14.1
laptop computer	笔记本电脑	bǐjìběn diànnǎo	n	16.1

Definition	Characters	Pinyin	Word Category	Lesson
laptop computer	笔记本	bǐjìběn	n	16.1
last time	上次	shàng cì	n	11.1
(a bit) later	晚点	wǎndiǎn	adv	11.1
to leave the country	出国	chūguó	vo	13.1
life; lifestyle	生活	shēnghuó	n	16.1
lively	热闹	rènao	adj	14.1
to love	爱	ài	v	11.2
lovely; pleasant (to the ear)	好听	hǎo tīng	adj	10.2
lover; sweetheart	情人	qíngrén	n	11.2

M

Definition	Characters	Pinyin	Word Category	Lesson
mad, angry	生气	shēngqì	adj	11.2
magazine	杂志	zázhì	n	16.2
to make (coffee or tea); to steep	泡	pào	v	13.1
to make friends	交朋友	jiāo péngyou	vo	15.2
manners; politeness	礼貌	lǐmào	n	15.1
martial arts	武术	wǔshù	n	15.2
to match, suit	配	pèi	v, adj	9.1
maternal grandmother	外婆	wàipó	n	16.2
may you have abundance every year (greeting used at New Year)	年年有余	niánnián-yǒuyú	ie	14.2
medium size	中号	zhōnghào	adj	9.1
to meet	见面	jiàn miàn	vo	11.1
melon seeds, dried seeds	瓜子	guāzǐ	n	14.1
Mencius	孟子	Mèngzǐ	name	15.2
method; means	办法	bànfǎ	n	15.2
Mid-Autumn Festival	中秋节	Zhōngqiūjié	n	14.2
middle	中	zhōng	adj	9.1
to miss (someone)	想念	xiǎngniàn	v	16.2
to misunderstand	误会	wùhuì	v	15.2
modern; modern times	现代	xiàndài	adj, n	15.2
modernized; modernize; modernization	现代化	xiàndàihuà	adj, v, n	15.2
modest	谦虚	qiānxū	adj	15.1
mooncake	月饼	yuèbǐng	n	14.2
more and more	越来越	yuèláiyuè	adv	14.2
most (used to describe superlative degree)	最	zuì	adv	9.2

Definition	Characters	Pinyin	Word Category	Lesson
Mother's Day	母亲节	Mǔqīnjié	n	14.2
mouth	嘴巴	zuǐba	n	12.2
movie	电影	diànyǐng	n	10.1
museum	博物馆	bówùguǎn	n	16.1
musical instrument	乐器	yuèqì	n	10.2
musician	音乐家	yīnyuèjiā	n	10.2

N

Definition	Characters	Pinyin	Word Category	Lesson
to need; to want	需要	xūyào	v	9.2
nervous	紧张	jǐnzhāng	adj	11.1
new year	新年	xīnnián	n	14.1
New Year's Day	元旦	Yuándàn	n	14.2
New Year's rice cake	年糕	niángāo	n	14.1
newspaper	报纸	bàozhǐ	n	16.2
next time	下次	xiàcì	n	11.1
nice, kind, kind-hearted	善良	shànliáng	adj	11.1
no wonder	难怪	nánguài	adv	13.1
nose	鼻子	bízi	n	12.1
not at all (a polite reply to a compliment)	哪里哪里	nǎlǐ nǎlǐ	ie	10.2
to not have expected or thought of	没想到	méi xiǎng dào	ie	13.1
not often; seldom	不常	bùcháng	adv	10.1
not only	不但	búdàn	cj	13.1
not wrong; (that's) right	没错	méi cuò	adj	15.2
nurse	护士	hùshi	n	12.2

O

Definition	Characters	Pinyin	Word Category	Lesson
to offend; to displease	得罪	dézuì	v	15.1
official	官员	guānyuán	n	13.2
often	常常	chángcháng	adv	10.1
OK, all right	行	xíng	adj	10.1
older male cousin	表哥	biǎogē	n	16.1
on the one hand; at the same time	一边	yìbiān	conj	10.1
oneself	自己	zìjǐ	pr	16.1
to open	张开	zhāngkāi	rv	12.2
opinion; perspective	看法	kànfǎ	n	15.2
opportunity	机会	jīhuì	n	13.2

Definition	Characters	Pinyin	Word Category	Lesson
or	或者	huòzhě	cj	9.1
orange	橙色	chéngsè	n	9.2
other people	别人	biérén	n	11.1
other than; except	以外	yǐwài	cj	16.1
otherwise	要不然	yàoburán	cj	15.1
outside	外面	wàimian	n	12.2
overcoat	大衣	dàyī	n	9.1
overcoat	大衣	dàyī	n	12.2

P

Definition	Characters	Pinyin	Word Category	Lesson
package	包裹	bāoguǒ	n	16.2
painful	痛	tòng	adj	12.1
painful; sore	疼	téng	adj	12.1
to paint; to draw	画画(儿)	huà huà(r)	vo	10.2
painting; drawing	画儿	huàr	n	10.2
pants, trousers	裤子	kùzi	n	9.2
pants, trousers (lit. "long pants")	长裤	chángkù	n	9.2
parents (formal)	父母	fùmǔ	n	15.1
park	公园	gōngyuán	n	11.1
passport	护照	hùzhào	n	16.2
to pay respect to (used for people)	尊敬	zūnjìng	v	15.1
to pay the bill	买单	mǎidān	vo	15.1
Peking opera	京剧	Jīngjù	n	15.2
to perform, to act	演	yǎn	v	10.2
to perform/have an operation	开刀	kāidāo	vo	12.2
to perform; performance	表演	biǎoyǎn	v, n	10.2
philosopher	哲学家	zhéxuéjiā	n	15.2
photograph	照片	zhàopiàn	n	16.2
piano	钢琴	gāngqín	n	10.2
ping pong	乒乓球	pīngpāngqiú	n	10.1
to play	玩	wán	v	10.1
to play (a musical instrument); to pluck	弹	tán	v	10.2
to play (an instrument with a bow); to pull	拉	lā	v	10.2
to play ball	打球	dǎ qiú	vo	10.1
to play the drums	打鼓	dǎ gǔ	vo	10.2
point, characteristic	点	diǎn	n	11.1

Definition	Characters	Pinyin	Word Category	Lesson
polite; to be polite	客气	kèqi	adj, v	15.1
pop music	流行音乐	liúxíng yīnyuè	n	10.2
popular	流行	liúxíng	adj	14.2
population	人口	rénkǒu	n	16.1
post office	邮局	yóujú	n	16.2
to prescribe medicine	开药	kāi yào	vo	12.2
pretty, beautiful	漂亮	piàoliang	adj	9.1
pretty; good-looking	好看	hǎokàn	adj	11.1
professional skills	专业技能	zhuānyè jìnéng	n	13.2
purple	紫色	zǐsè	n	9.2
to put one's mind at ease	放心	fàngxīn	v	15.2
to put; to set off	放	fàng	v	14.1
pyramid-shaped dumpling made of glutinous rice wrapped in bamboo leaves	粽子	zòngzi	n	14.2

Q

Definition	Characters	Pinyin	Word Category	Lesson
to quarrel; to fight	吵架	chǎojià	vo	11.2

R

Definition	Characters	Pinyin	Word Category	Lesson
to rain	下雨	xià yǔ	vo	12.1
really	真的	zhēnde	adv, ie	9.2
to receive (guests)	接待	jiēdài	v	13.1
to receive, to pick up, to meet (someone)	接	jiē	v	16.2
recently	最近	zuìjìn	adv	10.2
red	红色	hóngsè	n	9.1
red envelope	红包	hóngbāo	n	14.1
relation; relationship; connections	关系	guānxi	n	13.2
relieved; at ease; to rest assured	安心	ānxīn	adj, vo	16.2
to remember	记得	jìde	v	14.2
to remember, to bear in mind	记住	jìzhù	v	12.2
reputation; face; feelings	面子	miànzi	n	15.1
to resemble; like; similar	像	xiàng	v	14.2
to rest	休息	xiūxi	v	12.2
restroom	洗手间	xǐshǒujiān	n	15.1
résumé; curriculum vitae	简历	jiǎnlì	n	13.2
to ride a horse	骑马	qí mǎ	vo	10.1

Definition	Characters	Pinyin	Word Category	Lesson
rock music	摇滚乐	yáogǔnyuè	n	10.2
rose	玫瑰花	méiguīhuā	n	11.1
to row	划	huá	v	14.2
Russia	俄罗斯	éluósī	n	11.2

S

Definition	Characters	Pinyin	Word Category	Lesson
sad	难过	nánguò	adj	11.2
safe	安全	ānquán	adj	16.2
salary	薪水	xīnshuǐ	n	15.1
same	一样	yíyàng	adj	9.1
scenic spot	景点	jǐngdiǎn	n	16.1
to see a doctor	看病	kànbìng	vo	12.1
to send	寄	jì	v	16.2
to send (email, text message)	发	fā	v	16.2
to send a text message	发短信	fā duǎnxìn	vo	16.1
serious	严重	yánzhòng	adj	12.2
serious; conscientious; diligent	认真	rènzhēn	adj	10.2
to serve as, to be (a profession)	当	dāng	v	13.2
shirt	衬衫	chènshān	n	9.1
shoes	鞋(子)	xié (zi)	n	9.1
to shoot; to take (photos)	拍	pāi	v	16.2
short	短	duǎn	adj	9.2
to show filial obedience; filial	孝顺	xiàoshùn	v, adj	15.1
to sing	唱歌	chàng gē	vo	10.1
situation	情况	qíngkuàng	n	16.1
size	号	hào	n	9.1
size	大小	dàxiǎo	n	9.2
skill	技能	jìnéng	n	13.2
skirt; dress	裙子	qúnzi	n	9.1
slow	慢	màn	adj	10.2
slowly; gradually	慢慢	mànmàn	adv	13.1
small; little	小	xiǎo	adj	9.1
smart, intelligent	聪明	cōngmíng	adj	11.1
to smile; to laugh	笑	xiào	v	10.2
to snow	下雪	xià xuě	vo	12.1
socks	袜子	wàzi	n	9.1

Definition	Characters	Pinyin	Word Category	Lesson
software	软件	ruǎnjiàn	n	16.2
soon; quickly	快	kuài	adv	15.2
to sort out; to put in order; to arrange	整理	zhěnglǐ	v	13.1
to sound like	听起来	tīngqǐlái	ie	10.1
souvenir	纪念品	jìniànpǐn	n	16.2
special	特别	tèbié	adj	10.2
to spend (the holiday, an occasion)	过	guò	v	14.1
spring	春天	chūntiān	n	12.1
Spring Festival	春节	Chūnjié	n	14.1
stomach	肚子	dùzi	n	12.1
Stop it! (used when others are not being serious, poking fun at someone)	不要闹了	bú yào nào le	ie	11.1
studies; academics	学业	xuéyè	n	14.1
to study; to read	念书	niàn shū	vo	10.2
to succeed; success	成功	chénggōng	v, n	13.2
to suggest; suggestion, advice	建议	jiànyì	v, n	11.1
suit	西装	xīzhuāng	n	9.1
suitable	合适	héshì	adj	9.2
summer	夏天	xiàtiān	n	12.1
summer vacation	暑假	shǔjià	n	13.1
sunglasses	墨镜	mòjìng	n	9.1
surplus; superfluous	多余	duōyú	n, adj	14.2
sweater	毛衣	máoyī	n	9.1
to swim	游泳	yóuyǒng	vo	10.1

T

Definition	Characters	Pinyin	Word Category	Lesson
Tai Chi	太极拳	Tàijíquán	n	15.2
to take care (of oneself)	保重	bǎozhòng	v	12.1
to take care of	照顾	zhàogù	v	15.1
to take medicine	吃药	chī yào	vo	12.2
to talk	说话	shuō huà	vo	10.1
to talk, discuss	谈	tán	v	11.2
tea leaves	茶叶	cháyè	n	15.1
teaching assistant	助教	zhùjiào	n	13.1
tears	眼泪	yǎnlèi	n	11.2
to tell	告诉	gàosu	v	11.1

Definition	Characters	Pinyin	Word Category	Lesson
tennis	网球	wǎngqiú	n	10.2
Thanksgiving	感恩节	Gǎn'ēnjié	n	14.2
that is to say; in other words	就是说	jiùshìshuō	ie	15.1
the Internet	网络	wǎngluò	n	16.2
the West	西方	Xīfāng	n	14.2
these	这些	zhèxiē	n	10.1
to think	想	xiǎng	v	11.1
think highly of; attach importance to	重视	zhòngshì	v	15.2
thought, idea	思想	sīxiǎng	n	15.2
Tian'anmen (Gate of Heavenly Peace)	天安门	Tiān'ānmén	n	16.1
(to a degree)	不得了	bùdéliǎo	adv	11.1
to chat	聊天	liáotiān	vo	16.2
Tomb Sweeping Festival	清明节	Qīngmíngjié	n	14.2
tongue	舌头	shétou	n	12.2
to tour; to visit	参观	cānguān	v	16.1
traditional; tradition	传统	chuántǒng	adj, n	14.1
tragedy	悲剧	bēijù	n	10.1
to translate; translation; translator	翻译	fānyì	v, n	13.2
to travel; tour; tourism	旅游	lǚyóu	v, n	16.2
to trick, to fool, to cheat	骗	piàn	v	11.2
to trouble someone to do something; trouble; troublesome	麻烦	máfan	v, n, adj	15.1
to try and see, do something and see	看	kàn	v	9.2
T-shirt	T恤衫	T-xùshān	n	9.1
turkey	火鸡	huǒjī	n	14.2
tutor	家教	jiājiào	n	13.1

U

Definition	Characters	Pinyin	Word Category	Lesson
to be unable to remember	记不住	jì bu zhù	rv	11.1
to be unable to sleep	睡不着	shuìbuzháo	rv	12.1
uncle (polite term of address for a man of one's parents' generation)	伯父	bófù	n	14.1
to understand	明白	míngbai	v	9.2
to understand	了解	liǎojiě	v	15.1
(used after a verb to indicate a past experience)	过	guo	p	11.2

Definition	Characters	Pinyin	Word Category	Lesson
(used to express the manner in which an action is performed)	地	de	p	12.2

V

Definition	Characters	Pinyin	Word Category	Lesson
very infrequently; rarely	很少	hěnshǎo	adv	10.1
very, extremely	非常	fēicháng	adv	11.2
violin	小提琴	xiǎotíqín	n	10.2
visa	签证	qiānzhèng	n	16.2
volleyball	排球	páiqiú	n	10.1

W

Definition	Characters	Pinyin	Word Category	Lesson
to wait	等	děng	v	10.1
wait until; when	等	děng	cj	16.1
want; wish; would like	想要	xiǎngyào	av	13.2
to wear	穿	chuān	v	9.1
to wear (for glasses and hats)	戴	dài	v	9.1
weather	天气	tiānqì	n	12.1
webpage	网页	wǎngyè	n	16.1
website	网站	wǎngzhàn	n	16.1
week	周	zhōu	n	12.2
what kind/sort	什么样	shénme yàng	pr	13.1
what's wrong; what's the matter	怎么了	zěnme le	qph	11.2
white	白色	báisè	n	9.2
winter	冬天	dōngtiān	n	12.1
wireless internet card	无线上网卡	wúxiàn shàngwǎng kǎ	n	16.1
(wishing you) all the best	万事如意	wànshìrúyì	ie	14.1
wishing you happiness and property (greeting used during the New Year)	恭喜发财	gōngxǐfācái	ie	14.1
work objective	求职意向	qiúzhí yìxiàng	n	13.2
to work part-time, to temp	打工	dǎ gōng	vo	13.1
to work; to handle matters	做事	zuò shì	vo	13.1
writer, author	作家	zuòjiā	n	13.2

Y

Definition	Characters	Pinyin	Word Category	Lesson
yellow	黄色	huángsè	n	9.2

Definition	Characters	Pinyin	Word Category	Lesson
you can do it! (literally "add oil"; used when offering words of encouragement)	加油	jiāyóu	ie	13.1
young	年轻	niánqīng	adj	14.2
young people	年轻人	niánqīng rén	n	14.2
younger generation	晚辈	wǎnbèi	n	15.1

Z

Definition	Characters	Pinyin	Word Category	Lesson
Zhuangzi	庄子	Zhuāngzǐ	name	15.2